BALL
by
BALL

BALL
— by —
BALL

THE STORY OF CRICKET
BROADCASTING

Christopher Martin-Jenkins

GRAFTON BOOKS

A Division of the Collins Publishing Group

LONDON GLASGOW
TORONTO SYDNEY AUCKLAND

Grafton Books
A Division of the Collins Publishing Group
8 Grafton Street, London W1X 3LA

Published by Grafton Books 1990

British Library Cataloguing in Publication Data

Martin-Jenkins, Christopher
Ball by ball: the story of cricket broadcasting.
1. Great Britain. Radio & television programmes:
sports programmes. Commentating
I. Title
791.44

ISBN 0–246–13568–9

Phototypeset by Computape (Pickering) Ltd, North Yorkshire
Printed in Great Britain by
William Collins Sons & Co. Ltd, Glasgow

CONTENTS

ACKNOWLEDGEMENTS

My grateful thanks are due to Audrey Adams for her assiduous research and to the always co-operative John Jordan and his staff at the BBC archives department in Caversham; to Rex Alston, John Arlott, Peter Baxter, Leo Feord, John Ford, Robert Hudson, Brian Johnston, Charles Maxwell, Lord Orr-Ewing, E. W. Swanton, Michael Tuke-Hastings, Peter West and the late Norman Yardley for so willingly allowing me to tap their long and rich memories of BBC Outside Broadcasts during various conversations, all too relaxed to be called 'interviews'; to David Rayvern Allen for kindly loaning me correspondence relating to his books on BBC Talks; to Glenys Williams for research into MCC minutes; and to Tony Cozier, Charles Fortune, Iain Gallaway, Roy Lawrence and Alan McGilvray for answering my questions and writing with their helpful recollections of commentaries in their own countries. Special thanks are due to the BBC for kind permission to reproduce extracts from letters, sound archives and articles in *Radio Times*; and to ABC Books for kind permission to reproduce two passages from *The Game Is Not The Same* by Alan McGilvray.

Amongst books consulted, particular use was made of: David Rayvern Allen: *Cricket On The Air* and *More Cricket On The Air*; Peter Baxter et al.: *Test Match Special*; Richie Benaud: *On Reflection*; Asa Briggs: *The Golden Age of Wireless*; Brian Johnston: *Chatterboxes* and *It's Been A Lot Of Fun*; Johnny

Moyes: *Australian Cricket*; Roy Plomley: *Days Seemed Longer*; John Snagge and Michael Barsley: *Those Vintage Years of Radio*; E. W. Swanton: *Sort of a Cricket Person* and *The Barclay's World of Cricket*; various reporters: *War Report*; Teddy Wakelam: *Half Time*; and Peter West: *Flannelled Fool* and *Muddied Oaf*.

INTRODUCTION

A Personal Perspective

This is an attempt to tell the story of the development of cricket commentary from hesitant beginnings to its present state of happy popularity. I hope a self-indulgent introduction may be forgiven, for I consider myself extraordinarily fortunate to make my living out of talking about cricket.

Potent and nostalgic as the half-remembered smell of the music room which housed the old brown radio set on which I first heard cricket commentaries, the voices of the BBC commentators of the 1950s return to me now as I contemplate that good fortune. Sounds echo back into consciousness when I conjure up the scene of a musty room on the second floor of my prep school, St Bede's in Eastbourne, looking out across the playing field to the English Channel, a vacant blue plateau seen through a wide gap in the bank beyond the cricket pitch. Across that gap many a dirty British coaster butted its way through the mad March days, but on one particular morning I recall, the *Queen Mary* herself might have escaped my notice as I fixed my attention on the wireless perched on a cupboard opposite the tinny piano on which I never produced anything more original than 'Chopsticks'.

It must have been during the short break between lessons and lunch, which I would have normally spent outside with a bat and a ball. Word had got round that something of national importance was happening and I listened anxiously, along with other cricket-besotted boys, as the match-saving stand between Willie Watson and Trevor Bailey developed. Lord's, 1953: England v. Australia. It was the greatest salvage operation since Dunkirk and that had been three years before my time. The tension seemed all the greater for the measured nature of John Arlott's deliberate description, each word he uttered apparently savoured for a moment, like wine, on the tongue. That rough Hampshire burr was almost melancholy at times but it was fuelled by an agile mind with a seemingly limitless vocabulary at its disposal.

I had only been at the school for a month or so. Cricket had been my sanctuary from the start. I pity children who now have to start their schooling with the long Michaelmas term instead of the months of sun, ice-cream and cricket. Isn't it always the summer days that we recall when we think back to the best aspects of school life? I know that, when I was an eight-year-old boarder at St Bede's, the pain of being wrenched from home and parents had been eased, indeed forgotten, by a game of cricket with my elder brother and his friends on the first evening in my new surroundings. The passion for cricket remained throughout my schooldays and although, unlike Carlisle Best, the Barbados and West Indies batsman, I never actually commentated when I was playing in a serious match, informal games in the garden, on the beach or against school walls were always accompanied by a running commentary from me.

My reading for many years was, I am ashamed to admit, confined mainly to the cricket pages of *The Times* and the *Daily Telegraph*. My knowledge of first-class cricket was enhanced, however, by the BBC commentators – Arlott, Rex Alston, Jim Swanton and, a little later, Alan Gibson and Robert Hudson.

Moreover, my enthusiasm was sharpened when one of the school's joint headmasters, Rex Lord, occasionally took groups of boys to watch Sussex play at the Saffrons in Eastbourne. We used to sit on the grass by the boundary's edge, almost within touching distance of the players. I can remember gazing in some awe at Peter Richardson, rosy-cheeked like one of his Worcestershire apples and full of good cheer. I longed for a pair of the white 'sausage' batting gloves he wore. In the holidays I would sometimes get the chance to watch the all-conquering Surrey side at The Oval – Tom Clark, Bernie Constable, Peter May, the Bedser twins, Peter Loader, Laker and Lock, Arthur McIntyre, and later Micky Stewart and Ken Barrington. They were heroes to a man and it is quite a thought for me now that I was later to play cricket with some of them.

I am not sure when it was that I began to decide that I would like to become a commentator myself, but the idea was certainly crystallizing all through my schooldays. During matches in the garden at home my constant running commentary had become something of a family joke. When uncles or aunts asked what I was going to be in life the answer was unequivocal: a cricket commentator. Without specifying as much, I always knew that this meant being a radio commentator, although as time went on I watched just as much Test cricket on television as I listened to it on 'sound'. I had watched and listened as Jim Laker produced his amazing performance at Old Trafford in 1956 when he took 19 wickets against Australia; I had seen Ramadhin bowling England out in the first innings against the West Indies at Edgbaston in 1957 and May and Cowdrey's heroic second-innings stand. Then I had triumphed in spirit with Tom Graveney as he made 258 at Trent Bridge which rescued his Test career that same year, for Tom was definitely my hero of heroes.

These days schoolchildren approaching their 'A' level courses are encouraged to start thinking about what they would like to do for a living. In an ideal world the subjects chosen for study will lead on to a degree relevant to the selected profession. By the time that my own 'A' level studies were starting I was in the same Marlborough side as the future Sussex captain Mike Griffith and was no doubt aware, measuring my abilities against his, that a future life as a first-class cricketer was not to be my destiny. But I already had a firm idea that to write and broadcast about the game would be a most attractive alternative. I wrote to Brian Johnston, whose radio commentaries in those days were still

confined to overseas tours. Brian and my father had a mutual
friend, who was, I suppose, my original point of contact, but he
also seemed, and surely was, the most approachable of the
familiar voices.

Brian asked me to meet him at Broadcasting House in London
and immediately put a nervous young man at ease as we chatted
briefly in his office, characteristically decorated with risqué
holiday postcards, before he accompanied me to the BBC club in
the old Langham Hotel across the road for a salad and a glass or
two of white wine.

Brian did nothing to raise my hopes that I might fulfil my
ambition, but advised me to play the game to as high a standard
as I could at Cambridge and to practise commentating whenever
I could. Well, I followed the latter advice, taking myself off to
occasional matches with a tape-recorder and delivering private,
whispered commentaries. These sounded a bit like an amateur
Henry Longhurst, the hushed 'green-side' tones being due to the
fact that I was embarrassed at muttering into a microphone with
other spectators within earshot. On the field I played in three
final trials and one three-day match at Cambridge (subsequently
ruled not first-class!) but was never really more than a club
player and I failed to get a Blue. However, I did have a
marvellous three years, emerged with a reasonable degree in
history and managed to earn a couple of Half-Blues at Rugby
Fives. Within a few months of coming down, I began working at
the offices of *The Cricketer* magazine under the firm, kindly,
experienced eye of E. W. Swanton. Three years later I joined the
staff of the BBC and in 1972 shared a commentary box with
Arlott, Johnston and Jack Fingleton for the first One-Day
International played in England, against Australia at Old
Trafford.

I felt then, and I feel now, immensely privileged to have
become a small part of the great tradition of cricket commentary.
That it is a responsible job, especially when critical comment is
called for, was made very clear to me by the alarming reaction to
a report I delivered for the 'Today' programme's sports news a

few minutes after an incident late in the fourth day's play of the Barbados Test match during England's tour of the West Indies in 1990-91. What I said cut little ice in Britain because I had interpreted the incident itself, and commented on the issues it raised, in much the same way as several other cricket correspondents had done. But when the BBC World Service transmitted my comments, various journalists and radio personalities on the island whipped up what can only be called a hate campaign against me in a place where all I had ever received before was warm affection.

There is, however, a thin line between popularity and notoriety: in various phone-in programmes it was suggested that I should be deported, shot or – horror of horrors! – introduced to a bull-pizzle, for giving my opinion that both sides were cheating each other on over-rates and that an umpire had changed his mind on a decision under pressure from over-hostile appealing (the very thing for which earlier in the tour I had chastised both the England and Windward Islands teams – also on a World Service report).

I am in no hurry to make the acquaintaince of a bull-pizzle! It was apparent that my report had been heard at a time when relations between black- and white-skinned Bajans and between local people and the tourists on whom they rely were unusually sensitive. Moreover, many Bajans had been incensed by earlier comments in the British press and by commentaries on Sky Television by Tony Greig and Geoff Boycott, whose coverage of the series was taken by most of the cricketing islands of the Caribbean. Some of the local cricket writers were also furious at losing their normal seats to the visiting press corps.

Cricket has always aroused great passions in the West Indies and I came home still believing West Indians in general and Bajans in particular to be by nature both friendly and fair-minded. But the episode posed for me a dilemma which may not get any easier to resolve: how does a commentator speak his mind objectively about the game and its players if frank words and honest opinions have to be held back out of fear?

CHAPTER ONE

Australian Origins

Ball-by-ball commentary began, like Test cricket itself, not in England but in Australia. Broadcasting there was in its infant, almost embryonic stage when Len Watt, a former grade cricketer, was despatched to the Sydney Cricket Ground in 1922 to report on a testimonial match for Charles Bannerman between two elevens from New South Wales. Appropriately enough, Bannerman had been, 45 years before, the scorer of the first Test hundred in the inaugural match against England at Melbourne. Johnny Moyes, who wrote the history of Australian cricket and later became a well-known broadcaster himself with a chirpy, conversational style, relates that Watt 'was given a microphone and told to go on talking'. Whether he actually attempted to give a running commentary is not recorded but the clear implication is that he did. At any rate, two seasons later the experiment was extended to Test cricket.

During the series between the two countries in 1924-25, when England under Arthur Gilligan, later to become a popular broadcaster on Australian radio, were being defeated in four of the five Tests by Australia under 'Horseshoe' Collins, commentaries and scores were given on Sydney's local 2BL radio station. The pioneers, who may in this case have been more like reporters than actual running commentators, were Hyam Marks, a member of a well-known New South Wales cricketing family, and Clem Hill, one of the greatest of Australia's left-handed batsmen. They sat together during the Sydney Test and broadcast from the new scoreboard at the Sydney Cricket Ground, that marvellous board which told one everything about the game and, it almost seemed, the life history of all the players as well. (Sadly it is now idle, hidden by a new stand and replaced by an electronic board which tells one less but brings in more advertising revenue. Progress?)

The match was played either side of Christmas before huge crowds. Australia opened with 450, despite some heroic bowling by Maurice Tate, who took 6 for 130 in a little matter of 55 overs and one ball. Tich Freeman bowled 49 overs and took 2 for 124. Collins and Bill Ponsford made hundreds.

One of the talking-points for Hill and Marks was, no doubt, the fact that this was the first time that eight-ball overs had been bowled in Test cricket, which must have made the feet of Tate and Freeman all the sorer. One can picture them: Tate broad-shouldered, ruddy-faced and willing; Freeman tiny, wizened and nut-brown; and picture too the pioneer chatters, up in their lofty position at extra cover or wide mid-on, according to which end the bowling was coming from.

The England reply was initiated by the famous pair of Hobbs and Sutcliffe. Although Jack Hobbs was by then aged 42 and Herbert Sutcliffe 30, it was – remarkably – the first time they had opened the innings together against Australia. Hobbs made 115, Sutcliffe 59 and Patsy Hendren 74 not out, but England were still bowled out for 298 (Jack Gregory 5 for 111, Arthur Mailey 4 for 129). Australia then made 452, two better than the first time, and although the pitch held up marvellously well and Sutcliffe and Frank Woolley scored hundreds as England made 411 in the second innings, Marks and Hill were able to tell their listeners about an Australian victory on the seventh day.

This broadcasting experiment was repeated in February when the teams returned to Sydney for the last match of the series. Although Tate took nine more wickets to finish the series with 38 in all, Australia won even more convincingly, by 307 runs.

The service given by Marks and Hill was advertised as being

'commentary and scores'. From 1925, however, we see the first use of the term 'ball-by-ball' for descriptions of cricket. L. G. Watt was in the van again, in collaboration with H. P. Williams, later to become the first General Manager of the Australian Broadcasting Commission. In 1925 he was in charge of News and Sport at the 2FC station in Sydney and at his instigation Watt gave the first definite ball-by-ball commentaries (two years before the first such experiments were attempted in England) at the Australia v. The Rest Test Trial in December. He worked from near the sightscreen at the northern end of the ground, using a microphone suspended from the boundary fence, the 'picket' so beloved of Australian commentators.

From the start these broadcasts seemed both natural and attractive to Australian ears, in clear contrast to the reactions provoked by the first attempts to describe cricket in England, which, as we shall see, were treated with extraordinary scepticism for a long time. From 1926 it became commonplace in Australia for radio stations to carry descriptions of all grades of cricket. So much so that for the 1930 series in England, several commercial stations got together with the Australian Broadcasting Company, as it then was called, to give special coverage of the Tests. Amongst those involved were 2UW, 4BH, 3DB and 5AD.

I confess I have always been a little confused by these numbered stations, though they remain to this day as rivals to the ABC with different numbers in different states. Many are, in fact, owned by the same business magnate. As for the ABC itself, a form of national broadcasting was in force from 1929 to 1932, when the Government took over the so-called 'A' class stations. Technical facilities were provided by the Postmaster General's Department and programmes were let by contract to the Australian Broadcasting Company until, in May 1932, an Act created the Australian Broadcasting Commission, which two months later took over the national service.

Even before the Commission came into being there were signs of a different approach between the 'national' station and the more aggressive commercials. In 1930, for example, the ABC contented itself with a regular service of the latest scores from England, based on cabled reports, followed, at the end of the fifth Test, by a two-way telephone conversation at close of play with members of the Australian team. But H. P. Williams had the idea of using cables to provide a more imaginative coverage for listeners: a synthetic broadcast by which inventive commentators could give a running description of play (obviously some way behind the real thing) based on detailed cables of what had been happening on the other side of the world.

The commercial stations' service in 1930 was limited, of course, by the cost of the cables, but there was no doubting their popularity, and when England travelled to Australia in 1932-33 there was immense competition between the various stations. Players would be hustled into cars at close of play and hastened to the studio to record their impressions of the day's play. In England, meanwhile, all the BBC was providing, for the first Test of the series, was potted scores in the news bulletins. Shortwave coverage 'live' from Australia was not yet considered possible, but technical advances were swiftly being made by the dedicated band of engineers at Broadcasting House and it took a somewhat bizarre combination of French and Australian initiatives to force the hand of the cautious BBC.

Whilst Radio Paris upstaged 'Auntie' by transmitting two separate quarter-hour periods of scores and comment, another commercial station, Poste Parisien, imaginatively persuaded the New South Wales all-rounder Alan Fairfax, who had been a member of Woodfull's 1930 touring team, to travel to Paris. Seated in a studio in the Eiffel Tower he was fed with continuous cables giving considerable detail on the course of the play in the Tests taking place on the other side of the world, not forgetting such matters as the weather and the size of the crowd. John Arlott recalled in the book *Test Match Special* the effectiveness of Fairfax's almost instant translation of these cables into synthetic commentary: 'His background knowledge enabled him to put flesh on the hard facts and his use of the present tense and his strong Australian accent imparted an air of authenticity. Anyone with a radio set and an interest in cricket in that winter of 1932-33 will still remember the Fairfax broadcasts as both compelling and novel.'

Fairfax was helped, of course, by the intensely dramatic nature of the Bodyline series. It created an ideal climate for the development of cricket broadcasting on both sides of the world, especially, perhaps, in England where the deeds of Jardine, Larwood and Voce, and the whiff of controversy, stimulated a great demand for more detailed news of the Tests.

After the first Test the BBC responded to the growing demand for a better service by using the old Empire shortwave service to broadcast eyewitness accounts by Alan Kippax, that most stylish of batsmen who had been dropped from the Australian team after the first match in Brisbane.

This led immediately to the more comprehensive coverage of home Tests in England, as the next chapter will relate, but for the 1934 series in England the Australians still had to rely on ingenious synthetic broadcasts. This time, to cut costs, the ABC got together with the commercial stations, though all the stations used the cables in different ways, some merely giving scores, others developing the details into 'commentaries'. These were provided by Charles Moses, later to become the General Manager of the ABC (an indication, no doubt, of the higher status accorded to sport and sports broadcasting in Australia compared with England, where 'gross ignorance' was once described as being '144 sports commentators'), accompanied by several Test cricketers: 'Monty' Noble, the former Australian captain, Clem Hill, C. E. 'Nip' Pellew, Ted A'Beckett and Vic Richardson, another former Test captain. Dion Wheeler was responsible for sound effects and Wendell Bill for the essential task of sending the cables from England. Others involved in a team of fifteen specialists and technicians in the studios at Market Street, Sydney, were Bernard Kerr, P. C. Harrison, Mel Norris, John Chance, R. H. Campbell, J. L. Hall, J. Duffecy and A. Grey. The latter kept the score on a large black scoreboard, which recorded all essential details, including bowling figures. Bernard Kerr, who became the ABC's Sports Director and commentated in England in 1953, recalls: 'During the early broadcasts mistakes were frequent but quickly corrected. Slowly the team moulded itself into a splendid combination, heartened by the warmth and sincerity of the listeners. The receiving room was alive with tension, anxiety and concentration, and much the same anxiety existed in the broadcasting room, with the commentator ever glancing at the door through which the runner would appear.'

Although by the next Australian tour of 1938 shortwave coverage was possible, breakdowns were still common enough, and reception poor enough, for a similar synthetic operation to be set up. This time the team was Mel Norris, John Chance, Hal Hooker and Alan McGilvray, with 'expert' comments from Noble and Richardson. Eric Sholl sent the cables from England.

This was the year in which McGilvray, due to become the supreme exponent in Australia of the art of cricket commentary, first really made his mark. He had been invited by Charles Moses to make his first broadcasts in 1935-36 when, as captain of New South Wales, he gave close-of-play reports from studios at the end of matches in the Sheffield Shield. McGilvray was obviously a more than useful all-round cricketer and a man of some character, but his performances at first-class level were modest. Yet he became, as a commentator, one of the country's most famous and popular men, to the extent where the ABC, competing many decades later with commercial television, would market him with a catchy jingle, 'The game is not the same without McGilvray.' Alan himself still remembers that series of 1938 as the most exciting broadcasting experience of his long career.

He has described in his autobiography *The Game Is Not The Same* what it was like in the ABC studios in Market Street, Sydney:

Sholl was despatched to send back the cables according to an elaborate code.

Outside our studio, a team of five or six decoders would put the cables into readable form from which the commentators would operate. The cables covered everything we would need to paint a word picture of what was happening. Sholl would tell us about the weather, the crowd – even the traffic getting to the ground. He would keep us totally informed about where every player was on the field. Any time the field changed, he would fire off a new cable, and each over send a cable with a complete run-down on every ball: where it pitched, what the batsman did, where the ball went, who fielded – absolutely everything.

The inventive Charles Moses did all he could to help the commentators achieve an air of reality. The broadcasts would begin at 8.30 at night and Moses insisted on morning tea being taken at 9.30pm and lunch at 10.30pm, the latter consisting of sandwiches and fruit as it might have done had they been on duty in England. Knowing McGilvray I should be surprised if the repast was not helped down by a sensible amount of cold beer. A large photograph of the ground in question was suspended in front of the commentators' desk, and both a scorer and an expert on cricket records were supplied, plus, of course, the sound effects man. He had a series of recordings to use for each incident: loud cheers, polite applause, crowd annoyance in reaction to an umpiring decision. McGilvray drily remembers: 'In all my time I have never known a crowd like that which Australians knew through the England tour of 1938!'

But the most important sound effect of all, that of bat on ball, was not recorded: it was provided, farcical though it may seem now, by the commentator armed with a pencil. A cracking hook shot was signalled by a sharp bang on a round piece of wood on the desk; a stroke for one would herald a more gentle tap. McGilvray recalls that the co-ordination of the tapping pencil, a vivid description of the shot and the recording of the cheering crowd were not always perfectly synchronized. But this, as he recalled in his autobiography, was only one of the problems:

Sound effects were not the only area in which our enthusiasm initially made it tough for us. The information we were fed came at the end of each over, covering that over in entirety. We would work our way through the six balls, then look for the new cable and the new over.

At first, we were finding an extraordinary delay between the end of an over as we described it and the next cable.

'Where's the telegram?' we would plead as we thrust ourselves into long and arduous fill-in chatter, sometimes to take up several minutes.

Some simple arithmetic eventually forced on me the realisation that I was whipping through in two minutes an over that the bowler in England was taking four minutes to bowl. Since the cables couldn't come any quicker than the balls were being bowled, we soon learned to take more notice of our stop watch and spread each over to more realistic lengths.

But the mistakes and the rough patches were surprisingly few. As we grew accustomed to this rather revolutionary method of describing a cricket match, we became extremely polished at it. We got faster as time went on, and in the end I think it was every bit as colourful and comprehensive as the real thing became in later years.

The key to everything, of course, was the information with which we were supplied and the slick work of those who decoded it. The raw cables, sent at the end of each over, were masterpieces of improvisation.

A typical cable would begin: 'BRIGHTENING FLEETWOOD HAMMOND FULL FIRSTLY TWO HASSETT SECONDLY FULL FOUR STRAIGHT UNCHANCE BOWLER THIRDLY NO BALL FULL TWO OFFDRIVEN RUN APPEAL HUTTON FOURTHLY FOUR SWEPT BOWLER KEEPER OFFPUSHED.'

The decoders would get hold of that, and the message would come into us in slightly fuller form.

First of all we would establish that the weather was brightening and Fleetwood-Smith was the bowler. 'HAMMOND FULL FIRSTLY TWO HASSETT' would come back 'Hammond batting, first ball pitched up, driven, Hassett fielded, ran two'.

Then the cable continued, 'SECONDLY FULL FOUR STRAIGHT UNCHANCE BOWLER'. That would be interpreted as the second was full length to Hammond, driven straight but uppishly past the bowler for four. Almost a chance.

So we would work off that information, add a touch of atmosphere, try to imagine the scene, and come up with something like this:

'In comes Fleetwood-Smith, he moves in to bowl to Hammond and Hammond comes down the wicket and takes it on the full and he drives it beautifully past Hassett who moves around behind the ball and fields brilliantly just before it reaches the boundary rope, and meantime they've run through for two.'

The second ball we'd read: 'HAMMOND, FLEETWOOD-SMITH, FULL TOSS, UPPISH STRAIGHT DRIVE, ALMOST CHANCE, FOUR.'

We'd get that out something like this: 'Hammond again moves down the wicket and hits him beautifully past the bowler. My word, that carried. That was almost in the hands of Fleetwood-Smith, but it went just past him and although he put a hand out he didn't get near it and it raced past him for four. But it was certainly past him round about knee high.'

A fair bit of imagination was called for, although we were desperately careful not to be so carried away as to significantly risk the accuracy of the reports.

A cable which read 'HAMMOND SWEPT BARNES FOUR' might end up, 'Hammond sweeps him. He's really got on to that one and Barnes is tearing around the boundary to cut it off, but I don't think he'll get it, and he doesn't, and the ball just beats him over the boundary rope for four.'

Barnes's race around the boundary, of course, would be greeted with some enthusiasm by our sound effects man, who would bring an excited cheer from the crowd, reaching its peak as we nominated the boundary. He really became quite expert at producing a crowd reaction fitting for each event, and timed to perfection.

We could operate with quite remarkable efficiency on fairly skeletal information. We always knew where everybody was in the field, for instance, so with brief information on the rough direction of a shot we could assume a likely scenario as far as the fieldsmen were concerned. And the advantage of having men like Richardson and Noble involved, men who knew their cricket and their cricketers backwards, was that they could read the game with singular clarity.

Their knowledge of how the Australian players, particularly, thought and performed, their habits and their idiosyncrasies, allowed them to gauge reactions and assume trends of play with extraordinary accuracy.

There were, however, times when we were confronted with absolute disaster. Occasionally the flow of cables from the Post Office would be interrupted for one reason or another. When the delays were long we would simply announce a loss of communication and cease operations until they resumed.

But when the loss of contact was brief, or while we thought it would be brief, we tried to tough it out. We might slip in a few balls to mark time. We were always careful in such crises, however, never to advance the score beyond what we knew it to be. Any of these 'fill-in' deliveries would of necessity be insignificant, 'back-to-the-bowler' stuff.

And we filled the gaps with some of the most horrendous discussion. We used to get quite animated. We would be locked in heavy discussion and quite lively argument on subjects that were only imagined.

'He really should be moving forward to those deliveries that are pitched up to him and having a bit of a go,' Vic might offer. 'Well, I don't know about that, Vic,' I would reply. 'The bowling's pretty tight and I think the batsmen are quite right in being cautious and taking their time.' The verbal battle would ensue. We would argue the point hammer and tongs, completely oblivious to the fact that neither of us really knew how the batsmen were approaching it, or whether the bowling was good, bad or indifferent. But we became so involved in the broadcasts we almost convinced ourselves we were there. It is quite amazing how the mind and the imagination can take over completely in such circumstances.

Only once did an unsatisfactory cable lead to a really disastrous error:

I recall one occasion when the cable came through identifying one of the Australians simply as 'MC'. There were two 'Macs' in the Australian team, Stan McCabe and Ernie McCormick, and at this particular time both were batting.

The cable came through announcing that 'MC' was out. Which 'MC', of course, we had no way of knowing. I quickly switched off the mike and looked at Vic.

'Who'll I give it to?' I pleaded.

'Oh, give it to Stan,' Vic responded. 'He's got his hundred and he'll be throwing the bat at anything.'

In I plunged. 'McCabe steps into the drive. He's lofted it . . . it's in the air and I think he's gone, yes he's out, McCabe is out. And what a glorious innings it was.'

On I trekked into the unknown, rolling along valiantly as the picture unfolded in my mind. I described McCabe's standing ovation. I had him clapped all the way to the pavilion. The sound effects man had a field day.

Then came the next cable. It was McCormick who had gone, not McCabe. I could do nothing but launch into abject apology. I explained exactly how the error occurred. It was one of the more embarrassing moments of my broadcasting career, but explaining the error quickly and honestly served only to enhance the credibility of the broadcasts.

The ABC, and Moses in particular, were concerned that there should be no dishonesty involved. We were seeking only to inform in as colourful a manner as possible, not to 'con' people into believing the commentaries were the real thing.

The McCabe error was all the more unfortunate for the fact that it brought to a false and premature close one of the greatest of all Test innings: the immortal 232 not out at Trent Bridge which an awe-struck Bradman instructed his men to watch from the dressing-room balcony. Nevertheless, Alan McGilvray showed what he could do as a commentator by those synthetic broadcasts of 1938, and when Anglo-Australian cricket resumed after the war he was to join Vic Richardson and the former England captain Arthur Gilligan in an immensely popular combination of frontline ABC cricket commentators.

CHAPTER TWO

First Steps in England

It was 1927 when the first tentative steps in cricket broadcasting were taken in England – the first steps of any kind, indeed, into the unknown world of sporting outside broadcasts. Hitherto BBC sound output had been confined to studio-bound activities: talks, plays, music and discussions. The press viewed the still new phenomenon of wireless (the BBC had been founded in 1922) with grave suspicion: it was their refusal to print details of BBC programmes which led to the founding of the *Radio Times*, still today, remarkably enough in view of the now widespread coverage of the broadcasting media in the press, the biggest selling weekly in Britain. There was also an entirely understandable fear amongst sporting authorities, MCC included, that too much immediate information on a big match would adversely affect crowds. The reverse proved much later to be true, certainly as far as radio was concerned. Whether television has affected 'gates' is more questionable. What it has taken away in the form of 'bottoms on seats' it has put back by stimulating interest amongst viewers, especially young ones, and, of course, in the fees paid for broadcasting rights.

The miracle of being able to watch great sporting events without being there in person was beyond imagination, however, when in 1927 the BBC's new charter gave it the right to send reporters out and about to serve the public with news of major events. In Lance Sieveking, remembered by two of his old colleagues as 'a very strange, rather effeminate man', the Corporation nevertheless had an Outside Broadcasts pioneer of great imagination and ability. E. W. Swanton has referred to him as being 'versatile and highly talented'; John Arlott called him 'probably the outstanding and most creative pioneer of British broadcasting'. His model for the first commentaries came not in fact from Australia but from America, where Sieveking had recently been on a learning trip during which he heard some baseball commentary. The rugby season preceding the cricket, it was to rugby union that he first took the microphone, making a shrewd choice in H. B. T. ('Teddy') Wakelam as the first of all the English commentators.

Teddy Wakelam was a good games player at Marlborough – in the 2nd XI at cricket and outstanding in the rugby XV – and he went on to play both rugger and hockey for Cambridge University, though he did not get a Blue, and later played rugby with distinction for the Harlequins. In his entertaining autobiography, *Half-Time*, he described how, having survived the war in which no fewer than 40 of the 64 in his house at Marlborough died – a ghastly and incredible proportion – he received the phone-call from Sieveking which was to change his life: 'One afternoon (in January 1927) I was sitting at my table, working out some details of a tender, when my telephone rang. An unknown voice at the other end then asked me if I was the same Wakelam who had played rugger for the Harlequins, and, upon my saying "yes", went on to inform me that the owner of it was an official of the BBC, who would much like to see me at once on an urgent matter.'

The caller, Lance Sieveking, outlined the proposal that he should commentate at the England v. Wales Rugby International at Twickenham on 15 January. Wakelam was given an immediate voice test in the studio and then asked to take part with two competitors in a field trial the next day at the ground of Guy's Hospital. Here occurred possibly the first but certainly not the last BBC 'cock-up': neither engineers nor microphones were present, they having gone instead to another match in Greenwich Park. There the pioneers and their equipment were brusquely turned out by the park-keeper – again, not the last BBC men to be refused entry by a self-important gateman! An embarrassed Sieveking got his men together the following day – only two days before the Twickenham match – for an inter-schools' match at the Old Deer Park, Richmond.

The dummy run over, Sieveking decided that Wakelam was his man – posterity has not recorded who the unsuccessful candidates were – and off they went to Twickenham to examine their perch, a 'rickety-looking hut mounted on a scaffold platform at the end of the then single-decker West Stand'.

The inventive Sieveking had two brilliant ideas to make life easier for the fledgling commentator, in addition to keeping him on his toes by putting up a notice which spelt out in large red letters 'don't swear'. He produced the first squared plan of the field by which readers and listeners were enabled to follow more clearly the progress of the game (by looking at a chart in the *Radio Times* – hence the expression 'back to square one'). But his greatest piece of intuition was to get hold of a blind rugger enthusiast from St Dunstan's and to invite him to sit in front of the open window of the commentary box so that Wakelam could explain the game directly to him and so 'perhaps lose some of my very natural stage-fright'.

On 15 January Wakelam was one of the main attractions at Twickenham as press photographers recorded him sitting in the box with Sieveking, who made the opening announcement, a 'number two' called Charles Lapworth, whose job was to fill in the pauses (which he did with various prompts, some helpful, some – like 'Do they always play with an oval ball?' – fairly inane except to the uninitiated) and the listener from St Dunstan's. Ten minutes before the kick-off the first ever BBC sporting outside broadcast took to the air, and it is clear from all accounts that Wakelam rose splendidly to the occasion. His own description hints at his natural enthusiasm for his subject, a quality which all commentators need if they are also to enthuse their listeners: 'Straightway I forgot all my nervousness and stage fright, all my previously and arduously collected phrases, and all the, as I thought, snappy and pithy expressions which I had anxiously culled from the leading sports writers of the day. I was so wrapped up in following the flight and fortunes of the ball, and so desperately keen to keep my St Dunstan's man fully informed, that I raced away like a maniac.' . . . Or like a rugger player. When he turned his hand to the more sedate game of cricket he was to be, as we shall soon see, less content and less successful, but he had instinctively grasped, nonetheless, some of the essentials of running commentary. The first, as he implied when saying how all his preconceived ideas had quickly been forgotten in the heat of the moment, was to be himself and to react to events as they happened, using his own words. The second was to keep level with, or even marginally ahead of, the ball, starting to speak of the man passing the ball in the fraction of a second before he actually passed it. Likewise in cricket the good commentator will give the listener a moment of expectant silence between the delivery of the ball and its receipt by the batsman.

Arlott describes Wakelam as a 'natural talker with a reasonable vocabulary, a good rugby mind and a conscious determination to avoid journalese'. Swanton reckons him almost the equal of Howard Marshall as the best of the early commentators.

Neither of these two household names of the 1920s and 1930s was, however, the first to make a cricket commentary in England. That honour fell, not – as has always, with one exception, been reported before – to Pelham ('Plum') Warner, but to the cricketing parson from Essex, the Reverend, later Canon, F. H. Gillingham.

There was considerable, and general, scepticism about the whole idea of providing running commentaries for so 'slow' a game as cricket. Thus the *Manchester Guardian* of 1 April 1927:

CRICKET BY WIRELESS

A correspondent considers (and not without reason) that the BBC proposal to broadcast cricket matches during the coming season is one which suggests several difficulties: 'In sharp contrast to the sporting subjects hitherto selected, such as the Grand National and various football matches, cricket, being essentially a leisurely game, lacks the dash and wealth of incident necessary to sustain the listener's interest. How a succession of maiden overs or prolonged "sitting on the splice", producing somnolence in the actual spectator, can be made interesting to the unseen listener is not clear. Stoppages for bowling changes and at the fall of a wicket would be another problem. And what about bad weather? Perhaps some rainy afternoon this summer we may hear from 2ZY an announcement to the effect that, play being impossible at Old Trafford, the Station Orchestra will render "Jardins sous la pluie" or some other item appropriate to the occasion.'

On 14 April, the *Daily Herald* was rather more tongue-in-cheek:

BRIGHTER BROADCASTING!

The suggestion has been made that the BBC should broadcast a cricket match on the lines of the Grand National and Boat Race successes. But the BBC have turned it down. They may be inclined, however, to consider the brighter possibilities afforded by the Chess Championship, with its hair-raising gambit crises – or a billiards match, with all its accumulated excitements – the click of the balls, the controlled calm of the players as they ask for the rest, and the delirious palpitations of a miss-in-baulk!

(Or, as you say, possibly they may not.)

How uncomfortably surprised that writer would have been by the subsequent popularity not only of ball-by-ball cricket but also of televised snooker.

The BBC were, in fact, determined to experiment with cricket and, as the *Daily Telegraph*'s 'wireless correspondent' reported on 25 April, it was to Gillingham that the honour of being the first genuine ball-by-ball commentator on cricket in England fell.

The Rev. F. H. Gillingham, the well-known Essex cricketer, yesterday informed me that he had consented to broadcast a descriptive narrative on the cricket match between Essex and New Zealand at Leyton on 14 May. He had no idea yet, he said, as to the method of procedure to be adopted. The experiment will be watched with interest, for it is obviously impossible to broadcast anything but short periods of description of a three-days' cricket match. The problem will be exactly how to anticipate the most exciting parts of the game. I have already referred to the method adopted in Australia, where the narrator is stationed on the ground and telephones through to the broadcasting station at an interesting point in the game, the programme being interrupted to enable him to come on the ether for a limited period. This may be the method followed at Leyton; it is difficult to see how else such a broadcast could be made thoroughly interesting. I understand also that on Saturday evening 7 May, Mr P. F. Warner will, from the studio at 2LO, give an eye-witness account of the day's play between Surrey and Hampshire at The Oval.

Warner, so distinguished in other fields, was, as we shall see, something of a disappointment as a cricket broadcaster. The contents of his cricket talks seem, from those which survive, to be interesting and well put together, but by all accounts he had a quiet, apologetic voice on the air and his delivery was most aptly described as 'melancholy'. Whether he had inhibitions about doing running commentary, or the BBC after a voice test had any inhibitions about him, is not certain. But, as the *Manchester Guardian* reported, something more ambitious than a close-of-play report was planned for Gillingham:

The first cricket match to be broadcast in this country will be that between Essex and New Zealand at Leyton on 14 May. Recognizing that to attempt anything like a full description of the play, as in a football match, would be boring in the extreme, the BBC intend to deal with the event piecemeal.

From 2.10 until 2.20pm the commentator, the Rev. F. H. Gillingham, will give the names of the teams, describe the condition of the ground, and so on. After that there will be four five-minute descriptions of the actual play – from 3pm to 3.05pm, 4pm to 4.05pm, 5pm to 5.05pm and 6pm to 6.05pm.

At 6.45pm there will be a general summary of the play. In addition listeners may be switched over to the ground at any period when play is specially interesting. The microphone will not be placed in a hut, but will be fixed at the left-hand corner of the balcony outside the secretary's office in the pavilion. In this way a background of subdued noises will be obtained, though the noises will not be sufficient to interfere with the broadcast.

As the day approached the doubting voices continued to be raised. The *Morning Post*'s 'wireless correspondent' actually made a statement which would seem incredible to the listeners who 62 years later would be up in arms at the suggestion that ball-by-ball commentary might be interrupted by rival sports events. The lack of continued action in the game, not to mention its length, he roundly declared, made a running commentary 'impossible'. This gave the pioneer, he felt, several problems:

In Australia the difficulty is overcome by broadcasting only the interesting or exciting parts of the game, interrupting the ordinary programme, whatever it is, for this purpose.

Mr Gillingham's task, as the organiser of such a broadcast, is likely to prove difficult. He will have to bear in mind that the music-lover heartily disapproves of his music being interrupted by the voice of a cricket commentator.

The BBC may well consider the advisability of not attempting any running commentary, even on the lines suggested by the Australians. It would be appreciated by many listeners, particularly the music lovers, if the BBC arranged for a critic on the ground to give a talk at regular intervals of short duration.

But the national newspapers were saying nothing that the BBC itself did not believe. In an article in *Radio Times* designed to prepare listeners for the new phenomenon, an unnamed author described the idea of broadcasting the game as 'a new departure, an experiment and something of an adventure'. 'Cricket', he added, 'is one of the slowest games in the world. Obviously to broadcast a running commentary on a cricket match by the method used for Rugger Internationals, the Cup Final, the Boat Race or the Grand National would be impossible. What will be done is this. A microphone will be installed in the pavilion at Leyton and the BBC's narrator will watch the whole of Saturday's play from there. At fixed times (between dance band music) he will broadcast an account of the state of the game ... In this way, it is hoped, listeners will be given the gist – not to say the cream – of the match. They will not have to sit through descriptions of maiden overs and wait while the batsman sends to the pavilion for his cap.'

One can understand, I suppose, both the BBC's caution and the press's scepticism, which amounted almost to cynicism. After all, the newspapers would have seen the BBC as a potential thief of readers, and likewise cricket ground authorities must have feared what the new medium would do to their attendances. But it is odd that no one seems even to have considered the possibility that in the hands of a communicator of talent, knowledge, imagination and enthusiasm, the very slowness of cricket might actually lead to a more interesting 'listen' than is possible in hectic sports which call only for speed of eye and tongue on the commentator's part. The wheel was to turn a complete circle when, in the 1980s, Test Match Special was as popular (if not more so) when rain had stopped play and the familiar free-for-all of Brian Johnston and his team could begin with no interruptions from any play on the field.

Gillingham, though described by one of his Essex colleagues, T. N. Pearce, as a 'very nice chap and a terrific preacher who would have his congregations absolutely with him', was certainly no Arlott or Johnston. Perhaps, given the more *laissez-faire* approach to broadcasting which became rapidly evident after the Second World War, he might have become so; nevertheless, although he became a Canon and chaplain to the King in 1939, having been a curate in Leyton during his playing days for Essex, he was clearly only a limited success in his broadcasting role. He later seriously blotted his copybook by reacting to an interval for rain by filling in time with his observations on various advertisements around the ground, a heinous BBC sin in the days of Lord Reith. Nevertheless the newspaper comments about his inaugural effort were not all adverse. 'C.M.' of the *Edinburgh Evening News* reported on 16 May 1927:

So far as can be ascertained the broadcast on Saturday of the cricket match between the New Zealand XI and Essex from Leyton was particularly successful.

The three short transmissions, with the Rev. F. H. Gillingham as commentator, were excellent. Cricket broadcasts up to Saturday were of course only confined to results in the evening news bulletin.

Alas, on the same day, the *Western Daily Press* was less generous:

Those who were not out in the open on Saturday, and, either from choice or necessity, remained at home, were able to hear for the first time a wireless description of a cricket match. The game chosen was Essex v. New Zealand. To those particularly interested in either team the experiment might have had some interest; to the general body of listeners, however, it was deadly dull. Nor, in the writer's opinion, was the programme of dance music, comprising, in the main, fox-trots, of which a large proportion of wireless licence-holders are more tired than to the hackneyed tunes of a barrel organ [sic]. The experience has been useful, however. It has shown that a clergyman, though a good cricketer, is not necessarily the man for rattling off a bright, racy description of the game. It has proved, too, that unless there is a G. L. Jessop batting, running – crawling is the most applicable term – comment on a cricket match will be a waste of good ether. Unfortunately there is no player in first-class cricket able to emulate the deeds of Mr Jessop. The prevailing slogan is safety first – as, for instance, the display of Holmes, the Yorkshireman, against Gloucestershire on Saturday – 18 runs in an hour and three-quarters.

A DREARY PROSPECT

As already mentioned in 'Local Notes' the Cardiff station has arranged to broadcast the opening afternoon's play of the Glamorgan and Gloucestershire match in July. One almost shudders at the thought of a couple of hours' description of the game if Dipper and Smith settle down to a characteristic display of defensive batting. But even the two Gloucestershire men would present an easy problem for the describer when compared with some of the old stone-wallers of the past – Barlow of Lancashire, for instance, who once batted an hour and twenty minutes and then was out for a 'duck' and on another occasion, two hours for twelve runs; or Scotton, the Australian, who in a memorable match against England took five hours and three-quarters to score

90. If it had been possible for cricket to be broadcast 30 years ago, the man at the microphone would have had something worth talking about, especially if he had been at Harrogate when Mr G. L. Jessop scored 101 in forty minutes. There are, of course, occasions when a wireless account of a cricket match would be an irresistible attraction for people all over the country – a Test match with Australia, for instance – but the ordinary county game would, in the writer's opinion, appeal to a very small proportion of licence holders, and as it is, Saturday's experience proved, among other things, that all who are interested in cricket – and who is not? – will continue to look to the evening and morning newspapers for all they want to know about first-class matches.

Despite such forebodings, and perhaps agreeing with the Bristol paper's confident assertion that *everyone* was interested in cricket, the BBC continued to cover county matches in 1927, and the *Manchester Guardian* showed considerably more enthusiasm for the idea than hitherto when they learned that this was not just to be a southerly affair. Northern cricket enthusiasts, the paper reported in May, would be pleased to learn that it would not only be from Lord's and The Oval that cricket matches would be broadcast: 'The Manchester Station hopes to give the fullest possible expression to local cricket activities during the summer months. One such broadcast has already been arranged. On Whit Monday – the second day of play – special descriptions of the Lancashire v. Yorkshire match will be relayed from the Old Trafford ground. At intervals of half an hour listeners will be switched over from the studio concert to the cricket ground, where for five minutes at a time they will hear a description of the progress of the game.'

This prompted 'Cricketer', Neville Cardus no less, to a characteristically witty piece of anticipation on 25 May 1927:

'Good afternoon, everybody. This is Old Trafford calling. We are about to broadcast for you a few of the more enthralling episodes of today's Lancashire and Yorkshire match. Hallows and Makepeace are batting.

'Matches between Lancashire and Yorkshire are notoriously exciting. In these Homeric encounters we feel the blood flowing of the old feud between the rival roses. The Red Rose is for Lancashire and the White Rose is for Yorkshire.

'As you have already been informed, Hallows and Makepeace are batting. The score is Lancashire 51 for no wicket. The match has been in – ah, um – progress for two hours. A great crowd sits round the famous green sward and watches in silence whilst the run stealers flicker to and fro.' (The latter quotation, it may be known, is from a poem by Francis Thompson. No account of a cricket match is complete unless a reference is made to these soul-stirring lines.)

'Before lunch Hallows hit a boundary, and Lancashire are now 57 for none. The great crowd still sits in silence round the historic sward. Kilner bowls a maiden. Hallows and Makepeace are batting. Macaulay bowls a maiden. Rhodes relieves Kilner at the city end and bowls a maiden.

'Macaulay is attacking bitterly from the Stretford end. The state of the game is Lancashire 67 for no wicket. Waddington misses a catch from Robinson.' (! – !! And a voice: Will the listener in the Pudsey area kindly attend to his receiver which is oscillating badly?)

'Hallows, who hit a boundary before lunch, is taking off his sweater. He is apparently about to hit another. Listeners will be advised of the event in due course.

'Lancashire 76 for none, Hallows and Makepeace are still batting. The game is at the present moment delayed while Rhodes attends to a fly in the eye of Dolphin. The cheers you now are hearing announce that the fly has been successfully extracted. The match is being resumed.

'Emmott Robinson has just appealed for leg before wicket. You probably heard him. Lancashire 80 for no wicket. Tea.

'The players have come back to the field. Kilner bowls a maiden. And a no-ball. As I speak an aeroplane is flying over the ground. It is Captain Lindbergh, half-way through his flight round the world. He will be there long before this match is over.

'And now we have finished our broadcast of the Homeric contest between Lancashire and Yorkshire and are taking you from Old Trafford to London, where you will hear Jake O'Heim's Blue Bird Orchestra playing "Oh keep your heart a-beatin' for me, baby". Good evening, everybody.'

Such was his reverence for cricket, Pelham Warner would probably have considered Cardus's piece amusing but also a mite too cynical. Warner himself made the first broadcast from Lord's at the Middlesex v. Nottinghamshire match in June, an event thought worthy of the attention of the *North Mail and New-castle Chronicle*, which reported:

The BBC announces that Mr P. F. Warner will be the commentator at the Middlesex v. Nottingham county championship match played at Lord's county ground.

At 2.15 today, from a portable hut erected on the practice field side of the ground, Mr Warner will give a ten minutes' résumé of the morning's play. From 3 to 3.5, 4 to 4.5, 5 to 5.5 and 6 to 6.10 he will call the score and describe the progress of the game, which he will summarise when stumps are drawn.

In the intervals in the commentary music will be broadcast from the studio by the Wireless Military Band and two solo singers. If any especially exciting event occurs in the course of the game the description will be inserted into the afternoon programme, which will be broadcast from London-Daventry and other stations.

Warner made his broadcast from the roof of the 'bowlers' room' by the clock tower, which would hardly have been an ideal commentary position. An MCC archive of 25 April reports that the committee had been asked for a place in the pavilion or, failing that, the bowlers' room. Another minute on 4 May states that 'correspondence with the BBC was considered. Permission was given to use the position in June instead of May.' Presumably plans to cover a match before the Nottinghamshire one had been cancelled.

The following chapter relates Warner's experience as a commentator, but his first effort was successful enough for there to be further commentaries by him from Lord's in 1927 on the Eton v. Harrow and Oxford v. Cambridge matches.

Extensive perusal of the MCC archives has failed to unearth why, when Howard Marshall first made his reports from Lord's, he was obliged, unlike Warner, to do so from outside the ground. But in advance of his famous commentary on the Lord's Test of 1934, agreement had been reached for a more satisfactory broadcasting position. The MCC minutes reveal the following:

12 February 1934
The Secretary reported:

'That the BBC had applied for the use of a room in the hotel on the occasion of the Test match in which to broadcast accounts of the match. (Approved at a rental of twenty-five guineas.)'

12 March 1934
The Secretary reported:

'That the BBC had offered twenty guineas as rental for the room in the hotel on the occasion of the Test match. (Accepted.)'

The 'hotel' was, of course, the Tavern, erected at Thomas Lord's instigation in 1867-68 and dismantled, along with the adjoining dining room, clock tower, boxes and stand, exactly 100 years later to make way for the new Tavern Stand.

Another of the pioneer commentators of 1927 was Teddy Wakelam, who on 6 August joined forces with Alan Howlland, then on the staff of 'Children's Hour', for the Surrey v. Middlesex match at The Oval. It was to be in many ways a fateful broadcast, for although he was considered to have done well – and was rewarded with another commentary a fortnight later, Surrey v. Yorkshire, only for the match to be cancelled because of rain – Wakelam himself simply did not enjoy the experience. In his autobiography he no doubt recounts the mood of the occasion from his point of view more accurately than he does the facts of the match itself:

From the lunch interval up to six o'clock we were allowed the use of the air whenever we chose to demand it, the idea being that we should come over for periods of roughly 15 minutes every time play grew really exciting, we ourselves, of course, to determine the correct moments. It was a dull and cheerless looking day when Alan and I took up our position in the little cubby-hole adjoining the scorers' room ... and sadly the character of the cricket closely resembled the character of the weather. Surrey were batting, and having lost two or three quick wickets, including that of Jack Hobbs, they were not unnaturally putting up the shutters against a very steady and well-directed Middlesex attack. Andy Sandham was holding the fort, perhaps one of the best men possible in such a case, but the rate of scoring, from a broadcasting point of view, was most distressing, and the desperately exciting incidents on which we had gaily dwelt beforehand were absolutely non-existent. But we had to do something, for the commentary, of course, had been advertised, so every hour or so we went over, to recite with dreary monotony: 'Durston is now bowling from the Vauxhall end – there he goes, running up to the wicket, over goes his arm. Sandham has played the ball back to the bowler – Durston has fielded it, and is now walking back to his bowling mark – there he goes again, running up to the wicket', and so on almost *ad nauseam*. Actually Sandham that day played a great innings for his side, getting, if I remember right, 115 in four and a half hours.

He did *not* remember right and this is highly significant. Sandham in fact made 121 on a dead slow pitch which had been under water. Hobbs was *not* out all that cheaply and two or three quick wickets did *not* fall! Hobbs was actually out for 33 with the score at 50, whereupon Sandham and Andy Ducat put on 184 for the second wicket in two and a half hours – better than a run a minute. *Wisden* describes Ducat as giving 'a most attractive display'.

How can one explain such careless reporting by a man renowned for his accuracy in other sports? The painful conclusion is that Teddy Wakelam did not have, and probably never had had, his heart in that particular job. It is easy to judge him by modern standards, with all the received wisdom of inventive commentators like Marshall and Arlott, and to say that Wakelam really should have been capable of making something interesting to listen to out of what must have been an excellent stand by Sandham and Ducat. But he was working in a completely new field only a few months after the first outside broadcast commentary and his task was extremely difficult. Perhaps if the blind man from St Dunstan's had been there he would have found ways of varying his description of Durston running in to bowl: his eye would have strayed towards something interesting in the crowd; he would have commented on Sandham's technique against the rising ball; noted the contrast between the lofty Durston and the diminutive Sandham, or pondered the significance of the game in the context of that year's Championship. But it is obvious that he did not. That his exaggeration of the difficult nature of the cricket he had to describe that day, in an autobiography written only eleven years later, was a deliberate deception is highly unlikely. It is much more probable that he exaggerated the difficulties in his own mind and that his memory was being selective to ease his embarrassment.

Shortly after this, Lance Sieveking moved on to the drama department and was replaced as head of outside broadcasts by Gerald Cock. The following sentences by Wakelam strongly suggest that as the first established commentator he was decidedly influential in persuading the new incumbent that cricket commentaries were simply 'not on': 'That afternoon put paid to cricket for a long time as a real "running commentary" sport, and when it reappeared in the programmes, in the capable hands of Howard Marshall, the method of putting it over had considerably changed and the present system of several eye-witness reports interspersed with very short and very occasional ball-by-ball commentaries, was inaugurated. In Australia, of course, they do it ball by ball all day, but then cricket is a religion to almost every inhabitant of that great Dominion.'

Wakelam briefly returned to cricket when he took over from Marshall for the Tests of 1935. He relished the social side of the cricket 'circus' but disliked his onerous BBC duties. But for some years his deep reservations were shared by many, including a correspondent in the *Daily Record and Daily Mail* who, writing on 27 June 1927, may be said to have summed up the contemporary mixture of general apathy and hostility towards cricket commentary in Britain:

HOW NOT TO DO IT

It was pointed out to the BBC when the idea of broadcasting descriptions of cricket matches was mooted that only in very exceptional circumstances could such a 'stunt' hope to achieve popularity. With that charming disregard of the obvious which characterises the wireless authorities the broadcasts have been made so numerous that Saturday afternoons are nearly as boring as Sunday afternoons, which is saying a lot. Of yesterday's pathetic offering I will say only this – that the Radio Dance Band should be given a long holiday, and that the match grounds be given a miss while the holiday is being taken.

Such attitudes only make the later development of Test Match Special, to the point where it has become something of a national institution, all the more remarkable.

One thinks of the BBC as having a monopoly of the airwaves in the 1930s, but then as now they had considerable rivalry from commercial radio and this extended to the coverage of Test matches in Australia, which the BBC had been slow to exploit itself considering the immense public interest. Although in the 1936-37 series the BBC gave a daily résumé of each day's Test play at 8am, they were upstaged by Radio Normandy, who engaged Bill Ponsford to send two cables towards the end of each day's play. These were collected from Paris by none other than Roy Plomley, later to immortalize himself through *Desert Island Discs*. He, in turn, rang them through to Charles Maxwell, later the producer of *Take It From Here* and other successful BBC light entertainment shows, who was operating for Radio Luxemburg, equally eager to upstage the BBC. For Radio Normandy the cables were embroidered and broadcast down a crackly line from France by Bruce Anderson, an Australian cricket enthusiast on the staff of the IBC (International Broadcasting Company). Roy Plomley recalled in *Days Seemed Longer*:

At 7.45, when Bruce's voice came on the air from Paris, going down the line to Fécamp, the notoriously poor quality of the French line made it indeed sound as if he were speaking from 13,000 miles away. Of course, one snag was that he did not know the current score, and he had to keep skating round that until, at eight o'clock, I was able to give it to him by taking it from the opening of the BBC transmission, which I received on a radio in the next room. It was an innocent deception, which doubtless gave pleasure to many – and it certainly kept the Radio Normandy listening figures up.

Such 'innocent deception' is still practised today by commercial stations in Britain who simply monitor the BBC commentaries from overseas Tests for their own sports and news bulletins. In one sense the wheel turned full circle, however, when in 1989 the West Indies Cricket Board, through their agents IMG, sold rights for the 1989-90 series against England to Rupert Murdoch's Sky television and sub-let a package of highlights to the BBC.

CHAPTER THREE

An Uneasy Relationship:
Plum Warner and the BBC

Much has been written in recent years about Sir Pelham Warner, whose devotion to cricket during a long life became legendary. By general consent, the good he did by far outweighed the bad. The story of his association with the BBC demonstrates his determination and ambition as well as conveying a good deal about BBC attitudes in the pioneering days.

Never a wealthy man by comparison with many of the great amateurs of his time, 'Plum' Warner pushed his luck at the very outset of his somewhat mercurial and very occasional career as a broadcaster during a friendly exchange with his fellow Old Rugbeian, John Stobart, who was then the BBC's Director of Education. Writing on 20 March 1925, Stobart asked Warner if he would contribute a fifteen-minute talk on the 'prospects of the cricket season', on 9 May at 10.10pm. 'Our ordinary fee for Sports Talks', he added, 'is five guineas.' Warner replied immediately to say that someone of his expertise was worth more than that (and indeed, in theory at least, so he was).

Stobart's response on 25 March is a marvellously typical BBC letter. From the outset the great organization has always had to watch its expenses: the budget has been limited by the licence fee, and BBC administrators have always had something of the cost-conscious accountant in them. Moreover they have all been aware that the innate vanity of every broadcaster – at least of every willing one – enabled the BBC to offer employment at generally lower rates than Fleet Street, certainly until commercial television came along to broaden the market and force up the salaries of the best performers. In the circumstances, therefore, Stobart's reply represented a minor triumph for 'Plum':

Dear Warner,

If you won't tell anyone, I will make it eight guineas. But, as we have one or two Sports Talks every week, it won't do for us to make a precedent. We do, as a matter of fact, get the most tremendous experts in various departments of sport for five guineas, or even less. In fact, I confidently expect that you have [sic] once spoken to the microphone you will want to form the habit of it yourself.

Yours sincerely,
For The BRITISH BROADCASTING COMPANY Limited

Director of Education.

Like Ted Dexter, who resigned as *Sunday Mirror* cricket correspondent when he was appointed Chairman of the England Committee in 1989, 'Plum' Warner found himself faced with a possible conflict of interest in 1926 when as Editor of *The Cricketer* he also became chairman of the England selectors. His talk after the first day of the second Test against Australia warmly praised the achievements of the team he had chosen and not least those of the captain Arthur Carr, words which were to embarrass him later that season when he and his committee decided, in controversial circumstances, to dispense with Carr on the disputed grounds that he was not match fit and to replace him with A. P. F. Chapman.

Nevertheless he continued to be used as the BBC's most regular supplier of cricketing talks, and on 1 April 1927 – only two months after the successful experiment with running commentary at Twickenham – there came an invitation from Hugh Brennan, a senior director of programmes, which gave Warner (still somewhat unwisely insisting on a little useful publicity for

The Cricketer) his great opportunity to make the sort of impact which Wakelam had made in rugby union:

Dear Mr Warner,

I very much regret that I shall not be able to be present tomorrow night when you are broadcasting your talk on the Argentine Tour. I am, there-fore, writing to know if you could possibly lunch with me at Simpson's-in-the-Strand, at 1.15, on either Wednesday or Thursday next week, to discuss the question of Running Commentaries on Cricket matches.

We hope to broadcast a running commentary on the Surrey v. Hampshire Match at the Oval on Saturday afternoon, May 7th, and we should be very pleased if you could undertake to do this. It would take very little of your time, as the actual broadcast would only be from 2.30 – 3.15 and from 6.0 – 6.30, and there would be no continuous commentary. I can best explain the method we propose by discussing it with you.

Mr Young was here yesterday and said that, in the preliminary announcement of your talk tomorrow night, you would like to be announced as 'Editor of *The Cricketer*'. It does not seem necessary to us to give any such introduction, as you are naturally already very well known and, in fact, we generally make it a rule to avoid references of this kind. I could not quite gather from Mr Young's remarks whether you were really particularly anxious that this should be done. I feel that such an announcement would be rather like introducing Mr Winston Churchill as the author of a recent history of the War.

I should be very much obliged if you could leave a note for me on your arrival, letting me know which day would be convenient for you to lunch with me, and suggesting an alternative date if neither of my suggestions are convenient.

Yours very truly,

Programmes.

It would be interesting to know exactly what transpired at the lunch at Simpson's-in-the-Strand, which remains a favoured venue for cricket club dinners to this day. Brennan's letter is ambiguous on the question of running commentary. Such a term would in modern parlance mean what it says – continuous ball-by-ball description, but, perhaps aware of Warner's misgivings in this respect, Brennan in the same paragraph went out of his way to assure his mildly prima-donna expert that 'there would be no continuous commentary'. It was Warner's misfortune, since with his vast knowledge of the game he would have been a most interesting conversationalist, that no one in the BBC had the foresight at this stage to suggest that there should be two men in the commentary box to bounce ideas and observations off one another.

In the event a compromise was reached and the less ambitious idea of a close-of-play report, rather than any direct reports from the ground, was agreed. At 7.25pm on Saturday 7 May, two hours before E. M. Forster read one of his short stories in the series 'Writers of Today' ('In E. M. Forster', boasted the *Radio Times*, 'the list of notable writers who have broadcast from the London Studio gains a distinguished accession'), Warner finally gave BBC Radio's first eye-witness report of a cricket match. *Radio Times* gave him a suitably prominent billing:

7.25 THE START OF CRICKET

The first day's play in the SURREY versus HAMPSHIRE Match at The Oval, described by Mr P. F. WARNER

The first cricket match of the season began at The Oval today, when Surrey met Hampshire in the County Championship. The opening of the season at The Oval is always an event for Surrey supporters, whose number is legion and whose enthusiasm is unbounded, and for London's cricket fans generally. This evening all of them who could not enjoy the match from under the shadow of the historic gas-works will be able to hear it described by one of the most famous of living cricketers, who is also one of the most expert critics of the game. Mr P. F. Warner's playing career ended only a few years ago, and in the course of it he won a worldwide reputation as a batsman and captain. Besides captaining Middlesex for many years, he led MCC teams in South Africa and in Australia, where his teams won the Ashes in 1903-4 and 1911-12.

One has to read between the lines somewhat, so many BBC archives having been lost in wartime fires, to establish both why Warner himself was not asked to do running commentary again and also why the whole idea was shelved until the advent of the masterly Howard Marshall.

The correspondence between Pelham Warner and the BBC which survives shows that he continued to make life rather harder for himself than was necessary:

9th June 1927

The Editor,
'Morning Post',
Palmerston House,
E.C.

Dear Sir,

We received a telegram from Mr P. F. Warner early this afternoon saying that he could not broadcast on Saturday unless he was announced as the *Morning Post* Cricket Correspondent.

Subsequently Mr George Bigwood, of your Staff, came round to see us, and we informed him that there would not be the least objection to announcing, just before Mr Warner begins his commentary, the fact that he is your Cricket Correspondent.

Mr Bigwood asked us to let you know in writing that this would be done, and we shall, therefore, assume, unless we hear to the contrary, that you will not raise any further objection to our availing ourselves of Mr Warner's services.

Yours faithfully,

Programmes.

Such fastidiousness on Warner's part was unwise given that the BBC producers were beginning to come to the conclusion that he was not in any case doing much to further the art of cricket broadcasting. When Teddy Wakelam was used in his stead, Warner rang Lance Sieveking to protest that the game needed interpretation from someone of greater cricketing experience. Hugh Brennan tactfully begged to differ:

Dear Warner,

I have just come in and have been told the gist of your telephone conversation with Sieveking this morning.

In any case I was just about to write to you about the Cricket situation. Capt. Wakelam put up quite a good show last Saturday from the point of view of our people here, who seem to require not so much a critique of the game as an exact narrative of what is taking place. Whether the general public liked this or not it is difficult to say, as they so seldom express their views on this point. Capt. Wakelam has, of course, nothing like your knowledge of the game, but he is certainly an expert in the art of narrative, and as our people here seemed to like his work he is being given another trial on the Surrey v. Yorkshire match on Saturday week.

That will probably be the last cricket commentary of the season. We have taken up pretty nearly every Saturday afternoon with a commentary of some kind, and it is felt that the non-sporting section of our listeners should be given a chance. Besides, if we discontinue Cricket Commentaries for a time we shall learn if they were really appreciated by the ensuing correspondence.

I think that your commentaries appeal very much to a certain number of listeners, as the letters you received testify, but there are many people who object to Cricket Commentaries as such, no matter how well they are done. They feel that there is not enough excitement in the game.

This does not mean that we shall not require your services again for talks on Cricket, in fact I should very much like you to do a retrospect of the season on Friday, September 2nd at 7.25 p.m. I realise that the season will not quite be over then, but I have no other free dates until some time later. Also I hope that you will be able to do a talk on the South African Prospects just before the team starts.

In conclusion I should like to thank you once more for your kindness and hospitality to me on so many occasions.

Yours very sincerely,

Programmes.

P.S. At the moment of writing, a talk at 7.25 p.m. on September 9th has fallen through. Would this suit you better than the 2nd?

In May of the following year, the persistent Warner got in touch with Brennan again. This time the reply was unequivocal enough for there to be no doubt:

It has been decided not to do any running commentaries of cricket matches this year, as although there is certainly a demand for this sort of broadcast it is very small and hardly large enough to justify the necessary time and expense. As you will remember only Saturday afternoons are available, except in special circumstances, and most cricket enthusiasts are then either playing the game themselves or enjoying themselves out of doors in some other way. For the more important matches we may devise some system of reporting, but it is all rather in the air, so it would be best to fix up your arrangements without any thought of us.

Brennan then added unstated insult to the injury by continuing:

Colonel Philip Trevor is doing a few cricket talks for us as we have discovered that he has an exceptionally good broadcasting voice. I am afraid that this decision will more or less knock on the head my official visits to Lord's and The Oval, but still I hope that we shall meet there when I can get away merely to enjoy myself.

On Warner's file Brennan wrote the damning verdict: 'melancholy delivery'.

Characteristically Warner did not give up. He waited until he heard of a change in the BBC Outside Broadcasts staff and got in touch with Seymour de Lotbinière, then number two to Gerald Cock. With that fairness but firmness which was to make him such an outstanding head of OB's, 'Lobby', of whom much more will be related in the next chapter, spelt out the truth with some courage considering that he was writing to a former England captain of very high repute. Warner replied that 'if I am a good enough cricket authority to speak on cricket all this fuss about my dossier of four years ago seems out of place'.

Lobby agreed to 'abandon researches into the past' and asked

Warner, by now restored as chairman of selectors, to talk about the side he was planning to send to Australia the following winter. In June he did so, correctly mentioning Larwood, Voce, Allen and Bowes as the likely fast bowlers on the tour. Warner's broadcast was well received and he wrote to Lobby saying: 'I am glad my melancholy has gone forever. Everyone was very nice to me and I hope I will be asked again.'

Alas, the newly acquired BBC favour did not last long. A letter from Lobby marked 'personal' was sent to him at *The Cricketer* on 18 July 1933:

Dear Mr Warner,

Thank you for your letter of July 17th. I can quite understand how inopportune the 6.20 eye-witness accounts of cricket matches must seem to a great many people who have the chance of watching and playing cricket on a week-day afternoon. But the timing is not so awkward, perhaps, for the working man, particularly in the provinces, where he can very often get home by 6.15. In any case it is a matter of putting eye-witness accounts in at 6.20 or not at all.

I would rather leave your postscript unanswered. The fact is that we feel you do not quite do yourself justice in your cricket talks. You have such a unique store of material to draw on, and yet you do not make as much of it as we should like. A broadcast talk needs a special technique, and differs considerably from the literary article. This, I know, sounds rather unkind after all the help you have given us, and the anxiety you have always shown to meet our wishes, but I think it is best to be frank about the matter. I am afraid we were rather disappointed with the West Indies talk. We feel it was an opportunity missed.

I am sure you will realise that from the personal point of view I very much dislike having to say all that I have said.

Yours sincerely,

S. J. de L.

From time to time there continued to be contacts between the BBC and Warner, notably in 1937 when the OB organizer Roger

Wilson wrote to the MCC Secretary, Lt.-Col. R. S. Rait-Kerr, asking for guidance on how the Corporation might best commemorate the 150th anniversary of the premier club. A fifteen-minute talk on 28 May was suggested and Wilson was unwise enough to ask 'whether your committee would care to suggest a possible speaker or speakers'. 'We should also welcome suggestions from your committee', he added, 'about the kind of material that should be included. Probably the bulk of it ought to be historical retrospect, but you might think it worthwhile to get people with long personal recollections to contribute two- or three-minute pieces, for instance on the one hand a member and on the other a groundsman.'

Col. Rait-Kerr's response was described by Wilson in an internal memo as being 'cool and unhelpful', very different from the situation fifty years on when, with MCC's role diminished and the BBC's extended, the Bi-Centenary committee on which I sat was anxious to ensure that the Anniversary was given due prominence on radio and television.

At any rate, soon after the exchange between Wilson and Rait-Kerr, the possibility of a talk by Warner was raised, probably by Warner himself. Wilson sought agreement from the Director of Talks, Richard Maconachie, before turning Warner down on the grounds that comments on his broadcasting had been 'uniformly adverse' since 1932.

Poor 'Plum'! Unwisely persistent though he might have been, he was not a man to bear grudges and during his time as acting MCC Secretary during the war, when he devotedly battled to keep cricket going at all levels, he gave an interesting and illuminating scripted talk with Arthur Mason on Victor Trumper (1942). Later he was only too pleased to help Alastair Dunnett with suggestions as to who should contribute to a series of four-minute cricket talks. He himself did the last one on 'The Spirit of MCC'.

CHAPTER FOUR

Howard and Lobby

Hobbs and Sutcliffe, Larwood and Voce, Hutton and Washbrook, Trueman and Statham, Compton and Edrich, Lindwall and Miller, Gregory and McDonald, Lawry and Simpson, Rae and Stollmeyer, Hall and Griffith, Greenidge and Haynes: partnerships are an important part of cricket, and in cricket broadcasting it was the teaming of Howard Marshall and Seymour de Lotbinière which was to form the basis of ball-by-ball commentary in Britain. Each, Lotbinière as producer and Marshall as commentator, was both a pioneer and a master of his art.

Howard Marshall was born on 22 August 1900 and went to Haileybury – for whom he played at Lord's – and Oriel College, Oxford, where he won a rugby Blue. He became an inspired captain of the Harlequins, trained as a journalist and joined the BBC in 1927. He established himself quickly and within a decade, made famous by his cricket broadcasts, he was the premier Outside Broadcasts commentator, chosen to describe the Coronation of King George VI in 1937. Already he had held the post of Assistant News Editor of the BBC and he was held in such high regard that during the war he became first Director of Public Relations at the Ministry of Food from 1940 to 1943, then Director of War Reporting and a war correspondent. Amongst his most famous descriptions was the one from Normandy immediately after the D-Day landings. In a busy life he married

three times, also worked as a Director of Personnel and Public
Relations in the steel industry, wrote several books on subjects
including sport, housing and exploration, and co-founded
Angling Times and *Trout and Salmon*. A colleague at the
Ministry of Food spoke of his 'courage of conviction' and the
'wizardry of his personal charm' as he shaped public policy on
food and drink and taught Lord Woolton, Minister of Food in
1940–43, to broadcast 'with a professional flair equal to his own'.
A fellow member of the Savile Club, where 'amongst his literary
and artistic peers he held an honoured place', called him a 'shy,
immensely versatile man ... with a gentle compassion for
failures and down-and-outs'.

But his lasting fame rests in his deep, mellow, mellifluous
voice. Before Arlott it was the sound of summer, and one only
has to listen to those of his commentaries which survive in the
BBC archives (nine in all from 1934 to 1945) to know that he
would have felt entirely at home – and sounded entirely in place
– in the Test Match Special box today.

Burly and good-looking, Marshall was, as a broadcaster, very
much more than just a voice. For cricket and coronations alike
(he also described the 1953 coronation) he found exactly the
right pace of delivery. He was not, in fact, always up with the
delivery of the ball – which became one of the cardinal rules of
cricket commentary – but there was, as E. W. Swanton remembers, 'a balance in both his estimations and the language in which
he conveyed them'. He had a rich store of knowledge, both of
cricket and of life, an innate sense of when to use facts, or
'associative material' as de Lotbinière called it in his guidelines,
wit in both the sense of ready humour and alertness of mind;
and the observational qualities of a journalist and artist. (He
even drew some of his own illustrations for his fishing books.)

These were formidable gifts which he used to full advantage.
Above all they enabled him to go beyond the scripted broadcast
and to 'ad lib' – essential, of course, for any commentator.
Perhaps the main reason for the failure of Teddy Wakelam at
cricket was that he had insisted on writing down his reports. He

lamented in his autobiography that it was hard work writing down lengthy reports and very difficult to adjust if there was a sudden change of fortunes in the last few minutes before his lunch, tea and close-of-play reports. If he had trusted himself to 'ad lib' from basic notes, he would no doubt have found it easier. This is something which most broadcasters have to learn. But it is essential of course for the reporter to be knowledgeable; otherwise the 'ad lib' becomes an embarrassing series of 'ums' and 'urs'. Not so with Marshall, whom Swanton cannot imagine ever 'fluffing'.

Opinions about him are unanimous. Thus Arlott in *Test Match Special*: 'He was eminently suited to cricket: he had a deep, warm, unhurried voice, a respect for the hard news of event, and a friendly feeling towards the men who played the game.' Or Brian Johnston in *It's Been A Lot Of Fun*: 'His slow, deep, burbling voice came through loud and clear . . . I think it's fair to say that of all the pre-war commentators he would be the only one totally acceptable today, so good was his technique and his knowledge of cricket.'

The acid test of Marshall's genius was his ability to maintain the interest of the listener no matter how exciting or unexciting the cricket, made all the more remarkable for the fact that he was on his own, with no summarizer and, until he began to describe play for long periods, not even a scorer. It is an immense help, in dull or quiet moments of cricket (which, after all, is 'inactive' eighty per cent of the time), to have another person to bounce ideas onto or simply to give the voice a rest. Marshall had no such assistance but he did have the good fortune to describe, during the Lord's Test of 1934, one of the most remarkable of all days in Test match cricket history.

Interest in the England v. Australia Tests that summer was intense, not least, of course, because of all that had become known about the Bodyline series some eighteen months before. For the first Test at Trent Bridge, *Radio Times* had billed only three 'eye-witness' accounts by Marshall: at the lunch and tea intervals and at close of play. In one of these despatches he caused a minor furore when he emphasized the skill of Bill O'Reilly by parodying the old song: 'As for the O'Reilly, you value so highly, Gorblimey O'Reilly, you *are* bowling well.'

Marshall guessed that the BBC received some 300 letters complaining of his use of the word 'Gorblimey'. It was, at least, some indication of the size and interest of the audience, and by the time of the Lord's Test the *Radio Times* was giving the Test series front page treatment. Although the magazine's cover for 15 June only guaranteed the same three eye-witness reports, the following edition promised that for the last two days of the match 'the Daventry National Programme may be interrupted between 12.00 and 17.15 and the other National programmes between 12.00 and 18.00 by commentaries by Howard Marshall from Lord's in addition to eye-witness accounts'.

Previous books touching on the development of cricket broadcasting have wrongly reported that he was not allowed to broadcast directly from Lord's in 1934. In fact he described in graphic yet gently underplayed style the collapse of the Australians as Hedley Verity took 14 wickets in the day. A transcript of the last three overs is analysed in the following chapter.

As I have mentioned, there was indeed a time when Marshall was not allowed, along with the engineers and their paraphernalia, within the hallowed precincts and was obliged instead to go round the corner to a house in Grove End Road, one which, according to the memory of the MCC archivist Diana Rait-Kerr (daughter of the former MCC Secretary), belonged to Harold Craxton, whose sister was chief oboist of the BBC Symphony Orchestra and whose son Anthony became well known for his production of television Outside Broadcasts. The house had a musicians' gallery and it may be that the joint MCC/BBC decision to find a proper broadcasting point at Lord's had something to do with the embarrassment of a conflict between a Marshall broadcast and a music lesson. The incident was recalled by Marshall himself in the *Radio Times*:

It was all bound up, this particular broadcasting experience of mine, with a small girl and a piano. Stumps had just been drawn on a very famous cricket ground at the end of a Test match, and I rushed to a nearby house to give an account of the play.

A microphone had been installed there in the window of a semi-basement room, and just as the red light was about to come on we heard, with startling clarity, the tinkle of a piano in the room above. Someone was practising scales with the utmost vigour, and essential though scales may be in a musical education, they form an odd background to a cricket commentary.

It was zero hour, though, and I had to begin my talk while one of the engineers went upstairs to silence the piano. I must admit that the scales were a little distracting. 'La-la-la-la-la-la-LA!' they went, with a triumphant thump on the last note, but suddenly, abruptly, they ceased. My friend the engineer had done his job, either by peaceful persuasion or a show of force. Anyway, I could now concentrate on cricket.

Not for long, though; for a moment later there was a clatter down the stone steps outside, and an exceedingly irate lady appeared, brandishing an umbrella. She peered at me malevolently. I gave her a nervous glance and went on talking. She tapped peremptorily with her umbrella handle upon the window-pane. I waved my hands at her hopefully, and went on talking.

Then she could bear it no longer. *Rap-rap* went the umbrella handle again, and 'Hi, there!' she shouted, 'how much longer are you going on for? My little girl's wasting her music lesson!'

A year or two later, Howard Marshall was back inside the ground, in a room at the top of the old Tavern, with Wendell Bill at his side to send back his cables to the ABC for their synthetic broadcasts. In another article written for the *Radio Times* shortly before the Lord's Test, Marshall described his approach to the task. Although he was talking essentially about the art of giving ten-minute summaries, as opposed to running commentaries, many of the problems and principles he expounded were similar to those which de Lotbinière would himself be crystallizing in a year or two's time:

Some people seem to imagine that the life of the cricket commentator is one long Bank Holiday. 'Lucky devil,' they say. 'I wish I had your job, just sitting in the sun, watching cricket and talking about it now and again.'

Well, I dare say it does sound rather pleasant, and I won't deny that I like doing it. For all that, it has its problems and anxieties, and I hope you won't think me ungrateful if I enlarge upon them a little.

It is obvious that cricket, with its many complications and technicalities, must be one of the most difficult games to describe briefly and accurately. Put yourself, if you will, in my place at the microphone, and consider what the job of giving eye-witness accounts entails.

First you have to remember that you are talking to all sorts and conditions of people; to the expert, for instance, who expects to be told just what the bowler did when he took Bradman's wicket, and to the man who has never heard of a top-spinner, but simply wants a lively description of the run of play and the general scene. There are, moreover, so many essential facts to be crammed into your brief ten minutes – the individual scores, the state of the turf, bowling changes and the placing of the field, the rate of scoring and the fall of wickets. It may happen that batsmen come tumbling out one after another, and then the commentator has to become a lightning calculator to keep track of events; it may be, on the other hand, that Woodfull and Ponsford stay in all day, which would leave the commentator with an uneventful story to tell.

Let us suppose, though, that wickets are falling fairly fast. A batsman, apparently well set, is caught at first slip. You note the time, the batsman's score, the total, the catcher's name, and then you begin to wonder just why the batsman did make that fatal stroke. Is the wicket crumbling? Is the ball beginning to take more spin, or has the bowler found a length? Is this a critical moment in the course of the game, a moment to be expatiated upon in your account?

It is so difficult to tell what is really happening out in the middle. The commentator must do his best to find out the facts; he must not, for instance, lightly condemn the batsmen for being unduly cautious when they have their own good reasons for treating the bowling with respect. Some slight variation in the condition of the pitch, unperceived from the pavilion, may make all the difference. There are signs that will lead the commentator to suspect such variations, but he must try to verify his suspicions.

A complicated game, then, and the trouble is that unless the eye-witness watches every ball throughout the long day he runs the risk of missing an outstanding incident.

I don't know how you would set about preparing your accounts, but I like to watch the game from different angles. I shall have a microphone installed at a convenient place on each of the Test match grounds; at Lord's, for example, the

BBC has a room at the top of the Tavern, near the scoreboard there, and a very good observation post it is. But I like to spend part of my time somewhere behind the bowler's arm, so that I can see what he is doing with the ball. And I always make a point of sitting in the crowd for an hour or two, so that I can catch something of the true atmosphere of the match.

I suppose I ought to settle down and take copious notes as the game proceeds, but I find that such strict attention to business makes my account stiff and formal. I content myself, therefore, with occasional jottings in a notebook and a record of the score, and after that I trust to luck at the microphone, and hope that I may be reasonably fluent.

It's easy enough, really, once you know the points to watch for, and have evolved some sort of system of your own for keeping the main facts clear in your mind. With the score-card and your notes before you, the microphone is forgotten, and you chat as you would to a friend who is interested in cricket. If you do stumble and hesitate now and again – I know I shall, and I hope you will forgive me – you do at least preserve spontaneity and a certain colloquial freshness of expression.

This year for the first time at least three accounts are being given every day – at the luncheon and tea intervals and at the close of play. This will inevitably lead to a certain amount of repetition, and without doubt it will add to the commentator's anxieties! Still, the great interest which is being taken in the Test matches clearly warrants the innovation, and there should be plenty of excitement before the fate of the Ashes is decided.

In fact, of course, the public were soon demanding more from Marshall, alone as he was with his microphone with neither scorer nor summarizer. For the third Test at Old Trafford he was given equal billing by the *Radio Times* with lawn tennis from Wimbledon, which was jointly (but separately) described by 'Captain H. B. T. Wakelam and Colonel R. H. Brand'. A military title was obviously an aid to authority! For the fourth Test at Headingley, *Radio Times* published a diagrammatical guide to field placings and then (after A. E. Lawton had had his opportunity to give eye-witness accounts of the Roses match in August) Marshall returned for the decisive fifth Test with an even heavier schedule. Programmes could be broken into for running commentary at any time, and the number of fixed eye-witness reports was increased from three to five.

Howard Marshall's boss in 1934 was Gerald Cock, who had taken over as Director of Outside Broadcasts in 1927 and who paved the way for the even more inventive de Lotbinière. Cock greatly expanded the range of OBs, taking in events such as the service at the unveiling of the Memorial Arch at the Menin Gate at Ypres in July 1927 and the service of Thanksgiving at Westminster Abbey for the recovery from serious illness of King George V two summers later. He presided also over the first Promenade concerts from Queen's Hall and lighter entertainments such as the Royal Command Variety Performance, first broadcast in 1927, or a Gracie Fields performance from *The Show's The Thing* in January 1930.

Despite working with only one programme assistant at the start in 1927 and with only five before handing over to de Lotbinière eight years later, he was described by S. A. Moseley in *Who's Who In Broadcasting* as the man who had given 'many realistic touches' to broadcasting and by Roger Eckersley (in *The BBC And All That*) as 'an indomitable worker'.

It was Cock who first employed not just Wakelam and Marshall but also John Snagge, Freddie Grisewood, Bernard Darwin and the Arsenal stalwart George Allison. For a long time the BBC was not permitted, for fear of adversely affecting attendances, to report or commentate on Football League as opposed to Football Association (Cup) matches, but Cock was a very successful negotiator with other sporting and entertainment authorities.

Seymour Joli de Lotbinière (pronounced 'Lowbinier'), known quickly to all who worked with and for him as 'Lobby', took over as Head of Outside Broadcasts in 1935. Of Huguenot origins, he was a towering figure both physically and mentally. He had grown to six foot eight and a quarter inches soon after leaving school at Shrewsbury and qualified as a solicitor before joining the BBC as a 'Talks' producer. He turned a penetrating and analytical mind to the questions of how the BBC should be serving a public for whom sport was a way of life and how best the commentators and reporters should be bringing major sporting events into the homes of the millions of interested listeners.

Within a year he was announcing a much more ambitious coverage of sport, with 'flashes from every type of sport played in the British Isles'. This was hardly an exaggeration. In 1936 the menu included soccer, rugby league and rugby union, cricket (including, as we shall see, village cricket), tennis, golf, horse and greyhound racing, bowls, speedway, boxing and even darts and pigeon racing. The Sports Service on the second Saturday in August featured, as its main events, Howard Marshall on the Test between England and 'All India' at The Oval; Harold Abrahams, the Olympic sprinting gold medallist, on the athletics match between the Empire and the USA; and P. G. H. Fender and C. B. Fry on Gloucestershire v. Notts and Middlesex v. Surrey.

One Saturday the following summer, Lobby experimented with 'Three Aspects of Cricket': running commentaries from a Working Men's Club match at Leicester, a league match in Staffordshire, and New Zealand v. Notts. Generally Lobby was looking for experts, although they had to be experts who could broadcast – hence the cold shoulder given to Pelham Warner. He was enlightened enough to decide that two of the major events of the following summer, the visit of the German Ladies' Hockey team and that of the Australian women's cricket team, should be described by women. Having successfully passed a test – she had to give a running commentary on a film – Marjorie Pollard, renowned already as a fine cricket and hockey player, was chosen for the job. She was, by all accounts, a great success. A letter-writer to *The Star*, A. Kitchener of Primrose Hill, stated: 'It seemed to me that she had modelled herself on Howard Marshall, with that smooth, suave manner; at any rate she was a lesson in accuracy and clarity to certain other sports commentators who were performing on the same afternoon. As a man, I must say I never expected to find women's cricket at all absorbing. But Miss Pollard quite reconciled me to the idea of women with bats in their hands.'

An extant recording of Marjorie Pollard, describing the England v. Australia Test match at Northampton in 1937, does, indeed, reveal her to have been an enthusiastic, knowledgeable commentator. Thus encouraged, she applied gentle pressure on the Outside Broadcasts department in subsequent years. On 9 May 1939, Lobby's chief assistant, Michael Standing, wrote in response to two letters from her, mentioning that Miss E. E. Helme would be broadcasting on the women's international golf match at Bramshot on 2 June. He added:

We will certainly try to fit in a women's cricket match during the season, but unfortunately our programmes have already been planned up to the second week in July, and your principle [sic] fixture after that date appears to be the Australian touring XI v. The Rest of England, which conflicts with the Second Test Match, to be played by mere males at Manchester! There are, moreover, several other sporting events that weekend for which we shall have to find space in our programmes, but we might be able to arrange for an afternoon of composite sporting broadcasts, in which your Oval match featured.

I myself am responsible for the 'At Home To Sportsmen' programme and, as a matter of fact, I am planning to introduce women's sport into these broadcasts, as and when important events bring it into the news. Perhaps if the series is still running, July 19th might be a good opportunity for a contribution on the subject of women's cricket. If so, I hope very much that you would be ready to take part.

You may also be interested to know that we have made provisional arrangements to broadcast a commentary on part of the Annual Demonstration given by the Women's League of Health and Beauty at Wembley, on June 10th.

I hope you will realize from this that we are not completely neglecting 'women in sport', but you will appreciate at the same time that there are a great number of long-established events with very large followings to which we must give first consideration, and which tend to limit, during the summer particularly, our activities in other fields.

A less wise Director of OB's might have turned up his nose at the idea of broadcasting women's cricket, but Lobby was a great one for experimenting and he saw no reason why the OB microphones should be limited to great events. The man who had made such a success of organizing the Christmas Royal broadcast from Sandringham was soon sending off Commander Tommy Woodruffe to a village cricket match. Woodruffe was and will forever be famous for his intoxicated broadcast from his old ship, HMS *Nelson*, at the Spithead Review of 1935, which led to the title of George Black's West End show at the Hippodrome, *The Fleet's Lit Up*. Anyone who has not heard it should try to listen to that marvellous demonstration of the dangers of drinking and broadcasting. A brief extract will, however, give a flavour, so to speak: 'The Fleet's lit up. When I say "lit up" I mean lit up by fairy lights. Is lit up by fairy lights. It isn't a fleet at all . . . the whole Fleet is in fairyland. If you follow me through . . . if you don't mind . . . when I say the fleet's lit up I mean the whole ship's . . . I was telling someone to shut up. The whole fleet's lit up . . . the ships are lit up . . . even the destroyers are lit up . . .' and so on. Happily, the broadcast from the famous village green at Tilford in Surrey (where many years later the village match from *England Their England* was filmed), was more of a success. The *Farnham Herald* of 1 August 1936 reported:

This is cricket as it should be played. The game started like this on the village green, and that is the place to see it today. I would rather be here than at the Test Match at Manchester. I like the setting here, too, with the oak trees around.'

It was with these words that Lieut.-Cdr. T. Woodroofe [sic], the BBC commentator who put the Tilford v. The Bourne match 'on the air' on Saturday, described the game to a 'Herald' representative. At the time of the conversation he was standing outside the old forge at Tilford. Around were a number of small boys, anxious to catch a glimpse of the interior of the forge, where BBC engineers were working at the control panel.

The broadcast created considerable interest, and there was a larger attendance than usual of local spectators. Visitors from away also turned up in considerable numbers, and there were probably over a hundred cars parked around the green, and also numerous bicycles. Seven microphones were in use –

two on the flat roof of the Barley Mow, where the commentator had his stand; two outside the inn, where the local 'critics' were assembled; one at the scorer's table; one beneath a near-by tree; and another beside the river to pick up the sound of running water. As we have already intimated, the control point was at the forge. From here the commentator's remarks were taken to Broadcasting House by a land line. The preliminary work at Tilford had been done by Post Office engineers, and one of these was assisting the two BBC engineers on Saturday.

Although the spectators had the best impression of the match, those who chose to listen in had, of course, the best impression of the broadcast. They were the only ones, for example, to hear the Tilford ducks on the air. Indeed, so loud were the ducks at one period, that there was a special message from the BBC in London to reduce their volume. They also heard the commentator's remarks about P.-c. Spiers, who was directing the traffic, and about the cows which strolled across part of the green at milking time. Such asides as these had as prominent a place as did the actual cricket, for the intention of the broadcast was not so much to let the public know how Tilford and The Bourne were faring, as to convey the true atmosphere of village cricket.

Altogether, there were three broadcasts. The first was approximately from 3 o'clock until 3.15, the second, again of about fifteen minutes' duration, was round about 4 o'clock, and the third was for about fifteen minutes from 5 o'clock onwards. In the first something was said about each of the teams, and the opening play was given up to the time the first boundary was scored. At the 4 o'clock broadcast, the fall of the third Bourne wicket was described, and then the players left the field for tea. Cdr. Woodroofe was left with about seven minutes to fill in with no play in progress. However, he rose to the occasion nobly, and the minutes soon slipped by as he described the surroundings and related a few stories about village cricket, although he had an added embarrassment in that the players, on reaching the Institute, took the opportunity of listening in to his remarks. The final broadcast was confined almost entirely to a commentary on the play.

Cdr. Woodroofe's style was essentially light and humorous, and those who listened in will probably remember his amusing asides more than they will the actual game. For example, it will no doubt be some time before local people forget his encouraging remarks about Eddy's bowling (both as to its effectiveness, and the length of time for which he bowled), and his reference to Knight of The

Bourne ('a young fellow with curly hair, who doesn't wear gloves'). The 'flappers' who tried to photograph the commentator as he was speaking into the microphone, and who heard him tell the world of this little incident, will also remember the event. And so will those who heard him speak of the small boys who could be seen playing on the wicket with a tennis ball whilst tea was being taken, to say nothing of the friends of the young couple who had arrived by motor bicycle and instead of watching the game had their backs to the match.

Many people have been asking how Tilford came to be chosen for the broadcast. It came about through Mr S. Fry, son of the famous cricketer, C. B. Fry, and a member of the BBC staff. Having heard of the beautiful setting of the Tilford ground, he wrote to Mr H. Clifton (secretary of the Tilford club) and arranged the broadcast.

This unusual broadcast also survives in the BBC sound archives. It is amiable and slightly zany, with the sound effects including a motor bike as well as the ducks, but although his reputation as a general sports commentator was well founded, it is clear, from listening to recordings, that Woodruffe had less of Marshall's easy command at the microphone. Despite this, he was to share, with Aidan Crawley and Teddy Wakelam, in the television commentary on the 1939 West Indies Test at The Oval, a year after Wakelam had made the first ever television cricket commentary from the Lord's Test between England and Australia.

Incidentally Woodruffe was not the only accident-prone commentator in the 1930s. One hot day at Wimbledon Wakelam dropped a match onto a pile of old papers in the commentary box and the resultant blaze began to set fire also to the turn-ups of his trousers. He managed to continue his description of the Men's Doubles whilst stamping out the conflagration with his foot. It might have been really serious, for Wakelam later recorded that some rubber insulation mats had also started to ignite, causing the atmosphere in the tiny box to become almost stifling. The engineer just outside the box was blissfully unaware of the commentator's predicament, which says much for Wakelam's professionalism. 'I welcomed even more than usual', he wrote,

'Barotra's final smash which allowed me to close down and really sort things out properly again.'

On another occasion Michael Standing, an excellent club fast bowler whom Lobby began to blood as a commentator with Marshall (Brian Johnston remembers him as having 'a rather slow, languid drawl, well suited to the quieter periods of cricket'), was describing the Ceremony of the Keys in the Tower of London. He had just said 'And silence descends on Tower Hill' when a roar from half a dozen motor-cycles sent the sound effects needle off the dial!

Charles Maxwell, who got to know Standing well when he took over from the gregarious John Watt as head of Light Entertainments, remembers Michael Standing as a 'likeable, rather austere, very quiet man, a good broadcaster with a refined charm'.

Technical problems sometimes affected the cricket broadcasts too, especially, of course, from overseas. I well remember the reception from Australia in the 1950s and early 1960s when the voices of commentators like Alan McGilvray and Bob Gray would rise and fall like the breaking of the tide and one would often, indeed, feel like a swimmer submerged by the crashing wave, not quite sure where one was, whether the excited rise in the voice one had last heard heralded another four to Hutton or a wicket for Lindwall.

When transmissions broke down from Australia in the 1930s they made news. The *Manchester Guardian* of 2 February 1937, during the see-saw series in which England under G. O. Allen won the first two Tests only to lose the last three to Bradman's Australians, reported:

The failure of this morning's transmission of the Test match commentary from Australia was not caused by sunspots, as had been inferred in some quarters, but by interference from a telegraphic transmitter in Europe. This explanation was given to me at Broadcasting House today.

The increased prevalence of sunspots in the last few days has given rise to reports of interference with wireless reception, but a BBC official declares that

The pioneering days of cricket broadcasting: England v. Australia, 1934. Commentating at Headingley, Leeds, during the Fourth Test *(right)*, and the commentator's hut at Old Trafford, Manchester, during the Third Test *(below)*. The position (square-leg or cover-point) was far from ideal.

Above: Captain Teddy Wakelam, the first man ever to give a running sports commentary on the radio, broadcasts from Lord's in the England v. South Africa Test match in June 1935.

Below: The view from the commentary box during the same match: square to the wicket again!

Above: The television camera (right) on the roof of the Tavern 'hotel' at Lord's, England v. Australia 1938 (Second Test).

Below: Ground view of the cameras at Lord's, 1938. Here, Teddy Wakelam sat in the open on the top of the free seats at the corner of the stand at the Nursery End; his television audience numbered a few thousand.

Above: Television comes to The Oval, August 1938: England v. Australia, the momentous Fifth Test in which Hutton made 364.

Below: Sir Pelham ('Plum') Warner, of the 'melancholy delivery', gives a talk on the great Australian cricketer Victor Trumper in the 'Giants of Sport' series for the BBC Forces Programme, April 1942.

Above: A meeting at the East India Club, St James's Square, 1953. From left: C.B. Fry, D.R. Jardine, Rex Alston, G.O. Allen and A.E.R. Gilligan are planning a programme called 'Captains Confer' for the Light Programme.

Below: A Coronation conference, 1953. Round the table from the left: Audrey Russell, John Snagge, Howard Marshall, Henry Riddell, Charles Max-Muller (Head of BBC Sound Outside Broadcasts), Rex Alston, Jean Metcalfe and Alun Williams.

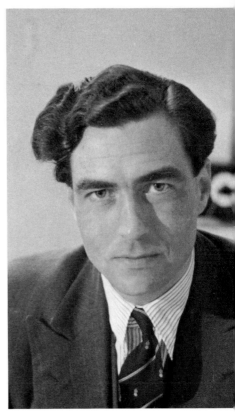

Above left: P.G.H. (Percy) Fender, one of the first television commentators, in 1952. He had already made a pre-war reputation as a sound commentator.

Above right: John Arlott at the BBC in 1946: 'a young man with flying black hair', in Rex Alston's phrase. A former Southampton policeman, he became a producer in the literary department of the BBC's External Services, where he succeeded George Orwell. His first commentaries described the 1946 Indian touring team's matches on the Eastern Service.

Left: Howard Marshall in 1953. Before John Arlott, his voice was the sound of summer. His cricket broadcasts in the 1930s made him famous and he was to become the premier Outside Broadcasts commentator and, later, Director of War Reporting and a war correspondent in World War II.

Above: The broadcasting team at The Oval (England v. South Africa) in 1951. From the left (standing): Steve de Villiers, Arthur Gilligan, Rex Alston, Charles Fortune and John Arlott. Sitting: statisticians Roy Webber and Arthur Wrigley.

Right: 'Meet the Australians', April 1953: Brian Johnston presents a kangaroo mascot to the Australian captain, Lindsay Hassett, 'on behalf of television viewers' at the Middlesex County Cricket School in Alexandra Palace.

John Arlott receives a message while waiting to go on the air with a running commentary on the Gloucestershire v. New Zealanders match in August 1949.

the situation has not found the BBC unprepared. The official explained that there are two distinctive sunspot effects. One is presumed to be caused by ultra-violet light radiated from bright hydrogen eruptions near the spots, which causes an abrupt 'fade out' of daylight communication except on the shortest of wavelengths.

To avoid this the BBC employs one of the shortest wavelengths in commercial use. The second effect is caused by the ejection of particles of the sunspots themselves. These particles are taken up by the earth's magnetic field and concentrated at the poles, and have the effect of giving good transmission of the daylight frequencies late into the night.

'In order to take advantage of the second of these effects, and anticipating the early February active group of sunspots,' the official said, 'we arranged ten days ago to decrease the wavelength used for Canada and the West Indies from January 31. This action has been more than justified, for there have been much better results than would otherwise have been possible.'

By means of simple equipment, and without in any way attempting to compete with Greenwich, the BBC makes its own investigations. The sunspots have nearly doubled their size in the last few days. They cover an area of about 3,500,000,000 square miles. This is less than one seven-hundredth of the surface of the sun, though it is eighteen times the area of the earth. They reach their maximum this year in their regular cycle of activity of 11.4 years, and this accounts for the prevalence of atmospherics and also probably for the world's heavy rainfall.

An official of the Government research station at Slough said to a reporter: 'A sunspot was due to pass over yesterday. It being a Sunday we were not on duty, but automatic recording apparatus was in use, and later today photographs will be developed, and we may learn something from them.'

Whether on duty on Sundays or not, the importance of BBC engineers to all Outside Broadcasts, from the earliest days to the present, cannot be underestimated. They are, of course, the *sine qua non* and from the start they were a group thoroughly dedicated to and interested in their work, striving always to produce broadcasts of the finest technical quality.

The chief OB engineer was H. H. Thompson, with R. H. Wood in charge of the London area, where most of the major events were held. He had a staff of twenty-five, easily the largest of the various OB regions.

Lobby, Thompson and Wood worked closely together. This was essential: in 1936 alone there were 2,857 outside broadcasts and a year later a typical week in Lobby's diary in June included:

Monday:	Yorks v. Kent, Bradford. Somerset v. Leicestershire, Frome (Michael Standing). Also pencilled in with a question mark was the Ladies' Open golf championship
Tuesday:	The same two county matches. (In fact they were not broadcast, which was a minor tragedy, for the match at Frome was the one in which Harold Gimblett made his famous début century.) King's College Madrigals – Regional (Freddie Grisewood, S. J. de L)
Wednesday:	Trooping the Colour. Regional TV and B Sussex v. Gloucester, Horsham (Howard Marshall/Michael Standing) Glamorgan v. Notts, Cardiff (P. G. H. Fender)
Thursday:	Sussex v. Gloucester, Glamorgan v. Notts Aldershot Tattoo, first night. John Snagge/Michael Standing
Friday:	Sussex v. Gloucester, Glamorgan v. Notts Richmond Horse Show Jumping. Major Faudel-Phillips
Saturday:	Women's Test Match, Northampton. Marjorie Pollard Belfast Athletics, Harold Abrahams Motor Racing: Nuffield Trophy, Crystal Palace.

Such events were carefully planned, although demanding much from all concerned, as Standing's quick journey from cricket at Horsham to the Aldershot tattoo later the same day demonstrates. He was the back-up both to Marshall at the county match and to John Snagge at the tattoo.

Lobby would himself either commentate or produce many of these events. He had shown his skill at the microphone when 'filling in' without repeating himself for forty minutes when Queen Juliana was late for her wedding at The Hague. But at the Coronation of King George VI in 1937 he supervised the entire six and a half hour broadcast from a control room behind the south wall of the Abbey, seeing nothing but hearing everything.

Every outside broadcast line had to be booked from the Post Office and tested by one of Thompson's staff in advance, once one of the hard-pressed OB staff had decided with the ground authority and the engineer a suitable broadcasting point.

By now the BBC had mobile vans from which broadcasts were possible, which came in handy at the Crystal Palace fire. It happened that Lobby himself had just returned to London in a recording van when the huge 300-foot twin-towered iron and glass building, constructed for the Great Exhibition of 1851, was seen to be on fire. The *Radio Times* related what followed:

At eight-thirty on a November evening the news came on the tape that fire had broken out in the Grand Hall. From Broadcasting House, the News Department telephones to de Lotbinière at his home. De Lotbinière telephones to Wood, also at home, arranges to meet him at an office at the other end of the Palace, goes straight there, and finds that their rendezvous has been burned to the ground. Also that all South London has turned out to see the fire and crowds are blocking the streets for miles around.

Meanwhile Wood has called at Covent Garden, where a broadcast has just finished, picked up two engineers with microphones and other gear. They get to Crystal Palace – ahead of the crowds. But it takes a lot to stop the OB engineers. They get their gear through to a café overlooking the fire; Wood begs the use of the telephone, gets on to the Post Office and arranges to use the telephone lines as a broadcasting line. Then the nine o'clock news sends more crowds to the Palace; de Lotbinière is somewhere among the crowds; he has already telephoned to Broadcasting House.

Even in a crowd it is easy to find a man six foot eight inches tall. Soon after ten o'clock everything is fixed up, and de Lotbinière and his microphone are established on the tin roof of a shed only a few yards from the burning Palace, ready to give Britain a first-hand description of the most sensational fire for years. Listeners who heard it will remember that it was a first-rate description, too.

A lot of hustle and a lot of worry, but as soon as it is over it is just another OB to be analysed and criticised at the next Monday morning meeting, and talked over between de Lotbinière and Wood, always looking back to see how things could have been better done. Though they have not much time for looking back, with plans still to be made for broadcasts two months ahead.

Lobby's description of the Crystal Palace fire is remembered by John Snagge as 'the model commentary for all time. He had a tremendous spectacle on his hands and like a good commanding officer he went straight in and carried on for about half an hour.'

The next Australian series in England, in 1938, demanded an even more thorough cricket coverage. By now MCC had granted the BBC a new commentary position, on the balcony above the visitors' dressing room, where W. W. Armstrong had carefully and irreverently carved his initials into the red brick. All five Tests were reported on the Home and Empire programmes, one of the six transmitters at Daventry being exclusively reserved for ball-by-ball commentaries each day from two o'clock until the close of play. The *Daily Telegraph* reported that special commentators were being sent from Australia and that Australian stations were co-operating with a large group of commercial companies to 'rebroadcast' the BBC's transmission. Running commentaries and reports of all the matches on the tour were broadcast on shortwave from Daventry.

Meanwhile Lobby and Standing were announcing an increased domestic service. The *Birmingham Post* reported:

General commendation no doubt will be accorded to the plans of the BBC's outside department for the broadcasting of commentaries on cricket. New methods of presentation of the national game are to be adopted, and the BBC hopes that in this fresh form the commentaries will be appreciated equally by the keen students of the game and its casual followers. Before the beginning of each Test match the microphone will visit several cricket grounds to enable followers of the game to get an insight into the form of both the Australian and the possible English players. The first match in this plan is Middlesex v. Gloucestershire at Lord's, on May 11, 12 and 13. P. G. H. Fender, the well-known ex-Surrey captain, will cover this, and on the same days A. E. Lawton, former captain of Derbyshire, will be stationed at the Aigburth Cricket Ground, Liverpool, to describe the play between Lancashire and Derbyshire. During the afternoon listeners will be connected alternately to the two commentators who will give a short appreciation of the situation and a description of the play at the time. Immediately following these matches, a more direct view of Test form will be given when P. G. H. Fender visits Lord's to report on the match between the Australians and the MCC. Also at Lord's later in the month a short visit will be paid to the tourists' encounter with Middlesex. For a final radio assessment of form there remains one important fixture before the first Test match on June 10, when England's 'Probables' and 'Possibles' face each other at Lord's on June 1, 2 and 3.

Howard Marshall will be chiefly responsible for the commentaries on the Test matches, but BBC scouts will be on the grounds to enlist the help of famous cricketers and well-known Australian supporters. No member of the Australian team is allowed to broadcast on the progress of the Tests. Cricket is a game of leisurely talk and endless reminiscence, and this aspect will be provided for by inviting celebrated figures in the cricketing world to the microphone. Should there occur a crisis, members of the general public, chosen at random from the crowd, will be asked to give their views on the situation. In short the radio impression of this year's games will give a sound picture of everything except, perhaps, the scenes in the refreshment tent.

The steady move forward towards the ball-by-ball commentaries on Tests which were to be expected and demanded after the war was not, however, universally welcomed. Witness the *Glasgow Herald* of 23 June 1938:

The BBC have apparently a touching faith in the geniality of British weather and in the 'brighter cricket' movement of which we hear so much and see so little. How else can one explain their decision to devote almost the entire National programme on Saturday afternoon to a running commentary on the second Test match at Lord's? For non-cricketing listeners there is, of course, the alternative Regional programme of orchestral and band music, serial reading, and the Children's Hour. Even the National programme is not to be given over exclusively to the mellow accents of the cricket commentator; Hurlingham and Wimbledon will be allowed to have their say, but not if the situation at Lord's is so exciting that it cannot decently be left to look after itself for a bare quarter of an hour.

It is possible, of course, that the play will be worthy of the honour the BBC have conferred on it. An innings by BRADMAN at his best or by McCABE in his Nottingham form might merit the undivided attention of commentator and listener alike. Perhaps – and this is a happier thought – VERITY may have another crowded, glorious hour such as enabled him to rout Australia in the corresponding match four years ago. But there is, on the other hand, always the grim possibility that the play will be more academic than exciting, that the batsmen, aided by the groundsman's art, will defy the bowlers' wiles, and not in any swashbuckling manner but in the stonewalling tradition of these matches. Then he will be a commentator of surpassing skill and persuasive eloquence and a listener of uncommon endurance who can maintain interest when even the crowd, with all their visual advantages, are growing restive.

The article reluctantly concluded that the non-stop commentary was probably worth trying 'as an experiment'.

A month later the *Glasgow Herald* was betraying its real interest in the commentaries:

Mr Howard Marshall very successfully dispelled one false impression on Saturday when he was broadcasting the Test match. One listener has often declared that if Bradman himself dropped dead at the wicket Mr Marshall would not allow even such a shocking happening as this to betray him into raising his voice or indicating that anything untoward had happened.

When Mr Marshall came on at 2.20 on Saturday he was describing an over by Farnes to McCabe, and the beautiful voice went easily on, soothing as sunshine to a holidaymaker taking it easy in a deck chair after a good lunch. And then there was a fearful shout as if Mr Marshall had swallowed his tonsils. 'He's out.' That said, Mr Marshall was his suave self again. But it was an astonishing moment. The prince of broadcasters had raised his voice.

In Australia there was no equivocation. The *Daily Telegraph*'s correspondent in Sydney reported feverish interest 'without parallel in recent years' and an increased sale of 20,000 for wireless dealers. The manager of Bunnerong power station, which supplied Sydney, said that forty extra tons of coal were being used each night to meet exceptional late-night demand for electricity from wirelesses. And a listener from Malvern, near Melbourne, wrote to the *Manchester Guardian* after the rained-off Manchester Test:

Sir, We in Australia shared your disappointment at the 'wash-out' of the third Test match. A large part of the population has been listening in on the radio to the Test cricket played so far. The time of the broadcasts is 8.30pm to 3.30am E.S.T. This covers Victoria, New South Wales, and Queensland and Tasmania. It is winter with us so fires and such-like are a necessary adjunct to comfort. It is quite an experience to motor home from a 'cricket sit-up party' in this city – almost every house well lit up, and smoke issuing from chimneys, and cars in hundreds getting home from similar festivities. All this round about 3.30 to 4am. The shortwave ball-by-ball broadcast from Daventry has generally been excellent from about 1.30am to 'close of stumps' here. Sorry the third Test such a wash-out.
Yours, C. Tyrrell Morres.

Come the fifth and deciding Test at The Oval, the nation, not to mention the Empire, was tuned in to Howard Marshall's commentary. It is no exaggeration to say that without it Len Hutton's 364 could never have become so famous.

Here was how the first master of cricket commentary described it:

And now Fleetwood-Smith beginning to bowl to him again. Here he comes, Fleetwood-Smith to Hutton. He bowls and Hutton just pushes it forward. This is the remarkable thing about Hutton. He's much more like an Australian batsman in a sense than an England one because he doesn't give in when he's passed a point, a hundred or two hundred or three hundred, or a record. He doesn't take liberties, and go mad and bang about. He just keeps steadily on. Here's Fleetwood-Smith again. Ah, there we are, there's the record, round the corner, and it's going for four down here, I don't think Hassett can possibly cut it off. Ah well, that's gone for four. And that is the record. The highest score ever made by an individual in any kind of Test match. It's beaten Bradman's record in England/Australia series, he's beaten Hammond's record in all kinds of Test matches and, there we are, he's on top of the world and the heartiest possible congratulations to him.

By 1938 Marshall had gained the assistance of a scorer, the Manchester accountant and former league cricketer Arthur Wrigley, so life became easier for him than it had been four years earlier when Verity whistled through the Australian batsmen on a drying Lord's pitch.

Otherwise little had changed other than the volume of cricket broadcasting and the gradual realization that cricket was, in fact, a sport which responded admirably to running commentary, its pace allowing for a discursive description which, in the right hands, was actually more subtle, interesting and enjoyable than the necessarily more frenetic commentaries on other sports.

The game was not confined to outside broadcasts. It appeared often under the heading of 'talks', involving luminaries such as R. C. Robertson-Glasgow, P. G. H. Fender and P. F. Warner. Amongst those who reported on matches for the news bulletins was Hugh de Selincourt, author of *The Cricket Match*, whose surviving scripted reports are models of their kind – succinct, lucid and informative.

Howard Marshall himself eventually opted out of cricket broadcasting but in his day, with no rivals from television, he was a bigger star than even his two greatest successors, John Arlott and Brian Johnston. The poet Edmund Blunden wrote thus of him during the war: 'And then on the air Mr Howard Marshall (his name may stand for all, the master name) makes every ball bowled, every shifting of a fieldsman so fertile with meaning that any wireless set may make a subtle cricket student of anybody.'

Marshall had that essential radio gift of taking the radio listener into his confidence and of simply talking to him or her: not preaching but passing the time of day. It was a secret handed down to the best of his successors, making radio the most companionable of media.

CHAPTER FIVE

Artists or Artisans?

At this point in the narrative, some remarks on the nature of commentary itself may be apposite. Cricket commentary, said the Head of Radio Three in the 1970s, the Austrian-born Stephen Hearst, 'has become an art form'. In truth perhaps some commentators – notably John Arlott – have been artists, others of us merely artisans. But all who followed Howard Marshall owe a great debt to the method he developed with Seymour de Lotbinière and which largely survives to this day. It might be interesting to look critically at one of Marshall's earliest and most famous broadcasts, the one from Lord's in 1934 when on Monday 25 June, after heavy weekend rain, Hedley Verity, who had already dismissed Bradman on Saturday evening for 36 as Australia replied with 192 for 2 to England's 440 (centuries by Leyland and Ames), bowled out Australia for 284 and 118, taking 14 wickets in the day.

The following piece of commentary lasts only six minutes 59 seconds for 18 balls, half of them by a fast bowler, emphasizing how much more quickly overs were bowled then than they are now. All alone in his box above the Tavern, with no summarizer, no scorer, the moustachioed Marshall, dressed no doubt in blazer and MCC tie, described the dénouement in a suave yet animated commentary, his deep voice at once both languid and urgent, with a sense always that, despite his relaxed tone, something exciting was just about to happen:

All the crowd seem to be making remarks. Naturally they are in high good humour: England are doing magnificently. Now here comes Bowes. He's running up, he's just going to bowl ... bowls ... Wall playing him with considerable difficulty but still playing him ... ironical cheering from the crowd, I don't know if you can hear it? Bowes walking slowly, purposefully back to his pile of sawdust ... just about to bowl ... Wall facing him ... up comes Bowes ... Wall shaping to play him ... Bowes bowls ... Wall staggers back on his right foot and plays a sort of nondescript cut at a ball outside the off-stump, misses it altogether and it goes thump into Ames's gloves.

This is desperate stuff. Wall doesn't seem really very likely to survive. Here comes Bowes again. Wall facing him. Bowes bowls and once more Wall lurches across his wicket at it, misses it altogether and Ames takes it.

Australia's chances are not looking very rosy at the moment.

Now we have Verity, who's done such great execution today, Verity bowling to O'Reilly, who has withstood the English attack for a considerable time and withstood it very nobly and in very difficult and depressing circumstances for him.

Ames is tapping his wicket-keeping gloves on. Here comes Verity from the Pavilion end up to bowl to O'Reilly. O'Reilly opens his shoulders and takes a crack. Bowes, as safe as a sandbank at mid-off, fields it. Verity going back to bowl. He's just going to run up to the wicket now. Ames crouching down behind the stumps. Great tension. Over goes Verity. O'Reilly plays him like a copybook. All in order with O'Reilly, he doesn't seem to be at all upset by the occasion. Perhaps he's regarding it now as rather a forlorn hope. Still he's playing very steadily, he's not beating about as he very well might being a natural hitter, he's playing very sound cricket. Leyland trotting up to retrieve the ball which O'Reilly had played gently and short to cover.

Verity is going back to bowl. Verity has got Hammond very fine and short on the leg-side close in. Here comes Verity bowling again. O'Reilly falling back into his natural habits, sweeps Verity away right round to the long-leg boundary, but Walters, racing in, just manages to stop the ball with his foot before it goes racing over by the Grandstand balcony for four and they only get two runs. That's more like the O'Reilly we knew at Nottingham, but if he does it very much to Verity I'm afraid it may prove fatal to him. He's waiting for Verity now: here comes Verity bowling. O'Reilly plays him perfectly correctly and safely. He's a difficult man this O'Reilly in a crisis as he showed this morning.

Verity. Verity had a very long spell. He's been bowling pretty well all day and bowling mighty well . . . hardly . . . hello, that was a near one, O'Reilly leant out to Verity, missed the ball altogether. It came off very quickly, Ames took it and whipped the bails off. There was a sort of universal appeal and once more the umpire shook his head; and Verity still remains to fight – O'Reilly I mean. Incidentally it's now over and Wall has to renew his somewhat tentative struggle with Bowes. Whether he will survive this over is a matter of considerable doubt, I should say. And Bowes is rolling up his sleeves; Bowes also seems to think it is a matter of some doubt. He's running up to the wicket now . . . Bowes is bowling – oh, and Wall has none of this sort of nonsense and plays him very steadily round to long-leg where Walters fields the ball and one run is taken. O'Reilly is now facing Bowes. The field is changing over. O'Reilly as you remember is a left-hander. The Australian total is 116 for 9 wickets, Australia have to get 156 to avoid the innings defeat.

Here is O'Reilly facing Bowes . . . Bowes is bowling . . . O'Reilly plays him perfectly safely . . . just goes down the pitch. Patsy Hendren doubles in, picks it up and throws it back to Bowes, who's walking back to bowl.

Well, this has been a day of surprises, and the tension is remaining until the last.

Now Bowes is coming up to bowl again. O'Reilly is facing him. Ooh, O'Reilly took rather a swing at that one. He didn't like the look of it very much. He missed it altogether. It was outside his off-stump and it went safely to Ames, who's standing in the pile of sawdust well back to Bowes. Now here comes Bowes bowling again, up he comes, one two three four five six seven eight, over he goes and . . . O'Reilly plays him quite safely square of the wicket and Walters runs in, picks the ball up and the batsmen take one run.

And now we return to the duel of the two fast bowlers. Wall facing Bowes. Well, Wall should know what a fast bowler can do. Perhaps he knows rather too well. Here he is, just waiting for Bowes. Bowes running up to the wicket, Wall facing him, left arm crooked, Wall plays this queer staggering stroke and plays him quite safely to extra cover. Bowes has Sutcliffe very close in at mid-on, silly mid-on and Farnes close in at short-leg. Wall is waiting, Bowes is bowling, Wall plays him quite safely to Geary in the gully – ah, to Verity I mean. Verity picked it up and is continuing from the Pavilion end.

Well, now the Australian total is 117 for 9 wickets. A very desperate position for Australia. They are surviving rather longer than we expected, as a matter of fact, after that sudden collapse between five and a quarter past when four wickets fell – four good wickets. Here comes Verity bowling to O'Reilly . . .

O'Reilly this time wasn't quite so sure – he played rather a half-cock shot off the edge to George Geary fielding at sort of backward point, rather deep. Now Verity is going back to bowl. Here he comes, O'Reilly facing him. Verity bowls. O'Reilly, with the straightest of straight bats, plays Verity towards mid-on but mid-on is very deep indeed and they get one comfortable run. And now Wall is facing the bowling and we rather wonder whether either Hammond or Geary or Sutcliffe, three slips very close in, may not snatch a catch off the edge ... Now here comes Verity bowling to Wall ... ooh he's out ... that's the end of the match. Players are pulling up the stumps. Wall played very gently and Patsy Hendren, at silly-point, took the catch and Australia are all out for 118; that is, if my arithmetic is not too bad, they are beaten by an innings and 38 runs ... The crowd are simply swarming onto the ground from all sides, the players have pulled up the stumps as souvenirs, the Australians are walking back and the police are trying to keep a line clear for the players to escape into the Pavilion. They're racing in. The crowd are swarming round the Pavilion gates there. An enormous crowd it is. Naturally they are very delighted. I'll just repeat that Australia are all out for 118 and England have won a most dramatic match. It's now ten minutes to six and we're having the usual demonstration in front of the Pavilion.

Listening to this commentary today a critic might notice that it took a little while for Howard Marshall to get round to giving the score, but, remember, he had no scorer to give such details as bowling figures, only the scoreboard opposite him on the Grandstand side of the ground with its limited information. There was a lack, too, of scenic description; we are not told from where the commentator was watching; what the weather was like, although the graphic mention of the pile of sawdust gives us a clue; how large the crowd was; or what Verity *looked* like as he ran in to bowl, though the speed with which he got on with the job gave the commentator less time.

Technically the commentary is also a little thin. We are not told that Verity was bowling left-arm orthodox or how much he was turning the ball, or that his success on this remarkable day owed so much to a drying wicket. But, remember again, there was no former Test cricketer at his side.

Where the commentary succeeded handsomely was in its general mien, and a typescript can only give a clue to this. There was, I repeat, an air of expectation throughout and the drama of a great cricket match has a much greater hold on the listener if it is under- rather than over-played by the commentator. Moreover the style was pleasantly conversational, a friend speaking to a friend not a lecturer to a pupil; and the voice was truly a mellifluous one.

It was in 1937 that Seymour de Lotbinière first put into print, in an article in *Radio Times*, his feelings on the art of sound commentary, and a warning that not all who felt called would be chosen:

The commentator's stock-in-trade is the spoken word, and as a normal person makes use of the spoken word every day of the week it is only natural that few people would think that they could not improve on the commentaries they hear. They might own that they could not write a waltz tune, or paint a picture, they might even own that they could not find a ready market for a written article, but as for commentary – well, a commentary, they would say, was quite different. After all, it was only a matter of describing what was actually happening and anyone could do that.

I, too, have sat at home and listened to a good many commentaries, and I have never heard one yet when I have not felt that I would have liked a little more of this or a little less of that, when I have not known that a comment or a word has been misplaced. But now I realize that it is no easier to do a first-class commentary than it is to write a first-class article. Just as a writer has to shape his words to his subject, so a commentary has to be built up in carefully chosen sentences, appropriately distributed between a description of the scene and the action, and an explanation of the occasion and of any sounds that may or may not be reaching the listener according to the quality of his set. And what is more, the commentator has no time to sit back and admire the finished product before submitting it to the public, any more than he has the chance of recapturing a word of anything he has once said.

I wonder what a painter would do if after painting part of a picture beyond recall, the rest of his canvas were suddenly to change its size. Yet that is a problem that is continually facing a commentator, and very often when the canvas is enlarging it is impossible to know from moment to moment how long the process will continue.

I believe that commentary work is as difficult as anything in broadcasting. It naturally demands a pleasant voice, a quick wit, an eye for the significant and a vocabulary with which to describe it. But the peculiar demand that it makes is for a brain that can cope with two or more things at once. A commentator must be able to describe one impression in neat smooth-running sentences, and at the same time he must be registering his next impression. He must be watching the broadcast as a whole to see that it is not losing shape, and he must be noticing what 'effects' are likely to be reaching listeners so that he can explain them and yet not talk through them.

It is true that a commentator must prepare a lot of material beforehand, but only so that he may have likely phrases ready to his tongue and a store of interesting associative material on which to draw. He should have plenty of notes – but he must have no script. For when a commentator begins to read, he might just as well be back in the studio. The only point of outside broadcasting is to bring the listener into touch with actuality – to transport him in space without any loss in time. The carefully prepared sentiment or the 'continuity' which, except for the state of the weather, is completed days beforehand is of no more use to the listener than a china egg to a pastry cook. Artificiality must find no place in outside broadcasting, however much room its absence may leave for the inept, the indiscreet and the insufficient.

So far I have tried to show that the task of the commentator is a difficult one, founding my arguments on theory rather than on practice. But consider that during the past ten years some hundreds of commentators have had the chance of actual broadcasts and several hundreds more have been tested and rejected.

Yet at the end of it all there are only, perhaps, half a dozen persons who would now be accepted generally as successful commentators. That should be practical proof that it is easier to criticize a commentary than to give one. But it is no sort of proof that all the available talent has yet been discovered. In fact, the discovery and training of new talent should be a first charge on the time of the Outside Broadcasts Department. But time is scarce and the Department wants all the help it can get from outside. The person who 'must look for something to do' or 'who played games at school', the person who has 'answered the office telephone satisfactorily for the past ten years', or who is 'chairman of seventeen committees' is no more likely to be a heaven-sent commentator than the man who can 'tell a good story' or whose voice 'carries clearly across the Serpentine'. Unless programme output is to suffer there is hardly time to acknowledge letters from all these aspirants, much less to see them and give them tests. As for the person who 'knows' that he could put across a first-class commentary, let him remember that that knowledge has probably been common to almost every commentator whom he has ever heard – however unsuccessful their performance.

If anyone wishes to become a commentator, let him first practise under broadcasting conditions – or the nearest he can get to them. He must set himself a time limit for his commentary and he must keep going for the full time. He must speak aloud, and he must be listened to 'blind' by someone who is not likely to be unduly sympathetic. And finally, his success with the 'blind' listener must be measured against the best commentaries heard on the air and not the worst.

If the would-be commentator proposes to broadcast a sporting commentary, he must be an expert on the sport concerned and, for preference, well known to its followers. His time must be more or less his own and he must be prepared to undergo at least one closed-circuit test before he can graduate to a real broadcast. If on this test he does not appear to be capable of anything out of the ordinary he must accept the verdict with a good grace and realize that whatever the circumstances of the test – whether they were unusually easy or unusually difficult – those listening will have made the appropriate allowances.

Every person who reaches the stage of a closed-circuit test can rest assured that if he shows talent he will be given a chance of using it. Good commentators are much too scarce and closed-circuit testing is much too irksome for the Corporation to allow anyone who shows promise to be allowed to go to waste.

The art of the 'sound' commentator is scarcely ten years old, and it still has a long way to go. But there may not be much time left for its normal development, as television will soon be making a different demand on the commentator, and, I believe, a lighter one.

In the meantime, if only for the sake of 'sound' listeners, commentaries must improve. Old-established commentators must adapt themselves to advances in technique and new commentators must be found to cope with the ubiquitous 'visits' of the microphone.

It was typically far-sighted of Lobby to foresee the different demands that television would bring, although curiously enough it is radio, not television, which has practised the art of 'lighter' commentary, certainly as far as the BBC is concerned. The point is proved by the fact that Brian Johnston was obliged (as we shall see later) to move from television to radio in the 1960s because his style was deemed to be too light-hearted and lightweight. Subsequent television producers have striven for a rather more informal approach in recent years, influenced not only by Johnston's immense popularity on Radio Three but also by the much chattier style which quickly developed in the Channel Nine commentary boxes when Kerry Packer moved into Australian cricket.

By the end of the 1930s Lobby had worked out a technique for radio commentary which has stood the test of time. He prepared notes for those applying for trials which his wartime successor Michael Standing also passed on and which, in turn, Robert Hudson crystallized into the following 'Notes For Would-Be Commentators'. These he gave to me when I was first given a test soon after joining the BBC in 1970, and they are still, I believe, handed out to would-be commentators who are dedicated enough to study their trade:

The BBC would like to be able to give 'auditions' to all would-be commentators. This is not possible, owing to the number of applicants. It is accordingly suggested that would-be commentators should begin by testing themselves under the nearest they can get to broadcasting conditions, i.e. they must describe something which is going on in front of them, they must speak out loud, they must give themselves a set period of anything over fifteen minutes for their 'broadcast' and for preference they should have someone listening 'blind'.

If after practising on half a dozen different subjects, the would-be commentator is satisfied that he (or she) has the necessary ability for the task, he should write to the head of Outside Broadcasts (Sound) at Broadcasting House, W1, and state what tests he has undertaken and how successful he believes himself to have been. Every endeavour will then be made to give him a test at an early date. This test will probably be given before or after an actual broadcast, and if practicable a recording will be made for subsequent analysis and discussion.

Applicants must realize that they cannot be given a definite standard by which to estimate their success; but at least it can be said that they should compare their performances with the best commentaries which they may have heard and not the worst.

Some of the essentials of good commentary may be summarized as follows:

1. The setting of the scene and the description of the action must be woven into a continuous story and should not be dealt with in separate pieces.
2. The commentary must not be allowed to lose shape, even though things may be altering unexpectedly. This means:
   (a) that essentials must be dealt with as early as possible;
   (b) that plenty of good associative material must be available to fill in gaps.
3. Associative material, whether historical, expository or personal, must be introduced in relation to what is happening, and must never sound as though it might just as well have come from the studio.
4. A catalogue of things seen rarely constitutes good commentary. Description is often at its best when it is subjective rather than objective.
5. It is often more important to 'put over' the significance of the event described rather than the details of everything taking place.
6. Human interest and suspense interest are useful ingredients in a commentary.
7. A dramatic beginning and a neat ending are important.
8. 'Effects' must be given prominence and an attempt made to satisfy both those who do not want the 'effects' interrupted and those who would like them explained.
9. A commentator must be honest in describing what he sees, and should not read from a script. But this does not mean that he should not give a good deal of previous thought to the sort of situation that he may be called on to describe and the sort of phrase that he is likely to find effective.
10. The commentator must be well informed and should never get himself into the position of having to admit ignorance.
11. Commentary should be fluent and informal.
12. The commentator should have a good microphone personality, i.e. one that attracts pleased attention whatever his subject.

Twenty years on from my first commentary test, genially supervised at The Oval by Rex Alston and kindly but realistically appraised later by Robert Hudson in some such words as 'a good effort for a first attempt', I shall conclude this chapter with a few observations from my own experience about the technique of the job, adapted from a contribution I made to *Test Match Special*:

It hardly needs saying that anyone aspiring to commentate on cricket needs a true devotion to the game. The fraudulent 'cricket lover' will always give him – or her – self away. To be able to interpret a match fairly, a commentator needs to have played the game a good deal – how else can he identify with those taking part? – and obviously the higher the level played, the better, so the would-be commentator should play as much cricket as he can. Any cricket is better than none and, although age eventually wins, that remains true for those actually doing the job. For instance, a few seasons ago I found myself invited to captain West Surrey in the festival for club cricketers held each September at the headquarters of the county's cricket, an excellent idea. Although only a limited-overs match, it was a valuable reminder to me of all sorts of things one ought to be bearing in mind when describing first-class cricket; for example, just how marvellous it can be to bat on a good, professionally prepared pitch; how difficult it can be to sight the ball on gloomy days in large grounds with seating all round the perimeter; how out-fields which look dry from a distance can in fact be sopping wet; and how captains rely on their bowlers. The opposition needed 30 to win off the last two 8-ball overs, 18 to win off the last one, and 1 off the very last ball. I am afraid they got them! During those two overs I twice foresaw the possibility of a 4 being scored in two particular gaps in the outfield but twice plugged the gaps only *after* 4s had been scored there. But if that was my fault, deserving of criticism had there been someone watching from the commentary box, the dropped catch in the outfield by the long-on who saw the ball too late and let it carry over his head with two balls of the match left, was crucial. And whose fault was that? It was a salutary reminder to be as sympathetic as possible when comfortably placed behind a microphone.

So, even to become a commentator – let alone a good one – you need luck, determination, a genuine love of cricket, and the will and ability to play the game as often as you can. You must also know and remember the history of cricket, if you are to place any performance you are describing into its proper context, as well as having a thorough knowledge of the laws of the game and of any special regulations applying to whatever match is being played. An awareness of the topical significance of the game in question and as close a knowledge as possible of the players, their characters, records, and methods are also important. This is another way of saying, really, that you have got to know what you are talking about. Again, the listener will soon spot someone who doesn't.

To know cricket inside out is essential, but in itself still not enough. Much more goes on at a cricket match than just the game itself, especially in a Test match, and the greater the education, both worldly and academic, of the commentator, the more interesting and rounded his description of events is likely to be. Good commentary is more subjective than objective: simply running an eye round a cricket ground and describing the landmarks in order to 'fill in' between the delivery of one ball and the next is often, for example, less effective than some relevant diversion, the type in which Brian Johnston specializes. Commentating is not just the ability to use words effectively to describe a scene; it is also a personal interpretation, a process of thinking out loud: the more interesting the thought, the more interested the listener is going to be. Above all, the process should be natural. If it suddenly strikes you that, say, St Paul's Cathedral is glinting in the sunshine in the distance, by all means say so, but *because* it has just struck you that this is so, not because a little voice inside says: right, now I will go round the ground and tell you everything I can see.

The art of 'natural' cricket commentary has been greatly aided in recent years by the more even flow between commentator and 'expert' summarizer who was once religiously called in at the end of each over, often to state the obvious about the six balls just past. Now he may take up, at any convenient moment, a theme or a technical point; he may be reminded of an anecdote, or digress on any relevant topic.

Some of these things will come only with experience, but the would-be commentator needs first to master the nuts and bolts of the job. It is, after all, the first duty of any ball-by-ball commentator to give the score, say who is batting against whom, to describe every ball and to up-date the score at least every time a run is scored and at the end of each over. Moreover, although the casual listener might not care too much whether Emburey is bowling off-spin with a five-four field or leg-spin with two slips and a gully, the knowledgeable listener does want to *know* what the bowler is trying to bowl, the length and direction of the ball being described, whether the stroke was played off front foot or back, etc, etc. Like all things in cricket, as in life, it is a question of trying to get the right balance – in the case of commentary the balance between correct, accurate description and entertaining and informative background material. So the requirement is not just to know cricket inside out, but also to know as much about as many other things in life as possible.

It would be easy to overlook the most important of all the necessities for would-be cricket commentators: a voice which is pleasing to listen to. Commentary stints are usually of 20 minutes' duration so the voice needs to attract and hold the attention – which does not necessarily mean it has to make you turn the volume down! A commentator needs to be easy to listen to over a long period and not therefore too monotonous, and he needs also to have some variety, some 'light and shade' in his voice. It is as important for the voice to be free of mannerisms that annoy as it is for the commentator to avoid clichés, constantly repeated phrases and whatever commentators' jargon happens to be in vogue at the time.

Recent ones to avoid have included: 'He's in all sorts of trouble'; 'We've got a game on our hands now' (or even 'a game and a half'); 'It has to be said . . .'; 'It's "day two" of the Lord's Test' (What is wrong with the traditional 'second day'?); 'Let me tell you something' (or 'I tell you what . . .'); 'He's giving 110 percent out there' (You can't give more than 100!); 'That's his third ton of the season.' (Cricketers *do* sometimes talk about a ton, but more often they refer to scoring a 'hundred', less often a 'century'. They also refer to getting fifty, never a 'half-century'. Hear 'half-centuries' from someone on the air and you may be fairly sure he has not played enough cricket to be talking knowledgeably about the game.)

It is very easy to criticize broadcasters, however, as any exponent of the 'art' is well aware. We all tend to repeat ourselves, usually fail to give the score often enough, too often have pet phrases which others may dislike, and, no doubt, all resort to the hackneyed from time to time. Therefore I shall now emerge from this glass-house and cease throwing stones!

CHAPTER SIX

◁▷

Wartime and Beyond: Arlott, Alston and Swanton

The value of cricket to British morale was fully appreciated by the nation's rulers, who allowed Lord's to remain a cricket ground, though the Nursery ground was requisitioned by the RAF throughout the Second World War. A great deal of cricket was played there, often before large crowds, with Sir Pelham Warner, acting as MCC assistant secretary, the presiding genius and inspiration. Although there were no more Tests on which to commentate, until the 'Victory' series between England and Australia in 1945, cricket remained a frequent subject of BBC broadcasts.

The main thrust of the OB department, both for engineers and reporters, was, of course, concentrated on the war effort and in particular, after D-Day, on the programme *War Report*, which went out nightly from Lower Ground Floor One Studio in Broadcasting House. Here all the skill which Lobby had encouraged came into its own and Howard Marshall, the man who had described Verity's triumph at Lord's in 1934, was heard, in the war in which Verity died, reporting from a Normandy beach: 'Our craft swung, we touched a mine, there was a very loud explosion, a thundering shudder of the whole craft, and water began pouring in . . . We were some way out from the beach at that point. The ramp was lowered at once, and out of the barge drove the Bren-gun-carrier into above five feet of water, with the barge settling heavily in the meanwhile. We followed, wading ashore . . . there was no sign of any confusion.'

Away from the action, however, cricket continued, not least as recreation for the fighting men, both at home and overseas in countries such as Egypt, where Squadron Leader Walter Hammond had been appointed to Cairo to promote sports facilities for the officers and men and where his own perform- ances at the Gezira Club were believed by Air Marshal Sir Anthony Selway to have done much for the morale of troops. In London the Australian Prime Minister, John Curtin, expressed a similar sentiment after one of his two visits to wartime matches at Lord's: 'Australians will always fight for those twenty-two yards. Lord's and its traditions belongs to Australia just as much as to England.'

The game's capacity to inspire nostalgia was reflected in frequent wartime talks by a variety of talented contributors. Bernard Darwin was amongst them, the distinguished golf correspondent of *The Times* distilling his wider biography of W. G. Grace into a short talk on the Home Service which ended thus: 'In 1914 just before the war he played his last innings of all. It was for Eltham against Grove Park on a fiery wicket. He made 31 and carried his bat. The last bowler who ever bowled against him could not get him out.'

In the same year, 1941, Sir Walter Monkton recorded a shorter piece on 'Fowler's match', the Eton and Harrow game of 1910, which began with as firm a punch as the one with which Darwin's piece had finished: 'It is 31 years ago this month that I made my nought in Fowler's match.'

Monkton did not mention that he had made a respectable 20 in the first innings, before Fowler, bowling slow right-arm off- breaks ('I can still see his tall, slight figure and the little moustache he wore, even as a schoolboy'), took 8 for 23 to win the match for Eton when Harrow had needed a mere 55 runs to win.

Harold Hobson, the theatre critic, was a particularly regular contributor of cricketing essays, usually with a historical slant and always with a nice, light touch. In one talk in 1942 he claimed Lord Frederick Beauclerk to have been the greatest cricketer who had ever lived, and in another he somewhat implausibly, but nevertheless charmingly, spun a theme round the phrase 'It isn't cricket', claiming that it had stemmed from a remark made in Pycroft's book *The Cricket Field*.

On the same Home Service in 1945 Compton Mackenzie contributed a masterly piece of cricketing nostalgia to mark the publication of the 82nd edition of *Wisden*. It was a brilliantly constructed broadcast, entertaining and accessible to all, despite its high-brow touches. He revealed how his own un-distinguished career ended when he split his hands in taking a catch at cover whilst playing for the Aegean Intelligence Service against HMS *Skirmisher* on the island of Syra in 1917.

Towards the end of the war a new voice began to be heard on Talks programmes, the voice of a Southampton policeman. Someone had spotted behind the strong Hampshire accent a well-read mind and sensitive character with an extraordinary flair for the English language; a born communicator.

John Arlott was born at Basingstoke in 1914 and brought up there. Clerk in a mental hospital and then a policeman, he left the force in 1945 as a Detective Sergeant to become a producer in the literary department of the BBC's External Services, succeeding George Orwell. His first commentaries described the matches of the Indian touring team in 1946 on the Eastern Service. At the age of 32 he had found his forte, and home listeners were introduced a year later for the first time to that deliberate Hampshire burr which was to become as famous to post-war cricket followers as Howard Marshall's mellower tones in the 1930s. To have an 'accent' was not the advantage to broadcasters which it may now be considered by some, and it once again reflected great credit on de Lotbinière that he should have spotted the touch of genius in the young poetry producer and without hesitation, it seems, given him the opportunity to commentate, in 1947, with Rex Alston and E. W. Swanton. From 1948 onwards Arlott was a fixture in the commentary box; he became the very voice of English summer.

Arlott retired from broadcasting in 1980, a figure of world renown. He was revered, even loved, for his extraordinary ability to find the right words to convey graphically the character of the cricketers as well as the drama and significance of the game they were playing. He retired to Alderney, in the Channel Islands, where he has lived happily with his devoted third wife, Pat, at a large and handsome house with the cellar and John's library-cum-study as the most important rooms, though kitchen and dining room come not far behind. It was part of the reason for his success that he was so well read; another, no doubt, that he was usually also well fed.

He recalls now with some awe the surprise he felt when he fell into cricket commentary at a time when his considerable wits were at their sharpest, though obviously he took time to mature in the techniques of commentary:

I'd just achieved my aspiration of becoming a poetry producer in the Eastern Service of the BBC when at a planning meeting of the Eastern Service in January 1946 the head of the Service, Donald Stevenson, said: 'Isn't there an Indian cricket team coming this summer?' (in a rather distasteful tone) and I said, 'Yes, there is.' 'Oh yes,' he said, 'I remember from your interview that you're keen on cricket. When do they start?'

I said: 'First Wednesday in May.'

'Where?'

I said: 'Worcester.'

'Where then?'

'Oxford.'

He said: 'How do you know?'

I said: 'Because I've got the fixture list in my pocket.'

He said: 'Have you ever done any cricket broadcasts?'

'Yes,' I said, stretching out the truth, because all I had ever done was a fifteen-minute talk about Hambledon.

He said: 'Would you like to do it?'

I thought someone had turned me upside down: it was impossible. So I gasped out, 'Yes'.

He said: 'Can you do your programmes as well?' and again I said, 'Yes'. So he sent me off to do them and when I got back on the Wednesday the Head of Service said, 'If you want to continue you can, you did all right, but you must get your programmes done.' So I missed about five programmes that summer and I ended up so broke it wasn't true but, you know for the others (Jim Swanton and Rex Alston) it was no great translation, they were somewhere about there but for me it was a sort of seventh heaven to be watching cricket and talking about it and being paid for it.

Rex Alston recalled that the Arlott style took some getting used to: 'At first I was not convinced by Arlott – nor was Lobby. He tended to talk too much. I remember on one occasion he got into a long dissertation about Jack Walsh (Leicestershire's Australian back-of-the-hand left-arm spinner) trying to explain the difference between the leg-break and the googly. But of course he had a gift for it and he was taken on full time after the series against South Africa in 1947.'

Arlott's contributions in 1946 for Indian listeners in the Eastern Service had consisted of short periods of commentary and summary, a task he shared with Abdul Hamid Sheikh, who did the same in Hindi. BBC World Service performs the same duty for its faithful listeners on the Indian sub-continent to this day. The interest there is immense and letters of appreciation are often effusive. Arlott must surely have received his fair share.

Television coverage of cricket, as a later chapter will relate, was now also to become a regular feature of the summer and for the first Test at Trent Bridge in 1946 commentary was in the hands of Brian Johnston and the multi-talented Aidan Crawley, although the latter was soon to become an MP and to move into a number of different fields in a varied, adventurous life. Indeed one can scan in vain his entertaining autobiography *Leap Before You Look* for any mention of his experience as a commentator on the Lord's Tests of 1946 and 1947, so insignificant a part of his life did it prove to be. Brian, of course, stayed to become an immensely successful and popular broadcaster, although, as we shall see, he crossed from TV to radio originally against his will. He also shared the TV box that season with E. W. Swanton, Dudley Vernon, R. C. Robertson-Glasgow and Percy Fender.

Rex Alston was the permanent fixture in the radio box in 1946, with C. B. Fry to provide erudite supplementary comments alongside the more down-to-earth Arthur Gilligan.

For several years after the war 'Jim' Swanton moved majestically from box to box, his wide vocabulary, deep knowledge of cricket and rich voice becoming as well known as his authoritative writing for the *Daily Telegraph*. He had already made his mark with Lobby before the war. Beginning his journalistic work for the *Evening Standard* in 1927 at the age of 20, he had by 1938 established enough of a reputation to write to Seymour de Lotbinière to ask whether, if he went to South Africa as a freelance in 1938-39 with MCC, the BBC would take from him some commentaries and reports and recommend him to the South African Broadcasting Corporation. Until then Swanton's broadcasting experience had been limited to occasional cricket talks on the Empire Service.

Lobby arranged a trial commentary under, as it were, match conditions and Swanton was assigned to the Surrey v. Lancashire game at The Oval, the two half-hour stints to be shared with P. G. H. Fender, who was covering Sussex v. Yorkshire at another of his old grounds, Hove. Swanton took the whole occasion in his confident stride:

It was the day when my old friend Henry Longhurst, whom I had once shared rooms with at King's Bench Walk, was being married and the service was at Dulwich, only about a quarter of an hour down the road from The Oval. After I'd shared my half an hour in the morning with P. G. H. Fender, who was at Hove, I took myself off to Dulwich to be an usher at my old friend's wedding. I got back to The Oval in good time and went and saw the captain, Monty Garland Wells, who, by prior arrangement, told me more or less what had happened. So I sat down in the tiny room by the scorer's box to the right of the pavilion and prepared to do my stuff. There was an engineer there but no scorer of course in those days and no one else to help one. I put my headphones on and in a mood of bonhomie I prepared to listen to Fender doing the first quarter of an hour. However, what he said was: 'Well, it's been raining here at Hove, and there's no point in staying down here, the score is this and now I'll send you over to the Oval.'

I had half an hour to do and even with a glass or two of champagne inside me it took some doing. Nine Surrey wickets were down and nothing was less likely than that Ted Brooks and Alf Gover would last out the time. I had no idea whether between the innings I should hand back to the studio or carry on. Well, there was some mild fun to be had from the last-wicket stand as there often is, before, inevitably, one of them got out and the field emptied before me. Ten minutes alone at the microphone seemed an awful long time, especially to a tyro, but out came what the OB people call my 'associative material' and I ended up by giving a couple of overs of the Lancashire innings. Typical of Lobby, by the time I came off the air the engineer had received a message of appreciation.

Many a contemporary appreciated the intense interest which Lobby took in all OB broadcasts. Each one was analysed and commented upon. Brian Johnston recalls him as 'a perfectionist. He used to record his impressions of each broadcast in a little black book. He was completely fair, never too excessive with his praise but also never unkind. "On the whole a brave effort" meant that you had done pretty well.'

Of Lobby's successors as head of OB's, only Robert Hudson has attempted anything like the same close analysis of what is now, of course, a vastly greater output.

A contract for Jim Swanton to work for the BBC in South Africa soon followed his own successful trial at The Oval. It is incredible that whereas these days a small army of media folk leaves home every winter to accompany the England cricket team on tour, only William Pollock of the *Daily Express* accompanied Swanton on the *Balmoral Castle*. Even then Swanton had failed to win many orders for reports from Fleet Street, his own paper included. But the BBC had offered him £126 for twenty broadcasts which, *mirabile dictu*, more than covered his first-class return sea fare.

On Christmas Eve, 1938, Swanton made the first live cricket

commentary back to England. He remembers the occasion as
somewhat anti-climactic, his first stint on the last half-hour of
the opening day of the first Test at the Old Wanderers ground
at Johannesburg coinciding with Paul Gibb, seldom a very
adventurous batsman, blocking some slow leg-breaks from
Bruce Mitchell.

The second day of the match was on Boxing Day and my luck really changed. At
first it was much the same story, with Mitchell himself doing the blocking this time,
against Hedley Verity. Alone in my hot little box I imagined people falling asleep
by the thousand after their second helping of turkey. But then, with about ten
minutes to go before the close of play, Tom Goddard caught and bowled Dudley
Nourse for 73. The nightwatchman, one Gordon, came in and was promptly
stumped first ball. Tom was on a hat-trick and I was very excited. Young Billy
Wade came in, a pretty good bat but a novice in Test cricket. He was obviously
nervous. He took some time to take guard and look round the field and then,
glory be, he was bowled first ball.

   It was only the fifth Test hat-trick by an Englishman and it was quite a story. At
the end of the match Michael Standing sent me a wire: 'Congratulations on
commentaries. Everybody pleased.'

By the end of the series, the South Africans had extended their
own commentaries from fifteen minutes to two hours a day and,
not least during the nine active days of the timeless (and
unfinished) Test at the end of the series, Swanton picked up more
valuable experience. He shared commentaries at home the following summer with Howard Marshall and Michael Standing,
though the bulk of the reports on the England v. West Indies
series went back to the Caribbean rather than to home listeners.

   After three harrowing years as a prisoner of the Japanese in
Siam, having been captured along with thousands of others in
Singapore, E. W. Swanton returned home to resume his outstanding broadcasting and writing career. His relatively late
marriage to the accomplished Ann Carbutt mellowed and
rounded him, by all accounts, and to me, as to many younger
men in cricket journalism, he was a considerate mentor, always

to be respected, occasionally feared. Jim and Ann have lived for many years at Sandwich in Kent, near the golf links, and still take an annual trip to Barbados, where they once owned and sometimes rent a house on the golf course at Sandy Lane.

Longevity has been a feature of the leading early post-war cricket commentators. Brian Johnston was still going incredibly strong in 1989 and Rex Alston, although a trifle lame from a rheumatic knee, was still mentally alert and generally spick and trim several years after *The Times* erroneously published his obituary in 1985. A schoolmaster at Bedford before the war, he had been a talented athlete, second string in the sprints for Cambridge, against Oxford and others, to the Olympic gold medallist Harold Abrahams, with whom he later shared many an athletics commentary. He was also an accomplished minor county cricketer and a rugby footballer for Rosslyn Park and East Midlands.

Now living at Ewhurst in Surrey, enjoying a devoted second marriage after the death of Elspeth, his first wife, from Alzheimer's disease, he recalled the chance meeting during the war which took him into the BBC:

I was forty when war broke out and was told that as a schoolmaster I was in a 'reserved occupation'. A chap called Leslie Woodgate, the BBC's chorus master and conductor, was billeted at Bedford and he persuaded me to have a go at joining the BBC as a billeting officer. I couldn't type but after two or three months I was told I had a 'nice clear voice' and was vetted as an announcer. I duly became an announcer in Manchester for eighteen months.

I was introduced to Raymond Glendenning at Maine Road one day. I liked the idea of becoming a commentator and Michael Standing arranged for me to go to Headingley for a fifteen-minute commentary test at a wartime match. I was considered adequate and as a result of that I was sent along to Abbeydale Park at Sheffield for my first live broadcast. No luxury like a commentary box or a scorer. The chap who came to help me in fact was the racing correspondent; didn't even look at the cricket.

But Rex Alston was on his way. He spent a year in Birming-

ham in 'Talks' as a producer under Dennis Morris and was there
when *The Archers* started a run longer than any cricket commentator's. He migrated to Outside Broadcasts towards the end of
the war and acted as 'number two' (general assistant) to Stewart
Macpherson on V.E. Night. His training continued when he
'trailed' the great Howard Marshall at the Victory Test matches –
standing in for him competently at Old Trafford when Marshall
was called to London for something deemed to be of greater
importance. When Lobby took over again from Michael Standing as Head of OB's (Standing going to Variety), Alston recalls
that he 'landed a job which was heaven-sent for me. I was put in
charge of commentaries on cricket, rugby, athletics and tennis.
Brian Johnston and John Ellison joined the department about a
year later and for a time Anthony Wedgwood Benn joined us
from the Overseas Service as a sports producer. I well remember
meeting John Arlott for the first time in the opening match of the
Indian tour at Worcester in 1946. A young man with flying black
hair introduced himself and presented me with a book of his
poetry.'

Johnston remembers Rex as being 'rather schoolmasterly' but
always good company and concerned to do things well. 'He was
precise, meticulous, fair and unbiased.'

It was Alston and de Lotbinière who together worked out the
post-war broadcasting schedule, with Charles Max-Muller
taking over as head of OB's when Lobby moved to be head of the
same department in television in 1952, in time for the momentous Coronation, which was to make television effectively the
senior medium overnight. The main outlets were 'Out and
About' on Saturday afternoons, and three days of midweek
cricket on the Home and Light programmes, mainly the latter. In
addition Rex had to organize rotas for the General Overseas
Service on matches involving the touring team.

For the series against South Africa in the hot summer of 1947,
C. B. Fry's summarizing role was also played by R. E. S. Wyatt
and George Duckworth. Except for Tests in London, radio had

the stage to itself until 1950, when the cameras ventured into the provinces for the first time.

The year 1948 saw the first appearance in England of Alan McGilvray, who with Arlott, Alston, Swanton and Gilligan comprised the regular commentary team on the Light programme throughout that famous Australian summer, augmented by C. B. Fry and George Duckworth. Alston describes McGilvray as a 'lovely broadcaster, even then', and to listen to him again nowadays on the surviving archive tape recordings is to be reminded instantly of his suave command at the microphone. His secret, I believe, apart from the obvious qualities – a deep knowledge of the game and an excellent voice – was the intimacy of his style, the way in which he spoke almost confidentially to the listener. His mouth used to be right up close to the microphone and it was hard to hear what he was saying if you were in the box with him, unless you were wearing earphones.

The tradition of inviting an overseas commentator or summarizer continued: in 1949 it was the former Test cricketer Roger Blunt for New Zealand; in 1950 it was Michael Laing of the Trinidad Broadcasting Company (billed in the *Radio Times* as being 'on holiday in this country') for the first Test and two more Trinidadians, the immortal Learie Constantine and Kenneth Ablack, who had played for Northamptonshire, for the remaining games. Another Test player, Gerry Gomez, and the genial Jamaican Roy Lawrence joined the next West Indies team in 1957, and another West Indian, Ernest Eytle, got a game during the Indian tour in 1952. In 1951 and on subsequent South African tours Charles Fortune represented the SABC and in 1953 and 1956, before McGilvray returned as the regular visitor, Bernard Kerr and Michael Charlton were here for the Australian Broadcasting Commission, with Bert Oldfield doing summaries. Charlton later made a bigger name as presenter of the TV current affairs programme *Panorama*. Visits were reciprocal, with Rex Alston and John Arlott making trips abroad on behalf of the BBC, later to be followed by Brian Johnston and myself.

The visitors to England generally fitted in well, but Johnston remembers Bernie Kerr, a small, red-headed man who later became head of ABC Sport, causing a considerable stir one day at The Oval in 1953 when he invited a girlfriend up to the box. 'She arrived in a huge flowery hat and made her way ponderously up a very sheer ladder on to the roof of the Pavilion, revealing everything to the spectators sitting below. As far as I remember women weren't supposed to be allowed in the Pavilion anyway.'

Although not then in the radio box, 'Johnners' got his training in radio cricket broadcasting, like all his contemporaries, in regional transmissions of county matches. Convinced of the popularity of the game, regional planners for London, the West, the Midlands and the North began to opt out of the Home Service to offer commentaries on the games in their region when there was no Test match. Alan Gibson, Peter West, Peter Cranmer and Robert Hudson were amongst those for whom half-hour commentary stints from 12 to 12.30, 3 to 3.30, and 6 to 6.35 presented great opportunities to learn the pleasures and pitfalls of live commentary.

By now it had been established that a scorer was desirable, if not essential. Arthur Wrigley, an accountant from Manchester, had been the first to make his mark in this field, at the behest of Howard Marshall. They had first worked together during the Old Trafford Test of 1934, sitting on beer crates at square-leg. The post-war men were lucky at least to have a reliable scorecard at their elbow, even if commentary positions were still fairly spartan in most cases, but these county sessions were otherwise performed unaccompanied and they represented, as Arlott recalled, 'sound training and experience'.

Few benefited more than Robert Hudson, a studious, meticulous broadcaster who prepared himself thoroughly for every broadcasting task and seldom uttered a false word. He had been a freelance operator between 1947 and 1954, when he was offered a job in Manchester. A future head of department, he became a senior OB producer, Head of Administration in the

North region, assistant Head of OB's in 1960 and a staff commentator on the retirement of Rex Alston (who, like many others, continued as a freelance) in 1961.

Rugby, special events and royal tours – he covered no fewer than ten of them – gave Robert Hudson a broader experience than most. It was he who wrote a momentous memorandum to his OB boss Charles Max-Muller in 1956 suggesting that it might be a good idea to broadcast a full ball-by-ball coverage of Test matches, rather than simply doing fixed periods, and suggesting the Third network as the most sensible medium. The Test Match Special era was at hand.

CHAPTER SEVEN

'Don't Miss a Ball'

Robert Hudson's personal experience had convinced him that non-stop commentary was what the public were demanding. He remembers to his slight embarrassment now that he began to feel his ambition to become a commentator might be realized when he heard John Arlott just after the war and thought: 'If they can use someone with an extraordinary accent like that I must have a chance!' Characteristically, though, he began to practise commentaries on a tape-recorder, sometimes taking his brother to Lord's and making him sit with his back to the cricket in the Mound Stand whilst Robert described all that was going on, a different version of Lance Sieveking's idea of talking to the blind man.

Arlott himself, incidentally, never felt he was talking to anyone in particular. He told Simon Jenkins in the BBC TV programme *The Editors*: 'Arthur Gilligan used to imagine he was talking to his mother. I always just thought I was trying to tell someone who was a bit interested and also that I was pleasing myself and talking about what interested me. Perhaps then it would interest somebody else. Everybody sees something different at a cricket match because you've got an infinite panorama and you're your own editor. You decide what can go in, because not everything can go in. So long as the commentator gets the score right I think most people will forgive him.'

This, of course, as John well knows, is not quite true. Giving the score is the *raison d'être* of the commentary, of course, but the idiosyncrasies of commentators can be nectar to some listeners, poison to others. Robert Hudson was always an absolutely straight-down-the-line observer of the cricket and no one was less likely to forget that giving the score is the first essential of the job. He had done some rugby commentary before giving his first cricket descriptions of the Northamptonshire v. Essex match at Northampton in 1951.

'We used in those days to have three half-hour periods of commentary,' he recalls. 'This was fine from the point of view of learning the technique of commentary and getting practice at it, but of course it didn't always coincide with the interesting bits of play and that's one reason why, little by little, it became fairly evident that what people wanted to hear was the continuous story of a match as it unfolded.'

If Robert Hudson was the first to express the public demand for a non-stop transmission of Test cricket on radio, the hitherto unsung producer Michael Tuke-Hastings was the man who put the idea into practice with the blessing of the programme planners.

A trainee journalist before the war, this large, bluff family man with a good sense of humour but a sometimes slightly supercilious air – certainly not a man to suffer fools gladly – was commissioned into the Reconnaissance Corps and invalided out of the war in 1944. He returned to the *Reading Standard*, briefly became a corn merchant, then joined the BBC as a Recorded Programme Assistant, dealing with discs. He progressed to become a studio manager, a useful training for any producer since these are the people who, in layman's language, twirl the knobs which put broadcasters on and off the air.

Tuke-Hastings joined the Variety Department before becoming a producer of Radio Newsreel, then splitting his time between Recorded Programmes under Arthur Phillips in the winter and Outside Broadcasts under Charlie Max-Muller in the summer: 'My first OB was at the White City as "number two" to Rex Alston. He taught me a lot. His first question was: "Have you got a pencil, a ruler and a pad of paper?"'

Cricket and, for a time, rugby union became Tuke-Hastings's responsibility. He shared an office with Brian Johnston and their joint secretary Penny Robins, daughter of the former England captain R. W. V. Robins.

Though a true blue Conservative with a very capital 'C', 'Tukers' had a flair for good broadcasting ideas. He introduced the first of several quiz programmes run by OB's *Sports Quiz*, with the cricket statistician Roy Webber, who had now taken over as Test match scorer from Arthur Wrigley, setting the questions and keeping the score, while Brian Johnston presided and Tuke-Hastings produced. The programme, with teams from industrial firms competing, was taken on by BBC TV for a 14-week run. It was the forerunner of *Treble Chance*, *Forces Chance* and *Brain of Sport*, all of which Tuke-Hastings produced in the winter months, the first two once the cricket season was concluded. *Brain of Sport* began shortly before his retirement, by which time he had handed on the cricket portfolio to the man who has held it ever since, Peter Baxter.

When Tuke-Hastings took over the production of cricket from Geoffrey Topping, the main headache for a producer was the constant need to switch commentary between the Light, Third and Home programmes and also the General Overseas Service. Reminiscing at his comfortable home on the island of Alderney, no more than a mile away from John Arlott, although the two seldom meet these days, Tuke-Hastings remembers the deft switching of cue lines from one service to another as being like 'handling a box of tricks':

We had a lot of fighting to do internally before we established the principle of ball-by-ball commentary. The idea to put it on the Third Programme of course offended the music lovers, so the main battle was between Charles Max-Muller and the Head of the Third Programme. Charlie was authoritative and genteel. He won the day and I came up with the slogan 'Don't miss a ball, we broadcast them all' before we started continuous transmission on the England v. West Indies series of 1957.

The pattern at first was to switch transmitters twice during the day. The bulk of the programme went out on the Third Programme but it was switched to the Light for the last half-hour before lunch and from 5.15 until close of play at 6.30. The following year the commentary actually went out on two of the three services – Light and Third – in the period before lunch, 1.00 to 1.34. In addition there was a five-minute summary of play on the Light programme at 10.40 every evening, usually by E. W. Swanton.

If there was any doubt about the success of the new venture, the cricket played during the 1957 series swiftly removed it. In the very first Test at Edgbaston, the commentators witnessed and passed on to an enthralled audience England's first-innings collapse against Sonny Ramadhin. Watching and listening between school lessons, I remember being fascinated by the way that Ramadhin bowled with his shirt-sleeve buttoned at the wrist, a rare thing in those days, to help the deception of his curious mixture of wrist and finger spin. Then came the famous stand of 411 between May and Cowdrey. It was a series of great individual performances after that: Cowdrey's 152 and Weekes's courageous 90 at Lord's; my special hero Tom Graveney's 258 at Trent Bridge to add to May's 285 not out at Edgbaston; Peter Richardson, 126 at Trent Bridge and 107 at The Oval; Frank Worrell 191 not out at Trent Bridge and Collie Smith 168 when the West Indies followed on; Peter Loader's hat-trick at Headingley; and Laker and Lock doing at The Oval what they had done to Australia four years before.

The Test Match Special Show was on the road and the principle of ball-by-ball coverage remained sacrosanct for more than thirty years until the idea of Radio Five was conceived and cricket's uncluttered stage was threatened, ironically enough, not by culture or politics but by the encroachments of other sports. Not that the interruption of music and the arts on the

Third Programme went unchallenged. There were plenty of objections from music-lovers, though they were a tiny minority compared with the cricket listeners, before the solution was found in the splitting of the network with the advent of VHF. No less a public figure than Spike Milligan wrote thus to the *Listener*:

With all the planning committees and debates about broadcasting in the seventies jazz [*sic*], I am stunned when the only channel that transmits classical music is the very one used to cover the Test matches. Couldn't one of the verbal pop music diarrhoea stations be used? In an age when the stress is on education, to terminate classical music for sports is a retrograde step.

P.S. I am a cricket fan as well.

No doubt Milligan spoke for many, but the general response to Test Match Special was enthusiastic and Tuke-Hastings was as pleased as anyone:

I saw my role as the representative of the listener. It is the main job of a producer to sit in the background and to come up with ideas. Originally I used to go round all the Test matches as the 'number two', but I became a sort of dogsbody, answering telephones and nannying the commentators, and I decided I wasn't really listening to the commentaries. I even tried sitting in a separate place on the ground with 'cans' on but it was no good, so I decided in future to produce from the Continuity Suite in London at Broadcasting House alongside the presenting announcer, with a television monitor beside me.

I chose the announcers. It helped if they liked cricket, like Michael De Morgan (now a spokesman for the South African Embassy in London). Gradually a team atmosphere developed in the Continuity Suite similar to the one in the commentary box. We always recorded the entire running commentary and then when a wicket fell or something dramatic happened we would mark it and eventually compile a tape of highlights for the Permanent Library.

What is now retained on disc by the Library is, in fact, a good deal scantier than most devotees of the programme would like, and it seems that a certain coldness has developed between the two distinguished residents of Alderney, Arlott feeling that Tuke-Hastings retained far too few of his finest phases of commentary but the latter maintaining that someone else must have thrown away portions of broadcasts that he had wanted to keep for the archives.

This was nothing new – only nine commentaries by Howard Marshall are extant – but it is a pity indeed that so little remains except in the memories of those who heard Arlott, the consummate wordsmith, in his halcyon days. Small examples have been noted down by his devotees – such as the time in South Africa when, on one of the three tours Arlott made for the BBC (one each to Australia, South Africa and the West Indies), England's captain George Mann was bowled by his namesake, South Africa's left-arm spinner, 'Tufty'. 'A case', said Arlott, 'of Mann's inhumanity to Mann.'

David Imlay, a retired major from Cheltenham, especially remembers two Arlott gems. In 1948, when the Gloucestershire left-hander Jack Crapp had bravely reached 19 not out on the Saturday evening in the second innings of his first Test, Arlott mused aloud: 'A very steady fellow is Jack Crapp; I wonder if he takes his pads off at the weekend?' Four years later, during a national cigarette shortage, Arlott remarked as play was about to get under way on a Monday morning: 'I'm told Jim Laker has spent the weekend looking for 10 Players.'

Though not so deliberate a humorist as Brian Johnston, these examples remind one that Arlott was not just a lyrical commentator but an extremely witty one as well.

Any lack of warmth between the outstanding radio commentator of that period and his producer was certainly not evident at the time, for although Brian Johnston had not yet brought across his marvellous freshness and *joie de vivre* from the television box (where, unwisely in my view, his irrepressible jollity was kept much more on a leash than it later was on radio) the atmosphere then, as now, was happy and convivial. Arlott recalled when he retired: 'To have observed only four instances of sharpness in thirty-five years argues a considerable communal good humour. There has, too, always been so much leg-pulling that pomposity is impossible.'

Not that Tuke-Hastings was above risking the temporary ire of one of the commentators if he thought it necessary for the good of the listener:

I used to infuriate commentators by asking them to give the score and to pick up on this and that or to cue to the Special Overseas Service or the Australian transmission or whatever it was. I used to get bloody bored at times, to be honest. I was never really a cricket *aficionado*. Mind you, that was no bad thing. I never expected to get any of the glory and I could ask for explanations if I felt the listener needed them. In practice that was seldom necessary. The commentators were all bloody good. I remember Arlott was particularly good at doing two-minute reports at the end of the day – a superb broadcaster. Fingo [Jack Fingleton] used to tease him and he got emotional at times, but his voice and his historical perspective were marvellous. You could smell the grass when he was talking.

We deliberately set out to get a balance of different types and the visiting broadcasters helped in this respect. The twenty-minute periods were ideal for both listeners and commentators. I worked very closely with Brian Johnston in later years and also with Robert Hudson, who was extremely conscientious. The combination of Arlott's serious approach and Johnston's humour was ideal and Swanton was a marvellous summarizer. Mind you, I think the standard is just as high now. It's still the same mixed grill, with something in it for everyone.

We got steadily more popular. Audience research discovered that many people were listening to our commentary and watching TV, especially, I think, after Brian Johnston joined us. The regular summarizers like Brown and Yardley and Bailey all added to the team.

They had many forerunners. Amongst those who joined the regular commentary team of Alston, Arlott and Swanton during the 1950s were Bill Bowes, Alf Gover, Billy Griffith and Crawford White (the *News Chronicle* and later *Daily Express* cricket correspondent, who covered one Test in 1955). Norman Yardley made his first appearance the following season at Trent Bridge in the year that the inimitable 'Fingo', with his distinctive clipped Sydney delivery and occasionally caustic wit, joined the commentaries for the last four Tests. Yardley recalled to me in a letter that Fingo and Arlott did not always get on, Fingo delighting in pulling Arlott's leg.

Although 1957 and the series against West Indies marked the first non-stop domestic coverage and the first official entitlement of the programme as 'Test Match Special', it was not quite as non-stop as it has been in recent years because in those days if it rained the rule was to hand back to the studio. Rex Alston remembers how that came to be:

We had fifteen minutes before the first ball was bowled at half-past eleven in one of the 1948 Tests. It was a nasty cloudy day and we started talking – I started and John was there and we went on talking and the umpires came out, had a look at the sky and walked back again and the covers came out. All this took a lot of time. There were five minutes or so and then the covers were removed and the umpires went out again, had a look and came back again. And we were still trying to talk. We had no idea what we ought to have done, partly because this was the first time we had done ball-by-ball commentary back to Australia, so in a sense we were serving more than one master. Anyway, I was wearing headphones and suddenly there was a frustrated voice coming up the line from Broadcasting House: 'For God's sake get back to the studio.' Which we did!

Many years later Arlott thought nothing of a twenty-minute monologue in which he managed to keep everybody spellbound simply by describing the covers being taken off at Lord's.

The former England captain Freddie Brown's first radio appearance was at The Oval in 1957 and for many years, certainly the early ones to which I myself listened, the two familiar voices at the end of each over were Brown's, rich and gravelly, and Yardley's gentler, polite, slightly hesitant tones with a characteristic little 'uh' punctuating his always charitable opinions.

Considering the fact that he had done his first radio commentary for the BBC in 1948 it took Alan Gibson a long time to be 'selected' for a Test match. That he was dropped after a Test at

Headingley in the 1970s when listeners noted that he was slow to keep up with play was hardly in the charitable tradition established when Tommy Woodruffe was merely suspended after his bibulous broadcast at Spithead in 1935, but like many with a touch of genius Alan always had a slightly rebellious streak in him and a healthy contempt for those of lesser intellect who might be laying down how he should approach his job.

He was a brilliant scholar who had spent most of his life in the West Country, though his roots were in Yorkshire. Always keen on games, he captained Queen's College, Oxford, at cricket, was president of the Union, and got a first in History in 1947, having interrupted his academic career to do his two years of National Service at the age of nineteen. He was a regular broadcaster in the West Region, on cricket, rugby and more intellectual matters, and his books and later his writing, for *The Times* and *The Cricketer* amongst others, was of the highest quality. As a broadcaster he had a mellifluous voice and an easy command of vocabulary and a twinkling sense of humour. One sensed always that he was feeling for the right word before he uttered it. It was characteristic of him that when one Saturday afternoon Neil Durden-Smith apologized for being late for a broadcast because he had been 'having tea with the Bishop of Leicester', Alan should have responded when he in turn was cued in: 'No episcopal visitations here.'

Brian Johnston also credits Gibson with the famous remark about the New Zealand bowler Bob Cunis being 'neither one thing nor the other'. Whether Gibson actually uttered the witticism or not, it was the sort of humour of which he was more than capable. Had he been more interested in worldly renown, more ambitious, more prepared to look after his interests in the small politics of the BBC, he would undoubtedly have become a celebrity. Recent years have for him been plagued by illness, both physical and mental, but those who have read and listened to him have recognized a man of quality.

The same could be said of Peter Cranmer. By no means an academic, but rather a hearty, robust character and an outstanding games-player who played centre three-quarter for England at Rugby and captained Warwickshire at cricket, he was a regular cricket reporter and commentator in the 1950s and 1960s. He had a good voice, a natural, conversational style and a cheery manner.

Another who has commentated on fewer Tests than he would have liked is Neil Durden-Smith, who joined the BBC in the mid-1960s after a naval career which included service as ADC to Lord Cobham when he was Governor-General of New Zealand, but eventually left the staff to make a successful life in public relations. An accomplished talker with a thorough knowledge of the game, it was only perhaps because he did not specialize in cricket that he did not establish a more regular spot in a necessarily small team for which many have been called but few chosen, especially once Arlott and Johnston had become what soccer programme writers used to call 'ever presents' from the late 1960s on.

Robert Hudson, another of the stalwarts of the 1960s – he had made his first Test broadcast at Old Trafford in 1958 alongside Arlott, Brown, Yardley and the former New Zealand Test cricketer Bill Merritt – became Head of Radio Outside Broadcasts in 1969 and it was he who, by appointing Peter Baxter and, above all, encouraging Brian Johnston, may be said to have shepherded Test Match Special into its modern and most widely popular era.

It was to Robert Hudson that Wilfred Rhodes, the great and long-lived Yorkshire and England all-rounder, who went totally blind in his old age and greatly enjoyed listening to sound commentaries, gave a characteristically sane and succinct summary of what a radio commentator should be trying to do. 'Paint a picture,' he said, 'and keep it the right way up.'

CHAPTER EIGHT

Adding to the Picture

It must be hard for anyone born after 1952 to imagine a world without television. It is a moot point whether the aeroplane or the television has changed people's lives more. Certainly both have changed cricket, bringing the first-class game and its players into the homes of every interested follower. The remarkable skill of the cricketers has been conveyed as never before, to such an extent that it is often taken for granted: worse, the advent of the video slow-motion replay has cruelly emphasized the smallest errors, often making batsmen look extremely foolish and sometimes falsely suggesting that the ugly-looking shot into which they may have been forced by the late movement of the ball was entirely their fault.

The intimacy of the camera has also brought the public much closer to the true character of players. Once they were distant figures viewed only from the boundary's edge. In the days of less frequent international cricket there was little danger of the familiarity which breeds contempt. A writer with the rare imagination of Neville Cardus could weave stories around cricketers with few people either able or willing to question their precise veracity. If someone had not said such and such a thing, Cardus would have argued, he ought to have said it. The camera has made that sort of constructive imaginative writing almost impossible and indeed has led indirectly to the worst excesses of tabloid newspapers which, needing to embroider what television has shown, or at least to find something new, have sometimes indulged in destructive writing and at other times revealed the private lives of players, however irrelevant to their performances as sportsmen. Who can say whether all the attention paid to Ian Botham's off-the-field activities in the West Indies in 1985-86 did not make it harder for everyone in the England team, their prime all-rounder especially, to give of his best? Who can say whether the wish to avoid that sort of intense scrutiny was not at least part of the reason for Botham's non-selection for the next tour to the Caribbean in 1989-90?

It may seem hard to lay any responsibility for this at television's door, especially when the BBC in particular has used the power of the camera so sympathetically in cricket. But the slow-motion replay has made life far harder for umpires as well as for players and has at times cruelly exposed their inevitable mistakes.

The fact is that television has enabled the public to get far closer to cricketers. This has increased their earning power in many cases but it has also increased their problems and their need to behave responsibly: when every peccadillo as well as every off-drive is examined in close-up by millions, that responsibility is great indeed, as is the responsibility of those who produce the transmissions and comment on the action.

The more sophisticated television equipment and technique become, the more this is true, but it was hardly a problem in the early days of the magical new medium in the late 1930s. Teddy Wakelam, the first man ever to give a running sports commentary on radio, was also the pioneer of television cricket commentary. He it was who was chosen to describe the scene portrayed to viewers, in the London area only, during the Lord's Test of 1938. Whilst Howard Marshall was reaching millions on the 'senior' service, Wakelam's audience numbered only a few thousand. He sat in the open on the top of the free seats at the distant top corner of the stand at the Nursery End, next door to the Mound Stand. (This stand was demolished at the end of the 1989 season.) From there Wakelam and the cameraman were looking into the sun for much of the day, with none of the sophisticated support afforded his modern counterpart.

Wakelam's producer was Ian (now Lord) Orr-Ewing, who had been a radio ham at school at Harrow and had studied physics at Oxford and who, with his great interest in electronic engineering, was an ideal recruit to the OB television team formed under the command of Philip D'Orté. Orr-Ewing was twenty-five when he joined the BBC in January 1938 to utilize the single OB unit made by EMI, who used the 405 line which superseded the Baird 240 line.

'I had already been involved with television,' he recalls. 'I was one of a team of three helping to build the first retail television set. It was a ten-inch black-and-white set – unswitchable, of course, because there was only one BBC service. It cost £90, which is equivalent to £2,700 today.'

Amongst his first duties when he joined OB's was to liaise with various sporting authorities to arrange the televising of the main events. 'Lord's and Wimbledon were easily the most helpful and accommodating; I dealt with Colonel Rait-Kerr, the Secretary of MCC, and another Colonel – Macauley – at the All England Club. Old Stanley Rous at the FA was helpful too but his League counterparts and most of the other sports weren't. In fact our right to cover most sport was restricted by an organization called "The Association for the Protection of Copyright in Sport."'

Orr-Ewing retained a close interest in cricket during his two decades in the House of Commons as MP for North Hendon from 1950 to 1970 and since 1971 as an unusually active Life Peer. He co-operated with Ben Brocklehurst, chairman of *The Cricketer*, to form an Anglo-Corfiot Cricket Association and in 1989 edited a large volume about Lord's and Commons cricket.

Wakelam returned to action a few weeks after the first transmission for the momentous fifth Test at The Oval. Hutton's monumental innings of 364 was viewed by the commentator from a platform atop a ladder underneath the gasholder at cover/mid-wicket. It was not exactly an ideal spot from which to offer authoritative opinion on how much the ball was doing through the air or off the seam, especially as any picture he might have had alongside him on a monitor was unlikely at this pioneering stage of the medium to be very informative. Mind you, on Bosser Martin's Oval pitch, firm as rock and true as a Bible oath, there cannot have been much movement to observe.

Lord Orr-Ewing remembers the Hutton innings mainly for the fact that it was so very hot in the big control van from which he directed:

We had all three cameras, all in a group, one giving long shots, one middle and one close-up. No zoom lenses then, of course. The cameras were so much string and ceiling wax, really: twenty-inch lenses which had to be changed frequently. Our operating van was huge, built on the chassis of a greenline bus. There was no ventilation and it was bloody hot. But we covered quite a bit of that match even though there weren't many viewers. Normal TV transmissions were only between three and four in the afternoon and nine and ten at night, but we were allowed to go on longer.

Not having many viewers didn't seem all that important, although we did once stop – on the way back from the 1938 Cup Final – because we saw a house with an aerial. We went in and asked the owner how it had come across and he gave us a cup of tea and was delighted to see us!

The Test match experiment was repeated the following year when Tommy Woodruffe and Aidan Crawley were the commentators for the two London Tests involving England and the West Indies. Orr-Ewing remembers Crawley as being 'a little bit stilted'.

For the first four years after the war the cameras were still restricted to Lord's and The Oval. The installation of a transmitter at Sutton Coldfield enabled the third Test at Trent Bridge in 1950 to become the first one outside London to be covered by television, and once Seymour de Lotbinière had moved to take charge of TV Outside Broadcasts in time for the Coronation of Queen Elizabeth II, the pace perceptibly quickened. Leeds and Manchester came into the television orbit with the opening of the

Holme Moss transmitter in 1952, so viewers as well as listeners were able to share in the extraordinary début of F. S. Trueman in the opening Test against India at Headingley.

After success in his second and third spells on a placid pitch in the Indian first innings, Trueman ran down the slope from the Kirkstall Lane end in the middle of Saturday afternoon before the most knowledgeable of Test cricketing crowds, as India sought to build on a useful first-innings lead. In the first fourteen balls of the innings he and Alec Bedser took the first four Indian wickets for no runs – the young Trueman's share being three, a top edge from a bumper and two balls of full length which uprooted the off-stump.

The television commentators who witnessed the unprecedented drama of this opening to a Test innings were E. W. Swanton and Brian Johnston, whose old friend Ian Orr-Ewing had rung him six years before, in his new post-war capacity as Head of TV Outside Broadcasts, to ask him if he would like to have a go at some cricket commentary on the MCC match against the Indians and the two London Tests. Johnston had joined OB's under de Lotbinière in their offices at 55 Portland Place only a few months before, and of course he leapt at this latest opportunity with that unselfconscious enthusiasm which was to characterize all his broadcasting.

'He was a natural,' recalls Ian Orr-Ewing, 'and even then he was disciplined: always punctual and prepared to accept instructions through the heavy earphones. Both Brian and Rex Alston, who also did some television for us, were delightful people to work with. So was Raymond Robertson-Glasgow – very light and amusing.'

Brian Johnston himself remembers it now as a step into unknown territory:

We were completely untutored in the technique of TV commentary. There was no method or pattern then of course. Lobby had set down the 'pyramid' method of radio commentary – that is, starting with the basic facts, like the score, who has taken the wickets, who is not out, etc., and then gradually working down from the point of the pyramid with other colour and information – but no one had written down any rules for telly and we just had to work it out for ourselves. The only advice we were given was, 'Don't speak unless you can add to the picture.'

That's easier said than done, of course, because you can't please everyone – in fact I don't think you can please *anyone* completely: you are either talking too much for the knowledgeable viewer or too little for the one who doesn't know the game well.

The other essential difference between a television and a radio commentary is that whereas at a radio microphone you are your own editor, in television you are constantly under the direction of the producer who, seated at the controls of the TV 'Scanner', the mobile van from which the broadcast emanates, has control of the pictures from however many cameras there may be and who is constantly giving instructions to his cameramen and also to his commentator. Johnston recalls how Percy Fender, inclined to be irascible, put his hand over his lip microphone when Orr-Ewing told him to stop reminiscing about his old days at Surrey and muttered: 'If he's so darned clever, why doesn't he come up here and commentate himself?'

Fender had already made a pre-war reputation as both a sound commentator and a masterly deliverer of cricket talks. Randal Davies, who played in a match at Lord's on 4 September 1937 for Welsh Schools Under 15 against their London counterparts, wrote to tell me how Fender good-naturedly implored the batsmen not to get out during his broadcast, because it was more difficult when there was no play in progress.

An internal BBC memo relating to a series of proposed instructional talks by 'P.G.H.' to schoolchildren in 1936 refers to his being 'in a class by himself when it comes to explaining cricket'.

Fender's fame was enhanced by those Tom Webster cartoons which exaggerated the length of his sweaters and of the huge nose which protruded beneath horn-rimmed spectacles. It was, indeed, larger even than Johnston's own distinguished proboscis, and Brian still chuckles at the memory of a director ordering Fender to put his lip mike closer to his mouth. 'But his nose was so enormous he couldn't do it!'

Of some of his other early companions in the TV box, Brian recalls Aidan Crawley causing something of a stir by referring to the South Africans as 'the Africans', an echo of an occasion when, in March 1948, John Arlott had annoyed C. B. Fry by interrupting him in the middle of a recording for the Eastern Service to suggest that his use of the term 'American darkie' was tactless in view of the sensitivity of Indian listeners so soon after Independence. The incident sparked Fry into writing to the Head of Eastern Services, C. J. Pennethorne Hughes, who wrote a tactful but firm reply, defending Arlott for his brave inter-vention. (Not many dared to cross the imperious Fry about anything, be it cricket or Greek pentameters.)

Neither Fender nor Fry was at his best on television, and Brian Johnston also believes that the brilliant wit of 'Crusoe' Robertson-Glasgow was rather wasted on TV: 'his voice had a rather sepulchral tone to it.' Crusoe too, sensitive and artistic soul that he was, could be irritable. He was the first to say, when a producer asked him to give the score a moment or two after he had actually done so: 'For those who weren't listening the total is . . .'

Commentary positions were soon more convenient than the ones from which Teddy Wakelam had had to operate before the war. At Lord's they were placed on the balcony outside the modern committee dining-room, over the visitors' dressing-room and below the present radio commentary box. Jim Swanton mentions that the names of some of the Australian team of 1921 are still carved into the red brick behind where the commentators used to sit. At Trent Bridge, Headingley, The Oval and Edgbaston (when Tests resumed there in 1957) the positions were much as they are today: at Leeds in the 'Football Stand' which divides the cricket and rugby league grounds; and at the other three in the pavilion, in the case of The Oval on the left of the roof of the pavilion as it faces the ground. (A new storey was added to house both the TV and radio boxes in the early 1980s.) It was from up there that Swanton once accidentally dropped his flask of 'tea' (in fact a drop of Scotch) and hit a spectator on the back of the head, an incident which Brian Johnston has never allowed Swanton to forget. The same is true of the time at Headingley when E.W.S. chose not to comment on a man walking in front of the camera with a lavatory seat around his neck, the sort of invitation to instant comedy which Johnners himself relished. Each to his own style.

Television transmissions in the 1950s were limited by the Cricket Board of Control because they feared an adverse effect not on Test match crowds but on the gates at county games during Test matches. Cricket was shown on Mondays, Wednesdays and Thursdays only in the half-hour before lunch and two hours after tea. On Saturdays coverage was limited to the evening session of play only, but on Tuesdays and Fridays, the third days of county matches which seldom drew large crowds, a maximum of four and a half hours' coverage was allowed. In 1959 a new contract was negotiated, with the BBC paying more money to gain unlimited coverage at their own discretion. In practice the demands of other programmes meant that it was rare for more than half the day's cricket to be televised, one exception being during the Ashes series in 1961 when the average was over four hours a day. It was one of the reasons, of course, for the popularity of Test Match Special after 1957 that – provided they could get a strong enough signal – anyone could switch on anywhere in the UK and find out the latest score. Even then, as a letter to the *Radio Times* in 1959 indicated, many people liked to watch television whilst listening to the sound commentaries.

Like most people Peter West, who became a versatile television 'front-man' in all sorts of programmes but whose great interests were always cricket and rugby – he had been an outstanding schoolboy performer at both – started on radio. He remembers his nervous, halting efforts at Test commentaries under Rex Alston's adjudication in 1947 and being 'thrown to the lions' that year for his first live broadcast on the Warwickshire v. South Africans match. He recalls that his loyal young wife, Pauline, was so excited at hearing his voice that she rushed upstairs from their basement flat in Weybridge to announce: 'My husband's on the air' – to which the old man upstairs replied: 'Oh, where's he flying to?'

In subsequent years West became a frequent commentator on county matches in the West Region, and he straddled the two distinct eras which might best be described as the Johnston and Benaud periods. From 1958 onwards Denis Compton became the regular 'expert' in the television box, his ready sense of humour making up for an obvious nervousness in his early days whenever he was in front of the camera. I remember his producing a delightful Spoonerism when he referred one day to the marvellous bowling with the new ball of 'Trayman and Stootham'.

West, who continued to be the engagingly smooth and relaxed anchor man of television Test matches until the end of the 1986 season, when he and Pauline retired to a cottage in the Cotswolds, remembers Johnston and Compton as being 'the greatest fun to work with' and he was sorry to see them depart the TV box. They did so when Bryan Cowgill, a tough north-countryman with an innovative, aggressive approach to the televising of sport born to some extent, no doubt, from the challenge of ITV, dropped the two stalwarts, apparently without a word of thanks or regret to either, and replaced them with others. Compton, in fact, carried on for some Tests after Johnston had gone but did not enjoy the new, sharper, less convivial approach. Indeed he once told me that when starting one day with 'Good morning, everyone!' the producer barked into his earphone: 'No "Good mornings" on television, Denis.' The two men who emerged as regulars in a more matter-of-fact team throughout the 1970s were Richie Benaud, who made his first radio broadcast in 1960 and his first for television three years later, and his old spinning rival Jim Laker, who had begun working alongside John Arlott on TV cricket commentaries on Sundays in 1968.

Laker was as unflappable in a broadcasting box or in front of a camera as he had been on the field of play. A Yorkshireman, despite his long association with Surrey, he had firm and perceptive views on the game and a nice, dry wit, which emerged more strongly as the television style reacted eventually from the rather rigid 'stick to the cricket and only speak when you've got to' approach laid down by Cowgill and his directors. His most characteristic idiosyncrasy was an inability to pronounce the 'g' on the end of words like batting, bowling and playing. Peter West recalled in his autobiography that it drew the following comment in verse from Mr Jack Cookson of Walsall in 1976:

> The English first innin's
> From slow, sure beginnin's
> Is takin' a turn for the worse.
> The wickets are tumblin'
> Supporters are grumblin'
> The captain should be in a hearse.
>
> What with Roberts and Holdin'
> And Holder, their bowlin'
> Is more than we English can stand.
> Excuses aren't heeded
> No alibis needed
> We're bein' emphatically tanned!

Jim Laker's sudden death on St George's Day 1986, the same day as Bill Edrich, deprived television viewers of a familiar presence, but the gap was eventually filled by the rougher tones of an even shrewder Yorkshireman, the former England captain Ray Illingworth. Other stalwarts of recent years have included the urbane Ted Dexter, the cheerful, versatile and generally charitable Tom Graveney, and the equally charming Tony Lewis, who moved from radio to take over from Peter West as the front-man, filling in with conversation and comment during breaks in play. More recently he has been joined by the former Warwickshire seam bowler Jack Bannister, an astute observer of cricket with an intimate knowledge of the game and its characters. Like Illingworth and Lewis, Jack started on Radio Three, although it was through his new medium that he informed viewers during a World Cup match between England and West Indies in Jaipur that Gladstone Small had just completed a fiery 'smell' at the pavilion end – quite possibly, in view of the unfamiliar diet there, an entirely correct statement.

In addition to the live coverage, evening highlights of the day's play have been regularly transmitted since 1971, following an experiment the year before in which edited highlights of the whole match were transmitted after the end of the game.

Producing a television cricket transmission has rapidly become a far more detailed and complicated business than is necessary for radio. Agreement has to be reached initially between the producer and the ground authority about the siting of cameras and the large control vans – the 'Scanner' and at least one other large green van from which vast amounts of cable stretch out like the roots of some huge tree. These days an additional position is required for the people who operate the computer statistics on behalf of Honeywell-Bull, the company Ted Dexter 'sold' to the BBC to enable the producer to bombard the viewer (if he chooses to) with a variety of up-to-the-minute facts about any given player.

The three cameras which were originally used for Test coverage have now multiplied to nine for most Tests in England and as many as thirteen sometimes in Australia, where the Channel Nine network added all sorts of sophistications and gimmicks when they 'seized' the right to cover cricket there from the ABC at the instigation of Kerry Packer after 1979. Some of the ideas of their producer David Hill were excellent – for example the score constantly appearing in the top right-hand corner of the picture and changing with every run, or the division of the picture to show the fielder haring after the ball on one side whilst the batsmen running between the wickets were simultaneously shown on the top left of the screen. Others, like the insistence on showing every ball from the bowler's end (an idea unfortunately borrowed by the BBC in 1989) and the strident hard sell of many of the commentators, took much more getting used to. The dangers of commercial television were demonstrated also when the catch off the first ball of an over, which clinched England's thrilling victory at Melbourne in 1982-83 after a heroic last-wicket stand between Border and Thomson, did not go out 'live' because an advertisement was still being shown.

These things are a matter of taste but, generally speaking, Channel Nine's coverage in Australia seems to have been as popular there as the BBC's less hectic, more straightforward approach has been in Britain. Richie Benaud has been common to both, a cool, faultless professional with a sure touch whether he is confronting the camera with unblinking eyes atop an immaculate suit or making clipped, perceptive comments about the game into his lip microphone. A brilliant Test captain who used the media to his advantage during his career, he has flitted to and fro across the world with the changing seasons for nearly thirty years and has made brilliant use of his decision, at the end of Australia's 1956 tour of England, to enrol himself in a three-week BBC television course.

Despite all the innovations of recent years, the basics of the coverage have not changed. One camera still points down the pitch, some thirty feet above ground level and plumb in line with the middle stump. The job of the camera next to it is to give a wider view, covering the movement of the ball when it moves off at a wider angle, so that, by the deft switch of a producer's button in the 'Scanner', the close-up of a perfectly struck hook will be followed by a view of the ball in motion over the top of square-leg's head and perhaps into the waiting hands of a spectator. Some other judiciously placed camera may then capture for the viewer the successful spectator's smile of triumph and perhaps his celebratory drink. The camera placed at square-leg or point may often be able to prove whether a stumping or run-out should have been given out or not, something which can never be said of lbw's and caught-behind decisions. It may not be long before a brave cricket administrator decides, with the support, one trusts, of the umpires, to allow the two umpires in

the middle to consult, during major televised matches, a third
official with access to the slow-motion replay of close stumpings
and run-outs.

All cameras nowadays have zoom lenses whereas originally
they had fixed lenses giving either a close-up or a wide-angle.
Instead of being produced on a computer, scorecards were
handwritten on copper plates, for many years by Maurice
Ryman. Action replays are immediately available for use at the
producer's discretion in either normal speed or slow motion.
The service is, indeed, comprehensive and seldom does anything
occur in a major match in either England or Australia that is not
'caught' by the cameras. Sometimes this creates for the producer
instant and awkward dilemmas: for example at Lord's in the
1989 Texaco International when a naked young lady ran dia-
gonally across the entire ground to the general enjoyment of a
packed house. No doubt the TV viewers enjoyed it too, but was
it desirable for the 'streak' to be shown and thus to encourage
future public exhibitions of this kind – or political demon-
strations as have also occurred from time to time?

The producers who have had to take instantaneous decisions
such as these have included David Kenning, highly respected by
those he worked with; Nick Hunter, who brought the eye of a
useful club cricketer to the job along with a quick, decisive mind;
and the present chief producer Keith Mackenzie, who recently
explained his working environment:

The nerve centre of any Outside Broadcast is the so-called 'Scanner', the main
van in the OB fleet. Working inside it are the Producer/Director, Production
Assistant, Engineering Manager, Sound and Vision Engineers. Although you may
see the cameramen, Stage Managers and various technical people with headphones around the ground, there are, in fact, a lot of people you will not see who
only work in the 'Scanner', or the mobile tape cans or radio links vehicle.

The 'Scanner' has three compartments: the vision control room, where the
camera pictures are processed and matched from camera to camera (this is also
the main technical centre of the vehicle, a mass of cables, dials and plugs,
controlling power and video distribution); at the other end is the sound control

room; and in the middle is the production area. This middle area is where the Producer/Director, Engineering Manager and Production Assistant operate from. In front of us is a bank of twenty-two screens showing every camera picture, videotape replay, computer scoring and statistics and any visual special effects, such as the main wicket picture squeezed down to $\frac{1}{4}$-size and then overlayed on the fielding camera picture. There's also the vision mixing panel operated by the Producer/Director to select the picture he chooses to go out on transmission.

In addition we have more panels of dials and switches for our two-way communications with the other sections of the 'Scanner', the cameramen, stage managers, computer operators, commentators and videotape personnel operating from various other vans or boxes around the ground. Everyone wears headphones, earpieces or listens on speakers to the Producer/Director and Production Assistant as they actually co-ordinate the overall Production of the Outside Broadcast. Everyone is in communication with everyone else. The Producer and his Assistant need to be able to talk to the Grandstand studio, if we're feeding our OB into them, or to the BBC1 or BBC2 network control rooms who switch from programme to programme. Sometimes on air we share time with horse racing, tennis or golf, so we have to co-ordinate between ours and the other OB or with a special switching studio. Although every element of the cricket coverage comes from the location, wherever we are in the country it has to be fed to Television Centre in London before going out to the transmitters.

The television commentator needs to be less single-minded than his radio counterpart. For a start he has to use the monitor not as a useful adjunct – a chance to see an incident again on the replay after he has described it 'live' – but as an essential tool. The monitor shows the commentator what the viewer is seeing at home, so his comments need always to be relevant to that. It is said that Henry Longhurst once forgot the rule and failed to see that whilst he was describing the difficulties of a particular green, the viewers were seeing a close-up from behind of a comely American lady golfer bending over and measuring her putt. 'I always think', Longhurst is reputed to have said, 'that this is one of the tightest and yet most satisfying holes in the whole world of golf.'

Skilled though BBC cameramen are they do not always capture the flight of what the Edwardians used to call the 'crimson rambler', and I was caught out on my very first TV commentary – on a Sunday transmission with only three cameras – when, in my determination not to ignore the monitor, I saw the batsman snick the ball in the direction of gully but could not see whether it had been caught and, if so, by whom. It was an early lesson to watch the ball with the naked eye at the crucial moment.

A good rapport between producer, cameramen and commentators is essential, although all producers are different. Some like to talk to their commentator a lot, often suggesting clichéd phrases which one would rather not use. Others may issue all sorts of oaths when something goes wrong. Needless to say none of this must be conveyed to the viewer. The whole business, because it is more complex, is perhaps necessarily less relaxed than it is in a radio box, although Sunday coverage, certainly when it was more copious than it has become in recent years, generally tried to reflect the 'afternoon out' atmosphere of Sunday League cricket. Peter Walker, the affable former Glamorgan and England all-rounder, used to conduct enjoyable tea-interval conversations, before handing over to Jim Laker as the programme's anchor man.

I succeeded John Arlott as one of the Sunday TV commentators for some years but, sadly, these games have been given scantier and scantier coverage as other Sunday sports have taken precedence. In recent years Ralph Dellor and the former Essex off-spinner David Acfield became Walker's main associates under the thorough and often passionate production of Bob Duncan.

The advent of the Sunday League, originally sponsored by John Player (the habit dies hard – their successors were Refuge Assurance and I referred one day to the John Refuge League), was the signal for the first of several disputes between the television and cricket authorities over coverage of the game.

Before the League was started by the TCCB in 1969 a series of matches was played on Sundays by a team called the Rothmans Cavaliers, mainly comprised of recent Test cricketers. Matches were usually played against counties, with most of the profits going to whichever member of the staff was having a benefit in the year in question. The games were televised by the BBC and were extremely popular, as indeed the new league turned out to be, both with spectators and viewers. There was considerable rivalry, however, between Rothmans and John Player, who had both been amongst the twenty-odd companies willing to sponsor this, the second of the successful one-day county competitions. There was also much bitterness when the BBC and not London Weekend Television, one of the interested ITV companies, won the exclusive right to televise the matches, at a price of course. LWT took the TCCB to court, using the future Foreign Secretary, Geoffrey Howe, QC, as their Leading Counsel, alleging breach of contract, but the Board won the case.

Since that day each new BBC contract, both for radio and television, has been ever more toughly negotiated by the TCCB. They have been aware that cricket has no divine right to be televised and that other sports will always jump at every chance to fill any gaps left by the game, but on the other hand they know they have an extremely popular product to sell. In 1989 Rupert Murdoch, the founder of Sky satellite television in the UK, looked to cricket to expand the tiny proportion of British viewers he had so far captured by buying the rights for the West Indies series against England in the early months of 1990. A separate company, Mark McCormack's TWI group, was engaged to produce the coverage, highlights of which were to be broadcast on the BBC each evening by an ancillary agreement. At the same time the TCCB let it be known that if the BBC wished to retain their exclusive rights to the coverage of Test and County cricket in England they would have to pay substantially more than the £1.2 million a year paid in 1987 for a new three-year contract. In the event the BBC decided to continue covering only the 'Cornhill' Tests and the NatWest Trophy. Sky has the rights to cover the Refuge Assurance League on Sundays, and a rival satellite company, BSB, made a successful bid for the Benson and Hedges Cup.

The chief negotiators for the TCCB, Bernard Coleman and Peter Lush, had for a long time been trying to open up the market in this way in order to push the BBC into paying more for their exclusive rights, but the reluctance of ITV to compete since losing the London Weekend case had weakened their hand. Adrian Metcalfe and Jeremy Isaacs did show considerable interest in taking the NatWest competition for the new Channel Four in 1984, offering what Coleman calls 'a reasonable fee', but the BBC countered by threatening not to televise the Test which England played against Sri Lanka at the end of that season. In addition negotiations did not reach the stage of a guarantee from the commercial channel not to repeat the disastrous experience of 1968 when, in the only year that ITV covered one of the major competitions – the Gillette Cup – they were too inflexible to alter their programme schedules in order to transmit the climax of the final at Lord's. Instead of a pulsating finish in which Warwickshire got up on the line to beat Sussex by four wickets, irate ITV viewers saw advertisements followed by the David Frost Show.

The TCCB employed the big advertising agency McCan-Erickson to produce a survey demonstrating what a full season of first-class cricket in England ought to be worth to a commercial television company, and the answer was that the advertising revenue would amount to some £12 million. The Board used this to try to press the Home Secretary to make the proposed new Channel Five a channel controlled by sport and the arts in order to reduce their reliance on sponsoring companies.

Until 1989, Bernard Coleman concluded, 'We had to accept that the BBC was the only feasible solution.' Late in 1989 the two parties were working towards another contract with the usual protests on both sides – on the BBC's that cricket is an extremely expensive sport to cover and that the Board are lucky that so many hours are devoted to it; and on the Board's that those hours are in fact being filled reasonably cheaply with a popular sport which ought to be better rewarded. But at the Board's autumn meeting that year Peter Lush was able to announce that at last he had succeeded in opening up television cricket to other companies. The overall fee was admitted to be 'well over twice as much' in 1990 as it had ever been before.

The hope for the future for Board officials such as Coleman, Lush and the chairman, Raman Subba Row, was that the Sky television transmissions of England's tour of West Indies in the first few months of 1990 would be popular enough to interest Sky, rival satellite companies and, in time, cable television, to continue to bid high for domestic cricket in Britain. But they must beware the Australian solution of selling to PBL Marketing, the company formerly owned by Kerry Packer, not just the marketing and televising of cricket in Australia but to some extent the conduct and administration of the game itself.

CHAPTER NINE

'TMS': The Brian Johnston Spirit

In 1970 Brian Johnston returned home from two months of commentating in South Africa to discover he was no longer wanted on television. 'The first person I bumped into on my return to Broadcasting House was Neil Durden-Smith,' he recalled in conversation nineteen years later. 'He said how sorry he was that I was no longer going to be doing TV commentaries. I was quite bewildered. I went to see Bob Hudson, who had quite recently taken over as Head of Radio OB's, and he confirmed it. But luckily for me he said he wanted me to be a regular member of the Test Match Special team.'

Hudson had not hesitated to invite his cricket correspondent to give his full time to radio. 'Brian being Brian,' he says, 'he injected a different atmosphere from the start.'

That atmosphere might be described essentially as friendly, even jolly, and from the moment that I first sampled it two years later I found it a wholly delightful environment to work in. Indeed it has truly very seldom seemed like work at all. Brian's bubbling enthusiasm and boyish delight in the cricket has uplifted the spirits over the years not just of the commentators and all involved with Test Match Special but with listeners as well. He attracts an extraordinary degree of affection because of his completely natural approach at the microphone, his honesty and his generosity of spirit. Although he is not a 'flowing' commentator with any great gift as a wordsmith, his natural

charm and optimism, his warmth of personality, reaches effort-
lessly across the air waves. A minority of listeners find his
humour childish sometimes and have objected to his tendency
to stray from the cricket to all sorts of things going on around
the ground or in the commentary box, including the arrival of
an ever-increasing number of cakes made by well-wishers who
know of Brian's delight in a good home-made chocolate
sponge.

Such frivolity has no doubt gone over the top at times,
especially perhaps when no cricket is taking place because of rain
and the commentary team has had to talk on through long
periods of inactivity. But shoals of letters testify to the popularity of the conversations, which are sometimes trivial, sometimes
funny, sometimes serious and absorbing. Certainly when cricket
is actually in play the essential duty of giving the score and
describing play has never been forgotten, by Brian or anyone
else.

I first worked with him in the winter of 1971-72 when there
was no winter tour and the OB and Current Affairs departments
came together under the direction of a genial producer called
Stephen Bonarjee to produce elaborately constructed commentaries on a computer Test match between the best post-war teams
from England and Australia. It was a great opportunity for me to
show such cricketing knowledge as I had and to try to make an
early mark as a commentator, having left *The Cricketer* to join
the BBC Sports News staff under the legendary sports report
producer Angus Mackay in January 1970.

Neville Cardus and John Arlott were also involved – it was a
chance for me to get to know both of them better – and we had
great fun constructing running commentary from information
sheets off the computer very similar to the cables used by the
Australians in the early simulated broadcasts.

The following year, having done several 'test' commentaries
for Robert Hudson with the blessing and encouragement of
Angus Mackay and his industrious successor, Bob Burrows, I
was asked to commentate on the first One-Day International

played in England, between England and Australia at Old Trafford. I relished the whole experience. I had had two years' experience on the staff in reporting, presenting, interviewing, writing scripts, even very occasionally producing, and, having lived the idea of being a cricket commentator since my schooldays, I felt completely at home in the friendly atmosphere.

Brian Johnston had made sure I was relaxed. I had joined him for dinner the previous evening with John Woodcock, the cricket correspondent of *The Times* (who in his own early days had acted as a television cameraman as well as a personal assistant to Jim Swanton) and Jack Fingleton, who was one of the summarizers during the match at Old Trafford. I remember Jack got extremely heated about the *fuserium* disease which had affected the pitch at Headingley earlier in the summer and produced ideal conditions for Derek Underwood, but he was in great good humour during the broadcasts the following day and he was great fun to work with.

My early opportunities to commentate were restricted to some extent by a rivalry between my department, Sports News, and Outside Broadcasts. The Head of Radio and later Director General, Ian Trethowan, had spotted that the distinctions between the two departments were blurred and in many ways unnecessary, and when the tough Scot Mackay, who had resisted any challenge to his personal empire, retired, it fell to Robert Hudson to organize the amalgamation of the two. I was encouraged to go as a reporter to home Test matches, however, for news and sports news programmes, and since the Tests of 1972 I have had the great good fortune to report and/or commentate on every home Test match.

Soon after his appointment as Head of OB's Robert Hudson was presented with a crisis which he and Mackay needed to face up to together. The BBC document *Broadcasting in the Seventies*, a blueprint for the future, virtually ignored sport, and Test Match Special was only pencilled in with a query as the music lobby took another opportunity to object to the interruptions to their programmes. But Hudson spoke with a voice of quiet

Below: 'Lobby' (Seymour de Lotbinière), an outstanding producer and Head of Outside Broadcasts, whose teaming with Howard Marshall was to form the basis of ball-by-ball commentary in Britain. He was made Controller of Programme Services, Television, in 1956.

Above: Robert Hudson, an accomplished cricket, rugby and Special Events commentator, who became Head of Radio Outside Broadcasts in 1969. It was Hudson who first suggested the idea of full ball-by-ball coverage of Test matches.

Below: Lance Sieveking at the BBC Drama Department in 1948. In the late 1920s and 1930s he had been an Outside Broadcasts pioneer of great imagination and ability. John Arlott called him 'probably the outstanding and most creative pioneer of British broadcasting'.

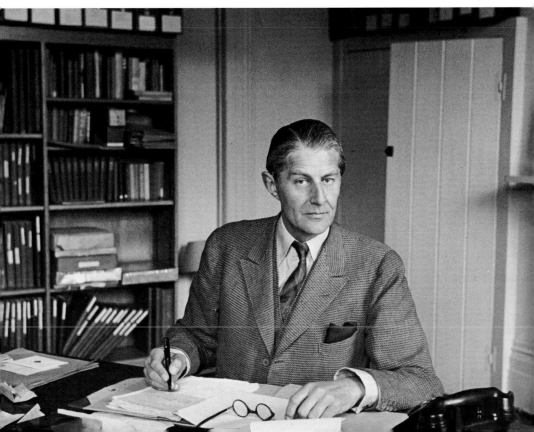

Left: Kenneth Ablack, a Trinidadian who had played for Northamptonshire, commentated on the 1950 West Indies series in England. He later became producer, BBC African, Caribbean and Colonial Services, and chairman of Trinidad and Tobago's National Broadcasting Service.

Right: Rex Alston, photographed in 1988 by Brian Johnston's wife Pauline. Three years earlier, *The Times* had erroneously published his obituary!

Below: Rex Alston in his heyday, commentating from The Oval in June 1949: 'precise, meticulous, fair and unbiased', to quote Brian Johnston.

Above: The BBC-1 *Grandstand* team of commentators at the Headingley Test (England v. Pakistan) in July 1971: (from the left) Jim Laker, Denis Compton, Peter West and Ted Dexter.

Below: A gathering of commentators at the *John Player Year Book* lunch in 1973: (from the left) John Arlott, Ted Dexter, Trevor Bailey, Denis Compton and Jim Laker.

Above: The BBC Radio 3 commentators at a lunch just prior to the start of the 1978 season: (left to right, standing) Bob Burrows (Head of Sport, Radio), Howard Newby (Managing Director, Radio), Tony Lewis, Stephen Hearst (Controller, Radio 3), E.W. Swanton, Trevor Bailey, Freddie Trueman, Don Mosey, Brian Johnston. Left to right, kneeling: Bill Frindall, C.M.-J., Peter Baxter.

Below: The commentary box at Headingley, 1980 (England v. West Indies): Peter West, Michael Fordham, John Edrich, Tom Graveney, Jim Laker, Richie Benaud and a young supporter.

His last Test: John Arlott bows out of the commentary box at the Centenary Test (England v. Australia), Lord's, 1980.

Right: With Keith Miller.

Below: Making television news.

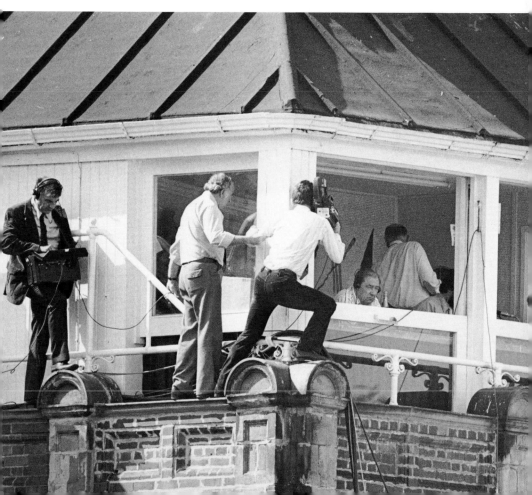

Above left: Alan McGilvray, the supreme exponent in Australia of the art of cricket commentary.

Above right: E.W. Swanton, 'who moved majestically from box to box, his wide vocabulary, deep knowledge of cricket and rich voice becoming as well known as his authoritative writing for the *Daily Telegraph*'.

Left: Colin Milburn, whose jolly Geordie tones enlivened the Test Match Special commentary box until his untimely death early in 1990.

Opposite above: The Test Match Commentary team in action at Lord's in 1981: (left to right) Alan McGilvray, Trevor Bailey, Freddie Trueman, Henry Blofeld.

Opposite below: The radio and TV commentary boxes at Trent Bridge, Nottingham (England v. New Zealand), 1983.

Above: The BBC Radio team at Old Trafford (England v. West Indies), 1984. Back row, left to right: Tony Lewis, Henry Blofeld, Ray Illingworth, C.M.-J., Peter Baxter, Bill Frindall. Front row: Don Mosey, Trevor Bailey, Brian Johnston, Freddie Trueman, Tony Cozier.

Left: The author and broadcaster at work in St Kitts, February 1990, being interviewed for Leewards TV.

authority, and Mackay was respected by most and feared by some (I always felt the same nervous unease in his presence as I had in that of my prep school headmaster, yet Mackay himself had encouraged me, having noticed my early freelance broadcasts, and I think had more or less seen to it that I should get a staff job). With such stout defenders, not only did TMS emerge unscathed but the output of both Sport and OB's actually increased, considerably so after Hudson had grasped the nettle and, with Trethowan's encouragement, amalgamated the two in 1973. He recalls with some pride the party held at his house in St Albans when hatchets were buried and new friendships sealed. The new 'Sports Unit' went from strength to strength under Hudson's successors, Cliff Morgan, Bob Burrows, 'Slim' Wilkinson, Pat Ewing and Larry Hodgson, although theirs was a difficult job with an increasingly young, ambitious, mobile staff to deal with.

None was in any doubt about the value of Test Match Special, which happily developed at its own pace whilst other sports programmes became, in reflection of the age, slicker, faster moving, flashier but also perhaps less flavoursome and substantial. Only in one case – the comprehensive coverage of the Wimbledon Championships under the direction first of Burrows, later of Mike Lewis – has any sports programme had anything like enough of the precious commodity of time to develop its character.

Cricket was always the game where, because of its time-scale, characters emerged through their play more thoroughly than in any other sport, and it is so, too, no doubt with the commentators who interpret and describe their actions. After myself, the new recruits to TMS during the Johnston era have included Henry Blofeld and Don Mosey in 1974 and Tony Lewis in 1977. Lewis moved to television when it offered him a regular job, but Blofeld's rich voice, unquenchable enthusiasm and quick eye for anything from a leg-break to the colour of the pattern on the red skirt of a watching lady in Row H, Section C, have made him as instantly recognizable as his deliberately cultivated catchphrase,

'My dear old thing' (originally conceived, I suspect, because he could never remember the name of the person whom he was talking to). Mosey has been an effective contrast, an authentic voice of the north. Inclined to be lugubrious, but as fond as anyone of a hearty laugh, he has a fine command of the English language and a firm belief in right and wrong, not least when it comes to broadcasting standards.

Fred Trueman and Trevor Bailey gradually emerged as the regular summarizers, almost by popular demand. Bailey made his first appearance in a Test Match Special box in 1967. He is a most sympathetic person to work with, letting one down lightly if ever he disagrees with one's judgement, unfailingly courteous and possessed of an excellent idea of when to speak and when to stop. His incisive analysis of the situation in a given game or of the abilities of players is seldom wrong, and although some listeners object to the bluntness of his judgements it is because he has such strong opinions and is prepared to give them that he is so good to listen to.

Fred Trueman was not 'discovered' as a broadcaster until 1974 but, although not without his critics, he has had a warm following ever since. He is at his very best during long periods of rain when it has become expected and accepted that we should fill the vacuum with cricketing comment and reminiscence. Few minds have stored so much in the way of cricketing fact and anecdote as Fred's and precious few tell a story better. He is a fierce critic of the modern player, some would say too fierce, but his relentless advocacy of the unchanging orthodoxies of cricket – a straight bat for batsmen, and line and length for bowlers – is repeatedly proved right.

A great many other former Test cricketers have joined the programme from time to time, for the sake of variety as much as anything else, including Mike Selvey and Robin Jackman, both closely in touch with recent playing trends, and the jovial 'fat man' Colin Milburn, whose jolly Geordie tones enlivened the commentary box much as his rumbustious batting once ignited matches in the middle.

Keeping a loose hold on the reins which bind these various talents together is the man appointed by Robert Hudson to produce the cricket as successor to Michael Tuke-Hastings in 1973. Peter Baxter was then only 26 and, as was the case with my own duties as cricket correspondent which I assumed in the same year at the age of 28 following Brian Johnston's retirement from the staff (he carried on doing as much work as ever as a freelance), he was not officially appointed to the job until he had done it for a while.

Baxter joined the BBC in 1965 as a clerk in OB Bookings, soon after leaving Wellington College and having spent four months in Forces Broadcasting in Aden producing a record requests programme. He had his first taste of Test cricket the following season as a 'number two' – assistant to the producer. Having had experience also of rugby and soccer OB's, he was plunged into the deep waters of TMS and quickly showed his conscientious approach and his capabilities as an efficient organizer as well as an easy-going nature which fitted neatly into the family atmosphere of the programme engendered mainly by Johnston.

'It was quite a responsibility, I suppose, for someone relatively inexperienced,' he reflects now, 'but the programme had its own momentum by then. I inherited a marvellous secretary from Michael called Brenda Davies, who knew the form with contracts and whom to deal with at the various grounds.'

At first he used to produce, like Tuke-Hastings, from the studio, except in the case of the two London Tests. Dick Maddock, a cheery, pipe-smoking former BBC announcer with an excellent, rich voice, was producer in the Midlands, aided by Joan Burns, his own extremely efficient secretary; and Don Mosey was very much cock of the north.

Baxter has introduced a number of new ideas, most of them unrelated to the essential business of the ball-by-ball commentary itself. 'I make no apologies', he says, 'for the family atmosphere or the fact that we try to convey an enjoyment of the game of cricket. Chocolate cakes, not to mention all the other goodies we receive from our loyal public – sweets, fruit, and, of course, the occasional champagne – are all very welcome, but the cricket has always been and always will be paramount. If I have a philosophy for the programme at all it is that there should be light touches on the tiller, not violent corrections.'

He has always been sensitive to public opinion expressed through letters or in the press. He had a stormy passage to steer for a while after Arlott's retirement in 1980 when, inevitably, there were some who said that the programme would never be the same again. In a literal sense this, of course, is true. Arlott had unique gifts and they could not directly be replaced once he had, with superb bathos, eschewed any rousing farewell speech and left the box at Lord's for the last time, during the Centenary Test between England and Australia, with the words: 'And after Trevor Bailey it will be Christopher Martin-Jenkins.'

Happily the programme survived the retirement of its poet and one hopes the same will be true when the time inevitably comes for its jester, Brian Johnston (78 in 1990), to call it a day as well, even though, initially, I do not doubt that there will be the same sense of loss and the same feeling that it will never be the same.

It will be Baxter's job as producer to keep the standards high. He has surely been wise to let events, to some extent, take their own shape over the years. It happened gradually, for instance, that instead of going back to the studio for music to be played whenever bad light or rain interrupted play, we began to talk about this and that for longer and longer periods until it became, without our fully admitting it, almost a challenge to keep going. In such circumstances Trueman and Johnston tend to be at their sparkling best and it is extraordinary how many people say that the programme is never better than when it is raining. Some might see that as an indictment of the cricket, but one man, an advocate of the 'talk about cricket and nothing else' philosophy, told me recently it was a sign that our commentaries were inadequate. Happily, his seems to be a minority viewpoint. Indeed he might be surprised to know that John Arlott wrote in 1961: 'Some listeners write to say that they only want to hear about the ball being bowled and what happens to it. We tried that once: the result was 75 per cent silence. There must be other material. Atmosphere varies from ground to ground. To describe it is surely part of the essence of cricket watching.'

Personally I often come off the air thinking I have not described enough of what has been going on in the theatre away from the centre of the stage. It is a comfort when some people say, 'Thank goodness you stick to the cricket', but it is not necessarily a compliment. The essential thing perhaps is that we all approach the job slightly differently, though we all stick to the basic framework laid down by Marshall and Lobby. Variety for the listener comes not just from the different characteristics of each commentator but also from the different accents and voice pitches. This balance has been deliberately sought by those – usually the Head of OB's in conjunction with his cricket producer and sports editor – who decide on the team for each match.

Other Baxter innovations have also been to do with the filling of available airtime. As early as 1953 Rex Alston began preparing programmes looking back at past Test matches, using archive material to fill in gaps caused by rain, but in the 1970s Baxter and I put together a number of more detailed programmes looking back at great games on the ground of the Test in question, which were originally transmitted during the lunch intervals. Other lunch and teatime features have included the answering of listeners' letters and of questions phoned in 'live'; the invitation to cricket-mad celebrities from outside the game to come in on Saturdays to talk to Brian Johnston about the game and their own careers; quizzes; and, more recently, a topical feature called 'Talking Point'. This last was my idea, designed to encourage young broadcasting talent and possible commentators of the future. Life will be easier for them if they are already familiar with the programme and not unknown to the listeners.

Peter Baxter's strengths as an organizer, and as a generally unflappable producer, have been seen at their very best during the planning and execution of overseas cricket broadcasts in many of which, from India, Pakistan, Australia and the West Indies, he has been involved at first hand, either as producer or as a reporter and occasional commentator with a light and civilized touch.

Until 1976-77, my third tour as cricket correspondent, there had only been commentary back to the UK in the winter from Australia, the few exceptions including 1938-39 from South Africa (E. W. Swanton) and the West Indies in 1967-68 (Brian Johnston) and 1973-74 (myself). The impact made, however, by the unexpected success of Tony Greig's team in India persuaded Baxter, with enthusiastic support from Bob Burrows and the willing co-operation of Jasdev Singh of All India Radio, to set up commentary on the closing stages of England's victory in the first Test in Delhi (John Lever's memorable 10-wicket début appearance) and at regular times during the thrilling third Test in Madras where, to my excitement, England wrapped up the series.

Since then overseas commentary on England matches has become an accepted part of the service to listeners, with Radio Three providing the willing home. Sometimes Baxter has, as it were, taken TMS abroad, familiar voices being joined by others like Mike Denness, Ashis Ray, Peter Loader, Paul Sheahan, Pearson Surita and Abbas Ali Baig. On other tours the BBC, as has been the case from the earliest days with the ABC in Australia, has merely transmitted the coverage of the home country's broadcasting authority, with the BBC man as the guest in the same tradition which allowed men like Alan McGilvray, Jim Maxwell, Neville Oliver, Roy Lawrence, Tony Cozier, Alan Richards, Omar Kureishi, Mushtaq Mohammed, the Nawab of Pataudi and the Maharajah of Baroda to be welcomed to TMS.

The late 'Jackie' Baroda, a delightful man inclined to giggle and possessing a deadpan sense of humour, was referred to, by directive from on high, simply as 'Prince', which I always thought sounded rather as though one were addressing a dog. He continued a princely tradition from India, following the Maharajah of Vizianagram ('Vizzy'), Pearson Surita, who sounded like a prince, and Pataudi. One of these days we shall employ a mere commoner . . .

⊏━━▆

CHAPTER TEN

Ball by Ball Overseas

The development of ball-by-ball commentary in Australia was outlined in an earlier chapter. Despite the advent of television, ball-by-ball radio commentary has retained a loyal audience and there have been fewer disruptions to running commentaries on Sheffield Shield cricket than there have been to county cricket in Britain.

These days a variety of commercial radio stations compete with the ABC, but the main radio service, which sometimes has to give way to live coverage of proceedings in Parliament, alone covers the entire continent, with its vast, sparsely populated country areas, and attracts an affection similar to that of TMS in Britain, especially amongst 'traditional' cricket followers, namely country folk or Australians of British origin. As with the BBC commentaries through World Service transmissions (until, to widespread protests from Asia in particular, the BBC's Special Overseas Transmissions were cut for budgetary reasons in 1989) ABC commentaries also have a wide following elsewhere in the world by means of Radio Australia, which reaches wide areas of Asia and the Pacific.

It has been the job mainly of commercial television – notably Channel Nine – and the commercial radio stations to 'sell' cricket to the newer Australians who have moved to the country in large numbers since the war from nations such as Greece and Yugoslavia. They have done so successfully; the popular Australian fast bowler Len Pascoe, for instance, was born with the surname Durtanovich of Yugoslav parents, and it is nothing these days to hear a Sydney taxi-driver pronouncing on the virtues and failings of Australia's team in accents curiously combining guttural Russian with purest New South Welsh 'strine'.

Whilst Mr Packer's television station successfully wooed the immigrants with hyped-up One-Day Internationals, 'Auntie' ABC, in many ways a more conservative organization than the BBC, stuck to traditional values. It has, for example, continued to have longer running commentaries on Sheffield Shield cricket than soccer-obsessed producers in England have accorded county matches.

I have had the privilege of joining ABC commentary teams throughout four Test series between Australia and England. I also helped out during both the Centenary and Bicentennial Tests (1977 and 1988) and the spurious 'World Championship of Cricket', which celebrated the centenary of the Victorian Cricket Association and the erection of floodlights at the Melbourne Cricket Ground following the successful tour of India by David Gower's team in 1984-85, ten years on from my first visit with Mike Denness's side. Wearying though these tours were at times, I generally found the experience delightful on each occasion, not least because of the friendly co-operation of everyone involved with the ABC cricket broadcasts.

One of the reasons why one always feels at home in an Australian commentary box is that the approach of the ABC is very much along the same lines as that of the BBC. Like their counterparts in England, engineers are dedicated and hard-working, if a little less formal. To a correspondent working overseas a helpful engineer is vital, and time and again I have been immensely grateful to someone staying on at the ground on the evening of a day's Test cricket long after everyone else has repaired to the bar or gone home. On many occasions these engineers have driven me to my hotel in their van long after some taxi I had ordered, or planned to share with a fellow journalist, has disappeared because my commitments have lasted longer than expected.

These days sports producers in London expect a multiplicity of reports of different duration and content for various outlets during the day, including general news programmes, not to mention frequent interviews with players and officials or 'opinion' pieces for current affairs programmes when something exciting or (more often) disastrous has occurred to the England team. Sometimes, however, the equipment being used at the commentary point on the ground is different from my own and considerable ingenuity is often required on the part of these willing technical wizards.

Life has become a little easier in the last few years as telephone lines have improved and it has been possible, to save time and money, to make reports or send interviews down telephone lines, often using one of a number of technical devices, including a 'Comrex' and a 'Muttebox'.

Tours were certainly more relaxed affairs for my predecessors as the BBC's 'Own Correspondent' overseas. Rex Alston, the first to travel with any regularity (he went to Australia, the West Indies and South Africa: tours to India and Pakistan were, he said, 'never seriously considered'), recalls that he would cover only the Tests for the BBC, not the matches in between except in unusual circumstances: 'Even for the Tests there was none of this hourly updating. I just got on the phone each evening and did one report. When Cowdrey made 97 in the second innings after scoring a marvellous hundred in the first I was quite unable to get through from Kingston to Ken Pragnell, the producer waiting at Broadcasting House, and that was that – my report never made it.'

Rex Alston, incidentally, denies the frequently alleged story that, during the riot at Port of Spain in the second Test of the 1959-60 series, he described a section of the crowd as behaving like 'animals', whereupon some of them, listening on transistor radios, started throwing bottles at the commentary box. But he does recall it as a very unpleasant experience, not least when the tear gas began blowing in his direction, whilst his wife Elspeth, watching on a different part of the ground, thought it the most exciting day's cricket she had ever seen.

Like Alston, Brian Johnston never visited India in his time as cricket correspondent, but he too witnessed a riot in Pakistan and he was, of course, a frequent visitor to Australia, touring there five times and attracting the same enthusiastic following.

The acknowledged master of the art of commentary in Australia until his retirement was, of course, the perennial Alan McGilvray who, though less amusing than Brian Johnston and less profound, literary and emotive than John Arlott, has nevertheless been bettered by no one in the world as a fluent, perceptive and intimate observer of the ebbs and flows of cricket. He was very much the central figure in the boxes of Australia and always a courteous and helpful companion. Just once in countless days of working with him I incurred his wrath by asking the producer if my own commentary period of twenty minutes might be changed in order to accommodate telephone reports required of me for another BBC programme. He muttered something about importunate interlopers from the Mother Country thinking they could lay down the law to their colonial cousins, but his irritation was entirely understandable and it was a matter quickly forgotten. As a regular traveller himself, as highly respected in England as he was at home, he knew something of the pressures on a commentator representing his country overseas.

Although he was once famously embarrassed by Brian Johnston when he endeavoured to answer a deliberately timed question with his mouth full of cake – an incident all the funnier because he prided himself on his dignity – and although on another occasion Brian innocently asked him something else and turned round to see him fast asleep in a chair, Alan was not usually one of those commentators who spend most of their time in the box. Certainly in Australia his habit, as soon as he finished one of his stints, was to leave for a smoke or a beer and a chat with one of his many 'mates', always returning in good time for his own immaculate twenty-minute period.

On my first few visits to Australia the regular summarizer was Lindsay Hassett, justly one of the most popular men ever to pull on an Australian sweater – or 'guernsey' as he would call it. The humour of this bright-eyed, poker-faced jockey of a man is famous. My favourite amongst the many stories of his playing days is of the time when, captaining the returning Australian Forces team in India in 1946, one of his players, Bob Cristofani, lost his temper when a catch-behind appeal was turned down. Lindsay told him to go and cool off for a while and Cristofani left the field in high dudgeon. When he returned, chastened, some time later he called to his skipper to ask where he should go in the field, a spinner having now taken over the bowling. Lindsay made an elaborate show of signalling him first one side of the pavilion, then the other and finally, to the great amusement of the crowd and as a firm lesson to everyone else about the need to accept the umpire's decision, he guided him back with hand signals towards the entrance gate of the pavilion and then back up the steps.

In the box his humour was revealed in occasional dry remarks as he summed the cricket up with shrewd judgement in a slightly monotonous voice. Off duty he twinkled with good humour. He is the only man, I am glad to say, who has persuaded me, over lunch at Melbourne, to drink more than was good for me during the course of a day's broadcasting. I got the giggles more than once during the afternoon session that followed – the occasion, I recall, was a relatively unimportant One-Day International – and Lindsay kept exploiting the situation with queries as to what I was laughing about, a mischievous look in his eye.

Norman O'Neill has taken over from the pipe-smoking Hassett as the most regular of the ABC summarizers. An exceptionally warm-hearted man with a great affection, like his predecessor, for the Poms, he is quick to praise and slow to criticize, always more than fair to the modern player, especially if he is an opponent.

Amongst many other colleagues, Dave Renneberg and Bob Simpson in Sydney, Peter Burge, Jack McLaughlin and Tom Veivers in Brisbane, Ian Brayshaw, Bob Massie, Keith Slater and Peter Loader in Perth, and Paul Sheahan, Bob Potter, Alan Hurst, Bill Jacobs, Frank Tyson (better known on television) and the marvellously loquacious Max Walker have all been enthusiastic, knowledgeable summarizers and splendid company.

It has often been remarked that the Australian style of radio commentary – supposedly a businesslike description of the game with no frills – is less interesting than the *laissez-faire* BBC approach, but I have always thought that a number of Australian commentators are very good, including Jim Maxwell, Dennis Commetti, Graham Dawson (particularly helpful and considerate to overseas travellers), Drew Morphett, Peter Mears and Neville Oliver. Several of these men have moved on to jobs in commercial radio and television having learned their trade in the Sports Department of the ABC under such dedicated leaders as Bernie Kerr, Dick Mason and Alan Marks, all of whom also did a good deal of cricket commentary.

Neville Oliver, a red-headed general sports 'caller' (the Australian word for commentator) from Tasmania, was chosen ahead of the respected cricket specialist Jim Maxwell for the tour to England in 1989 and made an outstanding success of his visit, his fluent, positive, amusing style being appreciated by TMS listeners at both ends of the globe. Another personable, experienced and efficient performer both as commentator and producer is Alan Marks, now high in ABC sports administration, who came to England in 1985 to share the load on Alan McGilvray's final tour.

I found much the same friendly attitude when at last I covered a tour of New Zealand in 1987-88. Alan Richards, a fine all-round sportsman in his youth, was for many years the NZBC's extremely competent travelling commentator and

reporter, based in Auckland, and he has been succeeded by a
bubbly character with an engaging sense of humour and good
eye for a story, Brian Waddle. For many years, however, the
doyen of the NZBC sound commentaries has been Iain Gallaway, a pillar of Dunedin society with a delightful, mellow voice
and a fine historical perspective. Apart from being a cricket and
rugby commentator of justly high repute, Iain is a greatly
respected lawyer with an old family practice started by his
Scottish ancestors.

During England's 1987-88 tour of New Zealand, Jeremy
Coney made as big an impact as a summarizer as he had as
captain of his country's Test team. A witty, whimsical character
with a great love of the game, he was extremely good company
throughout a dull series often interrupted by rain, when he
reminisced entertainingly and commented shrewdly.

The pioneer cricket broadcaster in New Zealand was Alan
Allardyce, who joined the Radio Broadcasting Company (forerunner of the present public service, Radio New Zealand) in 1926
and was soon broadcasting any sport he could. Allardyce himself
is on record as claiming that the first cricket broadcasts in New
Zealand were on two matches between New Zealand and the
Rest of New Zealand at the Basin Reserve Ground, Wellington,
and Lancaster Park, Christchurch, in November 1927. At the
first match 'Mr A. Varney' provided commentaries in between
races from Christchurch. Varney was Secretary of the Wellington Cricket Association and is thought to be Arthur Varney, a
former accountant from Eastbourne, Sussex, who emigrated to
New Zealand and died in Dunedin in 1942.

In June 1928 the RBC published a breakdown of its sports
coverage in the preceding year. Cricket had been allocated as
many as 29 broadcasts and a total of 58 hours, which suggests
coverage much along the lines of the early BBC approach,
namely reports and updates rather than running commentary for
long periods. This is confirmed by a notice that for the Otago
versus Wellington Plunkett Shield match 'short relays only are to
be given, the station passing back to the studio to entertain with

musical numbers and to announce the results of other activities to hand'. In the same year the RBC boasted that it could bring listeners the scores from cricket matches in Australia 'within three-quarters of an hour of the close of play'.

Life was enjoyable but hard working for the pioneers, here as elsewhere. Allardyce claimed in the New Zealand *Listener* of 6 October 1967: 'In those far-off days my task was to arrive at the ground, fir up the gear and be on the air from 11am to 6pm, without being asked about lunch or even afternoon tea, and to give a review of the play from the station at 7.30pm. My recompense was one pound, one shilling less tax, net 19 and 11.'

Modern commentators would no doubt aver that, apart from not having to 'fir up the gear', little has changed, either in workload or recompense.

Jim Sullivan of Radio New Zealand's Sound Archives recalls developments in the 1930s and 40s:

The Radio Company's successor, the Broadcasting Board, seems as usual to have been pretty pedestrian. Even as late as 1936 it was covering the NZ v. MCC Test in Wellington by giving hourly summaries of the state of play followed by light music – and they appear not to have relayed summaries to the other YA stations.

Under the NZBS cricket commentaries continued to be relayed from the local YA station, interspersed with musical interludes, and the wartime Mobile Unit sent back reports on Army cricket (one recording in Sound Archives is of the match NZ v. Australian Imperial Forces in the Middle East on 12 October 1941).

The first tour after the war was by an Australian team which played one Test at the Basin Reserve. The NZBS was adapting the wartime schedules to accommodate the new upsurge of sport once the troops had returned home. 2YA was now almost saturated with sport on a Saturday afternoon, so 2YC was put on air early to provide music for the non-sports follower.

Cricket coverage for the Australians was presented in quarter-hour blocks of commentary every hour and these relays were also broadcast by the other YA stations. This quarter-hour block schedule is unusual given the known interest in cricket. During the Australians' match with Auckland the 2YA switchboard was getting 250 calls a day from people wanting to know the cricket score, so continuous commentary might have been warranted.

The next major tour by New Zealand was to England in 1949. Walter Hadlee's team was covered by BBC reports prepared for rebroadcast in New Zealand – these were magazine programmes of eight minutes, 'with the boys on tour' sort of thing. Games were covered by commentary or reviews broadcast by BBC shortwave. (Many New Zealanders would have listened to BBC General Overseas Service direct.) The YAs broadcast the scores after news bulletins plus a review of the day's play.

The four Test matches earned energetic coverage. The BBC set up special transmitters in England and two new aerials were built at Singapore to ensure the success of the relay. Arthur Gilligan would introduce the broadcasts, which were ball by ball throughout the New Zealand night.

In 1953-54 New Zealand had her own version of 'synthetic' broadcasting when, during the tour of South Africa, Pat Earnshaw and Lance Cross 'commentated' all day from the post office in Wellington on the basis of cables sent every over by the South African commentator, Dennis Done. It took a cable of more than fifty words to do justice to the emotional and unexpected appearance at the crease of Bob Blair on Boxing Day, 1953, only a few hours after hearing of his fiancée's death in the Tangiwai train disaster.

Commentators on cricket in New Zealand in the 1950s included Gallaway (from 1953), Richards (from 1956), Jim Reid, Lankford Smith, the Test player Colin Snedden (father of Martin, another Test cricketer), Cyril Crawford and Noel Lawson.

Iain Gallaway was the first to cover an overseas tour for RNZ, travelling to India and Pakistan in 1955-56 as the sole representative of the entire media, an incredible thought considering the small army of press which now accompanies any tour. His job was to cover both for radio and for the NZ Press Association.

Other well-known cricket broadcasters in New Zealand in recent years have been Peter Sharp (Christchurch) and Trevor Rigby (Wellington), whilst a long line of distinguished players acting as 'comments men' has included Bert Sutcliffe, John Reid, Noel Harford, Bruce Murray, Bruce Taylor, Bryan Andrews,

Bob Cunis and, more recently, Coney, John Parker and Richard Hadlee.

Facilities have improved markedly in recent years, but Gallaway recalls broadcasting from a number of improvised 'boxes' including 'the front seat of motor cars, the tray of trucks, caravans or various precarious makeshift platforms'. These, however, are nothing compared with his experience in India in 1955-56 when he broadcast from the middle of a tree-trunk in Lahore and later shared a commentary with the Maharajah of Vizianagram: 'Although he fancied himself as a commentator he had not been appointed by All India Radio, so he arranged a three-day game against his own XI at Benares so that he could broadcast it – which he solemnly did with me for three days. I have no idea how vast our audience was!'

My own first experience of commentary abroad was in the West Indies in 1973-74 when the main matches in each island were covered, as they still are, either by the Caribbean Broadcasting Company or by commercial companies. In some cases they transmit rival commentary services side by side and there are few households on the main islands which do not have the ball-by-ball commentary ringing loudly out all day long. Cricket here is truly an essential part of the way of life.

The first-ever radio commentary in the West Indies was performed in Trinidad by Ken Loughlin in 1937. He covered a cricket tournament in a rented transmitter, working alone, he told me during 1989, from 11.30am to 6pm. Here indeed were shades of Howard Marshall. No wonder Loughlin was awarded the 'Humming Bird' medal in 1987 for fifty years of service to sport in Trinidad and Tobago. Other early commentators in Trinidad were Trevor McDonald and Ken Gordon. Ernest Eytle, of the BBC's Caribbean Service, covered the famous Worrell v. Benaud series as a freelance with the ABC.

For many years the outstanding journalist and commentator on Caribbean cricket has been Tony Cozier, the genial Bajan who first joined a BBC team in 1966 and who has covered the game fairly, fluently and with growing authority ever since.

He first toured with a West Indian side to England in 1966. Immensely hard-working, he became Editor of the Barbados daily newspaper *The Nation* in 1989, but showed no sign of reducing his workload as the freelance cricket pundit whom all the world trusts on West Indian cricketing affairs. The son of another well-known journalist, Jimmy Cozier, he was a keen and useful club cricketer for the Wanderers, and his beautiful wife Gillian has organized many a club cricket tour in her capacity as a travel agent.

Cozier's predecessor as the best-known West Indian commentator was Roy Lawrence, a tall, amiable Jamaican who left his native land, disenchanted with its politicians and its horrendous social and economic problems, in the 1970s to settle in Yorkshire. His memories go back to his first broadcasts in 1946 when Overseas Rediffusion Ltd came to the West Indies and started commercial broadcasting. He recalls:

There was radio and Rediffusion in Jamaica, Trinidad and British Guiana but only Rediffusion in Barbados. I was sports announcer, disc jockey and sales representative, and my first Test match was at Sabina Park against Gubby Allen's team in 1947-48. George Headley was to have captained the West Indies but was injured the day before and so Everton Weekes, who had been dropped from the side, was sent for. The West Indies fielded the first day with a substitute, and when Weekes went in to bat Godfrey Evans dropped him twice before he made ten. Weekes went on to make a century, the first of five consecutive centuries in Test cricket. The commentators were Ivan Barrow, Crawford White and myself, with Jim Swanton doing comments. (I was terrified at Jim's manner as he was so abrupt by our standards, but I certainly appreciated his accuracy in summing up a day's play.) There was no transmission of commentary to the other islands of this series. Winston Place of Lancashire got a hundred, but the West Indies won the Test by 10 wickets.

Next came the West Indies tour of 1950 on which, through Cable and Wireless, we were able to carry commentary. I can assure you that Ramadhin and Valentine were as much of a surprise to us as they were to England. I tied everything up at our studios, and it was interesting to get commercials adjacent to the commentary, without commercializing the BBC. After this tour we entertained British Guiana under Peter Baillie, who told me the night before the match that he was going to show the Englishmen how to play Valentine. The next day I apparently said: 'Trevor Bailey has been batting for just over an hour and he gets a single off Valentine which takes him to 10, nine of which are singles.'

The 1952-53 season saw India paying their first visit to the West Indies, and for the first time commentary was sent to all the islands through Cable and Wireless. The West Indies won the second Test in Barbados and the other four were drawn. Berry Subadicari joined Ivan Barrow and Lawrence as commentators, and Allan Rae, who had been dropped from the West Indies team, was the summarizer.

Len Hutton's side of 1953-54 had to suffer a riot when J. K. Holt was given out lbw to Brian Statham during the first Test at Sabina Park. Roy Lawrence describes the scene as 'intense, dramatic and furious: the poor umpire, Perry Burke, was beaten up that night – so was his wife – and they had to have police protection for the rest of the match'.

After the West Indies had won the first two Tests and England the third, Lawrence became the first commentator to be invited to work outside his own island when he joined the team in Trinidad for the fourth Test. This was, he recalls, the last Test in the West Indies to be played on a matting wicket:

I experienced a bit of insularity when a spectator came up to me and said: 'Are you Roy Lawrence of Jamaica?' I said, 'Yes' and he said: 'Go back to Jamaica: you are no damned good.' I believe I won him over in the end. It was a very heavy-scoring match and I remember Graveney catching Holt in the slips off Compton. After Holt was walking, Puss Achong the umpire gave him not out. Holt was out soon after lunch but Weekes got a double century and Worrell and Walcott centuries. For England May and Compton got centuries and Graveney ninety. I remember Laker being hit a dreadful blow in his face by Frank King. When I went to see him in the hotel I recall Jim saying that it was his fault as he should have got out of the way. The Test was drawn and back to Jamaica we went. I remember George Headley meeting us at the airport and saying that they had had a two-inch rainfall the day before and he hoped England batted first.

Well, the West Indies batted first and I saw the greatest piece of bowling from Trevor Bailey, who took seven wickets. Hutton then played a wonderful innings of 200-odd and England won the Test and tied the series. I'm told that it was in this match that I said: 'It's another beautiful day here at Sabina Park, the sun is blowing and the breeze is shining all over the ground.'

It was in that Test match that Gary Sobers made his début for the West Indies. He replaced Alf Valentine as a bowler and I well remember him being booed all the way to the wicket when he went in to bat!

In 1954-55 the Australians made their first visit to the West Indies and on this occasion I was invited to cover the whole tour. How I enjoyed it! Working with Alan McGilvray was a real pleasure. Australia, led by Ian Johnson, were too strong for the West Indies, but the highlight for the West Indies must have been in Barbados when Australia in their first innings made over 600 and had the West Indies 147 for 6 when Depeiza joined Dennis Atkinson. They put on 347 – a truly remarkable partnership.

Lawrence remembers that reception from New Zealand on the 1955-56 tour – captained by Atkinson and managed by John Goddard – was so poor that they had to get the scores from Radio Australia. But there was no question of such haphazard coverage of the 1957 tour of England. England dominated the series once Ramadhin had been tamed by May and Cowdrey at Edgbaston, but Lawrence has happy memories of this inaugural season of complete ball-by-ball coverage.

It was my first trip to England as a commentator and I was contacted by the shipping company T. Geddes Grant Ltd. to do ten-minute summaries on every first-class match – quite a chore.

It was a most enjoyable tour for me and great to be working with John Arlott, Rex Alston and Robert Hudson. Our summarizers were Freddie Brown, Norman Yardley and Denis Compton. The commentary box was a happy one and our scorer was Arthur Wrigley, whom I became friendly with and was able to invite to Jamaica for a Test match against Pakistan. Indeed he was scoring for us when Gary Sobers broke the world record by making 365 not out. It is peculiar that this was his first century in Test cricket; he was ably helped by Conrad Hunte, who got 260: they still hold the West Indies record of 446 for the second wicket.

When Gary made the 365th run, the crowd broke the fence down, ran on to the field, picked Gary up, carried him to the pavilion and told Gerry Alexander that that was enough and he must declare. Gerry had no alternative, though he said in an interview with me that he had every intention of letting Gary make 400. This was not the end of the excitement of the day as Kardar, the Pakistan captain, helped the crowd to damage the wicket and refused to continue playing on it, so there was no more play for the day and the wicket had to be repaired. But the West Indies won the next day. It is not often remembered that Gary went into the next Test and made a hundred in each innings and never looked back. What a wonderful cricketer he was and how I enjoyed touring with him.

Gerry Alexander was a fine captain and it is not generally known that when the West Indies Board invited him to captain the team to Australia in 1960-61 he reminded them that Frank Worrell had returned to the West Indies from university in England and was available to tour and that he, Alexander, would be happy to play under him. I had a disappointment on the next tour to Australia in 1968-69, as my wife was expecting and was not keen for me to be away for that length of time, so I had to phone Alan McGilvray and cry off. I told him that I thought Tony Cozier would do a good job and he had me ask Tony to send a tape, and that was Tony Cozier's first trip to Australia.

After that amazing tour to Australia there was great excitement in the West Indies over our tour to England in 1963. Things I remember of that 1963 tour include, of course, Charlie Griffith. The English press were quite satisfied that Charlie 'chucked' and so were some of us from the West Indies. Barely a day went by that Charlie didn't get a roasting in the papers. I remember having dinner with Frank Worrell during our Lancashire match and saying to him how worried I was over Charlie. Frank said: 'Remember the umpires are in charge and if they no-ball him I will deal with it.' The last day was coming to an end and I and Maurice Edelston were broadcasting on the General Overseas Service when Arthur Fagg from square-leg no-balled Charlie. Frank took him off and brought him on the other end and he was passed. I drove that night to Fenner's for the University match and bought every morning paper and could find no mention of Charlie being called! At the ground were Syd Buller and Charlie Elliott, who would not believe me, but thank goodness when the bus with the West Indies team arrived, Jeff Stollmeyer, the manager, confirmed it. When the Lancashire players arrived at Lord's for their match with Middlesex they gave the press hell for not reporting it.

The other thing which will live with me all my life is that remarkable Test at Lord's when Colin Cowdrey had to come in to bat with a broken arm. Wes Hall had bowled unchanged from the start of play and Frank Worrell asked me if I would drive him to Southampton as he was so stiff he didn't want him to ride in the bus. We stopped half-way down at a restaurant for dinner and I had to help Wes out of the car. I also remember saying to him what would he have done if he had had to bowl to Colin and his reply was: 'I would take the chain of the Virgin Mary which I wear round my neck and pray to her that I wouldn't hit him and then I would have bowled as fast as I could.'

On the following tour to England in 1966, my station allowed me to go providing I returned to Jamaica for the Eighth Commonwealth and Empire Games, so I missed the fourth Test at Headingley, but as Rex Alston had retired from the BBC I was able to invite him to join our commentary team and it was good fun working with Rex on athletics.

Roy Lawrence retired after the 1966 tour to England and left the stage to his outstanding successor Tony Cozier, but a host of former Test players act as summarizers in the West Indies. Gerry Gomez is the most experienced of them all, a fair, balanced and always serious observer with a fine deep voice and the unique perspective of a man who has been at different times Test cricketer, Test umpire, coach, selector and administrator.

Tony Cozier vividly portrays in *Test Match Special* the significance of Test commentaries throughout the Caribbean:

Pedestrians scurry about their business, one hand holding the transistor tightly to an ear. Bicyclists pay more attention to the commentary emanating from the box on their handlebars than they do the oncoming bus, whose driver is probably tuned into the same wavelength. Company executives and parliamentarians couldn't care less how silly they look at their desks with an earphone securely plugged in, so long as they can follow Viv Richards's latest escapade stroke by stroke.

Nowhere, however, is there such a concentration of radios as at the matches themselves. It may turn out to be of some promotional advantage for one of the Japanese manufacturers to take a survey of, let us say, Kensington Oval in Bridgetown or Queen's Park Oval during the Saturday of a Test to determine just how many of their products are in use. It has now reached such a state of affairs that the size, value and volume of the transistor brought into the ground have become very much status symbols. The spectator with the pocket model (and they seem to be fewer and fewer) will conceal it shame-facedly in deference to the owner of the twin-speaker, four-band radio cassette recorder resembling some satellite earth station.

Constantly during a day's play, the producer will stick a card in front of his commentator who will go through the ritual of asking spectators to 'kindly turn your radios down as the quality of the broadcast is being affected by feedback'. It makes not one iota of difference, mind you. Only when a batsman, who can no longer stand the comments on his strokeplay or lack thereof clearly audible in the middle, pulls away and begs for quiet does the noise temporarily abate.

It is, at one and the same time, a flattering and dangerous situation for the commentator. On the one hand, it is pleasing to know that even crowds as knowledgeable as they are in the West Indies feel that their understanding of the game can be embellished by the radio broadcasts. On the other, it is worrying that they are waiting for every mistake and every comment which does not meet their favour to let you know all about it. A leg-bye inadvertently called a run, or a dropped catch given when the ball may have bounced, or any one of the hundred and one little traps designed to ensnare the commentator, is guaranteed to bring whistles and cat-calls from spectators who are listening. I have actually heard a Guyana crowd boo a certain, perfectly reputable broadcaster whenever it was his turn to take over the microphone, but I believe there was a political motive for that.

Politics, of course, is never far from the surface in the Caribbean and neither are fierce inter-island rivalries. Naturally, any commentator needs to be above these and relate the cricket as he sees it. Yet the pressure can be great.

When the West Indies were winning their first Test for ages at The Oval against England in 1973, the large West Indian section gathered in the south-western bleachers were understandably ecstatic. I made the comment that I felt their spirit had been helped in no small measure by the consumption of large volumes of a Jamaican beer and a Barbadian rum, both of which I identified by brand. Within a few days, two letters arrived from competing bottlers in the Caribbean angered that I had not included their products in my observation!

The BBC decision to mount Test Match Special from the West

Indies in 1985-86 seemed a popular one on the whole, although we did run into some problems on Antigua where a middleman with a chip on his shoulder insisted on charging us for services which the BBC had willingly supplied free to overseas broadcasting authorities over the years. I went to try to sort things out at 'Broadcasting House', St John's, and was surprised to find that this impressive-sounding building was little more than a hut in a field with a flag on top and goats grazing outside. What did it matter? It is silly and unfair to judge tiny countries like Antigua by the standards of older and bigger ones, but it was disconcerting to find from the one person on duty in the building, a large, smiling, languid, bespectacled lady, that the only person who had answered the many telexes from London about our technical requirements for the Test match had moved to another job.

There was nothing for it but to return to the self-ordained Mr Fixit. Once money had passed between myself and this hostile middleman things began to move, but I had to start my commentary on the first morning of the match on the telephone from the press box.

South Africa, where I did a little radio commentary in 1989 during the centenary celebrations of the first Test at Port Elizabeth, has ever presented an enormous challenge as broadcasting terrain. The country is close to half a million square miles in extent: the size of West Germany, France, Italy and Portugal all put together. There are two official languages – Afrikaans and English – and half a score of languages spoken by the African people of which Xhosa, Zulu and Sotho are the most widely used. These were fundamentals to be met in establishing first a comprehensive radio service and, still more formidably, a nationwide TV service available in numerous languages. Thus not until 1956 (the visit of Peter May's MCC side) did South African radio embark on regular ball-by-ball cricket commentary, and the country was late – partly perhaps for political reasons – in its first launch into television in September 1975.

Once Walter Hammond's party hastened out of Durban in 1939, after the England XI's marvellous rearguard action to score

over 600 runs for victory in the fourth innings of the 'Timeless
Test' had fallen just short of success, leaving the match drawn,
little cricket broadcasting was heard until the 1939-45 war had
run its course. The tour to England in 1947 by the South Africans
under Alan Melville brought with it the novelty for South
African listeners of enjoying direct cricket broadcasts from the
Test match grounds.

George Mann brought his successful MCC touring team to
South Africa a year later (1948-49), but the South African
broadcasting facilities could manage no more than short relays at
long intervals and even so managed its first colossal howler when
cutting John Arlott's commentary from Durban sharp on six
o'clock with the last over of the first Test about to be bowled and
England wanting just one run for victory. A year later, with
Australia in South Africa, the cricket commentaries were but
small affairs and still largely restricted to the English language
and a smattering of broadcasts in Afrikaans. In fact so little
interested was the Broadcasting Corporation in cricket commentary that when in 1953-54 a New Zealand touring team came
to South Africa the Test broadcasts became part of the commercial radio service. Mostly at the instigation of Norman Filmer,
later to become the Corporation's Director-General, both an
Afrikaans- and an English-speaking commentator went with the
tourists for the South Africans' visit to England in 1951. Steve de
Villiers in Afrikaans had two fifteen-minute sessions each day of
the Tests while Charles Fortune joined Rex Alston and John
Arlott as the running commentary trio for the ball-by-ball from
the Test matches. South Africans enjoyed the long relays from
England, but when next year a South African team visited
Australia, no representative of the South African Broadcasting
Corporation went with Jack Cheetham's team for a tour that
revitalized South African cricket standards. By contrast, the
Australian Broadcasting Commission engaged the freelance
Fortune to cover every match of the Springboks' tour.

A schoolmaster, he was rapidly establishing himself as the
voice of his country's cricket: a precise, articulate, cultured

English voice with a tendency towards the flowery description
and the literary quotation. He became well known not just in
South Africa but also in England and Australia and was still
upright and sprightly when he retired as a commentator in the
late 1980s. His natural home in the minds of his listeners was the
commentary box at the Wanderers, which he well remembers
being built:

A major concern for South African cricket over the years immediately following
the 1939 war was the loss of the Old Wanderers' ground in the very centre of
Johannesburg. Appropriated by the United Party government (Jan Smuts was
Prime Minister) the rugby ground at Ellis Park and the Transvaal Rugby Union
helped out by laying a cricket pitch at the middle of the rugby pitch and very well
(often excitingly) did that temporary wicket play. Meanwhile, re-establishing
itself in the Johannesburg northern suburbs, the Wanderers' Club laid down a
fine string of playing fields and from virgin ground set up a new Test match
arena. The new playing field (Alec Hastie in charge) has proved admirable for
the game.

The press and broadcasting accommodation, hoisted very high and directly
above the boundary, looks down the wicket and thus for viewing and describing
the game is second to none. Originally the plans allowed for just one commentary
box and that in a land with two official languages and a dozen indigenous tongues!
And that commentary box in a land of endless sunshine was hermetically sealed
with a plate glass front, fixed and immovable.

This fine new venture was first put to the test on Christmas Eve 1957 when
Peter Richardson and Trevor Bailey opened the innings against Peter Heine and
Neil Adcock: First Test – South Africa v. England (under Peter May) 1956-57.
Nowhere else did radio commentators sweat it out as did those who came to
broadcast at the 'new Wanderers'; all attempts to persuade the Broadcasting
Corporation engineering department to remove that glass front came to nought.
Then on a rain-sodden Sunday, their cricket washed out, two Wanderers' players
sought relief from inaction with a number four iron and a few old golf balls. From
the middle of the playing field they aimed to strike a golf ball over the top of the
towering main grandstand. The first up – a former 'light Blue' cricket captain – had
no problem and easily cleared the grandstand. Second up – a scratch golfer and
Transvaal batsman – did not make the altitude and instead found the exact

intersection of the diagonals of the plate glass sheet that sealed the English commentary box.

The effect was superb: a hole circular and of six inches diameter with the remainder of that glass sheet traversed by a dozen major cracks that ran from point of impact to window frame. It was a spectacular violation that meant immediate relief from the glasshouse incarceration of cricket commentary staff. And the most effective Hole In One of all time!

During the first Test to be played at the Kent Park Wanderers' Club – a match that England won by 131 runs – Charles Fortune and his scorer, John Landau, introduced what they tend to think was a new dimension in cricket scoring and reporting and one now universally accepted. Before the Test, Fortune had asked Landau – a professional accountant – if he thought he could tack on to his scoring data details that would show to whom among the batsmen each ball was bowled. This, could it be done, would make immediately available the number of balls bowled to a batsman (and by whom) and thus provide a far more specific assessment of scoring rate than did the long-established 'scored his runs in so many minutes'. Fortune, a science graduate, had long been unhappy with scoring rates being assessed against the clock for individual batsmen and was anxious to have scores equated against the balls bowled to him in the course of the batsman's innings. Participating in both BBC and Australian Test broadcasts (England 1951 and 1955, Australia 1952-53 and 1954-55) he had heard no mention ever made of balls faced and now with Landau's immediate and totally accurate compilation these statistics became available. A scorebook still in Landau's possession shows that he first used the new method in the second innings of this game.

From that first Test of 1956-57 all official Tests in South Africa were covered by ball-by-ball commentary. Rex Alston, moving on from the 1956 Olympic Games in Melbourne, joined the South African team at New Year 1957 and the Second Test at Newlands, Cape Town. Later tours to South Africa brought with them Brian Johnston from England and Alan McGilvray

from Australia. On the occasion of Bill Lawry's Australian visit
the SABC commentary team included both McGilvray and
Johnston, making a truly international (and totally 'neutral')
broadcasting panel. No official Tests have been played in South
Africa or by South Africans since 1971, but broadcasting in
South Africa has vastly widened its listenership with matches
today covered on both TV and radio in numerous African
languages.

Fortune apart, the best known of the South African voices is
the former Worcestershire and Gloucestershire batsman Martin
Young, a longstanding resident of Cape Town and a jovial,
relaxed performer at the microphone.

Commentary in the most recent of the Test-playing nations,
Sri Lanka, also follows the lines laid down by the BBC and the
ABC, and listeners there have always tuned in to the overseas
services provided by the two original Test nations, as frequent
letters to the BBC World Service have testified over the years.
One such listener, Alan De Silva, now resident in Portugal,
vividly recalls how he escaped a severe beating from his
Yorkshire-born headmaster when, shivering in the corner of the
fearsome schoolmaster's study, he also listened in awe to
Howard Marshall's leisurely description of the build-up to Len
Hutton's breaking of the Test record in 1938 at The Oval. De
Silva remembers his headmaster sitting close to the wireless with
his eyes closed and his fists clenched and then, when the runs
came, jumping to his feet with hands upraised and crying out
'Thou'st dunnit, lad.' De Silva's description continues: 'He was
prancing around his study like a dervish – fist pounding palm,
eyes shining in ecstasy and feet beating a tattoo on the wooden
floor. He struggled to regain his breath. "Ah yes," he said. "We
have – er – some unfinished business to settle. We-ell in the
circumstances perhaps not. Push off now and behave yourself!"'

Posted to The Hague in Holland in 1962-63 De Silva also
recalls the BBC transmitting the ABC coverage of the Ashes
series from 6am via their Vancouver transmitter, prior to which
they apparently tapped Radio Ceylon's commercial service

which was itself relaying Radio Australia. This required, De Silva recalls, some imaginative interventions by a BBC announcer whenever Radio Ceylon were transmitting advertisements, explanations which, he says, 'ranged from the simply factual to the downright rude'.

I did some broadcasting as a guest of Radio Ceylon on my only visit to that beautiful and now sadly troubled island in 1976-77 and much enjoyed the experience, although seeing all their players for the first time and having to make instant attempts not just at identification but also pronunciation was something of a nightmare.

Even in the non-Test playing countries there has been occasional ball-by-ball commentary. In Rhodesia, now Zimbabwe, there was a good deal, and still is, with Bob Nixon, who now commentates for one of the modern phone commentary services in England, the best known exponent.

A less regular performer, Freddie Greenop, recalls the occasion when he pioneered the art in Kampala in 1953. Uganda were playing Tanganyika:

The recently inaugurated Uganda Broadcasting Service was prepared to run what would be the first outside broadcasts on cricket in Uganda at various times during the three-day match, and it was assumed that the OB position would be located in or on the pavilion. This was acceptable up to a point, but bearing in mind that we would have been side-on to the wicket the limitations were obvious. An approach was made to the ground authority and the Uganda Cricket Association to see if some form of structure could be erected that would have the advantage of being behind the bowler's arm.

By good fortune a member of the UCA was not without influence on the local council (Kampala was a municipality in those days) and after he had talked to the people concerned it was arranged that a certain amount of council timber should be stored, temporarily, at one end of the ground and that the best way of storing it was in the form of a commentary point.

Thus it was that I clambered up a ladder and in due course arrived on a platform way above the sightscreen. It was what it was meant to be, a commentary point that had been assembled by using uncut and unplaned timber and right behind the bowler's arm. We enjoyed the luxury of an awning, but the structure was definitely temporary and rickety.

The whole venture received the seal of approval when the then Governor of Uganda, the late Sir Andrew Cohen, himself a keen cricketer, asked if he could watch the game from our commentary position as it 'gives a much better view'. He was quite happy to perch himself precariously aloft with us although anyone who knew him will remember that he was a large, not to say huge, man.

Nowhere has cricket commentary expanded more quickly than on the Indian sub-continent. When I first went there, with Tony Greig's MCC team in 1976-77, All India Radio had the show to itself with a variety of commentators speaking at different times in different languages. It was quite a shock to me, in my ignorance, to realize that there were so many different languages in that vast, teeming country and that although English was in theory the common one it was not understood by everyone by any means.

Apart from the occasional 'guest' appearance on All India Radio on that tour I worked exclusively for the BBC because my old friend Alan Richards, who had just finished touring the country with the New Zealand team, had done me the favour of dissuading the producers from inviting overseas commentators to join them in future: it seemed that Alan had been more frank than they would have wished about the standard and integrity of some of the umpiring.

I was myself a little embarrassed when, after we had mounted our own commentary team at Madras, as explained in the previous chapter, Robin Marlar, never a man slow to speak his mind, disagreed with good-humoured violence with my description of an lbw decision against Tony Greig when several yards down the pitch against Prasanna, the off-spinner. Choosing my words carefully, as one always should in such circumstances, I mentioned that with the batsman so far up the pitch there must have been some doubt. 'Doubt!' thundered the former Sussex captain. 'That was a ghastly decision, outrageous!' Actually, it was no more than the truth.

We did further commentaries during that series from Banga-lore and Bombay. I was very concerned on arrival in Bangalore two days before the fourth Test to find that my commentary box was an unfinished mixture of plywood and wet concrete hanging perilously in space. Yet by the morning of the match it had been transformed by characteristic Indian industry into a smart new commentary booth with a high, commanding view.

On subsequent tours of India and Pakistan, Test Match Special has produced its own commentaries, with willing help from a host of engineers. Meanwhile the sub-continent has 'discovered' limited-overs cricket and television. It was the unexpected World Cup victory over West Indies at Lord's in 1983 which was the catalyst for a revolution in the cricket-watching habits of Indians in particular. Whereas the man in the street would beg, borrow and steal to get a Test ticket it is now the One-Day International which is all the rage, and although the two home countries were beaten in the semi-finals of the World Cup in 1987 the tournament was superbly staged and thoroughly covered on radio and television.

Commentary boxes proliferated on all grounds, many of them like mine at Bangalore in 1977, erected almost overnight – never a problem in this part of the world with so much willing labour – and everywhere one looked there seemed to be a famous former Test player commenting wisely for one station or another. The BBC was well catered for, with only the occasional technical hitch wherever we went, although Peter Baxter and I did spend nearly two hours in roasting sunshine one day at Jaipur whilst a small army of bare-footed engineers tried to work out how to put us through to London. The line was working perfectly from London to Delhi and also from Delhi to Jaipur, but the mile or so between Jaipur Post Office and the cricket ground seemed to be an insurmountable problem. We got there in the end. In India and Pakistan, unlike in the West Indies where time means little to some engineers and tomorrow will usually do, there is never any doubt about the willingness to please and the determination to do a good job, even if some of the equipment is very old-fashioned.

My worst experience came in 1976 at Jullunder where the studio from which I was trying to despatch reports one Saturday evening was being 'modernized'. There were wires everywhere, some of them looking dangerously live, and it took hours of trial and error by the studio manager to make contact with anyone, let alone London. Precious minutes were ticking away and I could imagine the producers in Broadcasting House thinking that this idle so-and-so of a correspondent was letting them down and probably living it up in the bar.

Eventually on a thin, echoing line I heard a distant voice in London answering me, with about half an hour of the sports report still to run. In India it was about 10.30 in the evening. I begged them to settle for whatever quality they were getting my voice at and to start a tape running so that I could unburden myself of my reports and interviews. At that very moment the studio door opened and an important-looking Sikh of athletic build and proud demeanour dressed in a smart safari suit with a royal blue patka strode towards my seat. Behind him came the anxious-looking engineer, muttering apologetically: 'Please stop at once, Mr Jenkins. Chief Minister of Punjab must make party political broadcast.'

I knew from one further look at the Minister's quite unyielding countenance that there would be absolutely no point in arguing.

CHAPTER ELEVEN

They Also Serve

Test Match Special in particular and cricket commentaries in general are family affairs. Those who feel a part of them are not just the commentators but also the engineers, the producers, the scorers, the presenters in the studio and the very listeners themselves: indeed without any one of these the whole happy structure could not function.

Those who were involved in the technical side of cricket commentary from the earliest days still remember these broadcasts as being amongst the happiest experiences of their working lives. John Ford, who joined the engineering staff of BBC Outside Broadcasts after the Second World War and became head of the department when it moved out of Broadcasting House to Concorde Road, Acton, in the early 1980s, recalls:

My boss then was the famous R. H. Wood, Head of Engineering from 1935 to 1965. He had been in the Services and he ran his department exactly like a military unit. We had a bigger staff then than now, upwards of sixty people. Radio was king in communications of course and the BBC had colossal muscle.

Wood was quite clear about the sort of people who should be working for OB Engineers. There was no opportunity for anyone in T-shirts or jeans. Respectable dress was essential, ties *de rigueur*. After all, we had to go to places like Lord's and be accepted – or to the Palace of course.

The cricket matches always meant meeting interesting people. I wasn't a particular fan of the game but I always enjoyed going to lovely grounds like

Fenner's or Hove or St Lawrence. The pace was always leisurely. I remember once at Oxford one of our engineers – a bit eccentric – suddenly said to me: 'Listen, hear that bird? I think it's a robin.' And he promptly put the effects mike up so that it almost drowned the commentary.

My memories are chiefly of sitting in the sun with amiable people like Brian Johnston and Rex Alston. We used to get to know the idiosyncrasies of the various broadcasters. E. W. Swanton always used to insist on sitting at the end of the balcony at Lord's, which meant climbing over everyone else. It was a bitch to get the equipment up to the top of the Pavilion at Lord's. It was heavy stuff: great big amplifiers like Lego blocks. There were no sophisticated effects microphones until directional parabolic mikes came out in the 1950s and made life easier.

We had great problems on some grounds in getting post office lines. Great long cables were necessary. Sometimes we had to pay the post office for putting up telegraph poles especially for our broadcasts. We used ordinary telephone lines which had to be repeated every thirty miles or so with a BBC engineer at each point to re-amplify the wires, the so-called 'lines engineers' who sat in post offices linking the control room at Broadcasting House to the site. We sometimes did this on Saturdays just for a single one-minute report for Angus Mackay's *Sports Report*.

Things are much more flexible these days because of the invention of a device originally called a SOOBE, now changed to COOBE – Self, or Commentator, Operated Broadcasting Equipment. These are black boxes, the size of an overnight suitcase, inside which is a small control panel, batteries, microphones, earphones, cables and a check receiver (radio) for use as a cue to broadcast should the incoming line go down. New broadcasters of a non-technical mind are inclined to be frightened by the thought of putting themselves on the air and there are certainly pitfalls, but provided the lines have been booked the COOBE is in fact extremely useful, cheap and simple to use. The most serious problem I have ever had with one was on my first solo visit to the Lord's commentary box when I could not find the hole into which I was supposed to insert the plug – a familiar problem for novices.

COOBES are frequently used for cricket broadcasts by the low-budget BBC local radio stations, which usually cover their local county team with a mixture of reports and commentaries. The quality of transmission is inevitably inferior to a full Outside Broadcast. For all network radio in England when commentaries of any length are envisaged – which these days means Tests and major limited-overs matches – the engineers still get their chance to spend several convivial days at a cricket match, sharing, in the case of TMS, in the plentiful supply of cakes and ale.

'I can't think of any area of broadcasting which has changed less,' remarks Leo Feord, second in command of Radio Engineering. 'Maybe it's my age or maybe it's a fact, but the broadcasts seem a bit less relaxed than they used to be. My memory of the past is of long summer days and no hassles but perhaps that is because when I first joined we would do three days of a county or touring team's match whereas now it is just the major occasions and it all tends to be a bit more frenetic.'

Certainly the outlets these days are more numerous, with engineers responsible not just for the transmission of the running commentary, which requires one man to be constantly monitoring the output, his hands hovering over the 'level' controls to keep a satisfactory balance between the commentator's voice and the background noises, but also for reports to News, Sports News and World Service Sports News. Traditionally radio commentary has been delivered through big 'open' microphones, but increasingly in recent years it has been essential to use lip microphones because the level of crowd noise is so great that otherwise the words would be lost.

Feord also has fond memories of R. H. Wood: 'We always addressed him as "Sir". He was a north countryman with an oddball view of life. He had a strange way of misquoting proverbs. He would refer to "niggers in the ointment" or a "bird in the bush". Of course he had great influence and always took charge of royal broadcasts. He became quite a friend of King George VI.'

Wood would be proud, no doubt, of the continuing high

standards of the OB engineers of today, many of whom have started at the BBC as studio managers before opting for a more exciting life on the road.

If engineers are the *sine qua non* of the Test match broadcasts, the scorers have become almost as indispensable. Wendy Wimbush, Malcolm Ashton, Peter Byrne, Keith Downer and other present-day regulars in BBC radio and television boxes have had many predecessors, the best known of whom were Arthur Wrigley, Roy Webber, Jack Price, Michael Fordham and Irving Rosenwater. Easily the most famous of this peculiar breed, who require many special qualities, including the ability to concentrate, accuracy, quick-thinking, neatness and coolness under pressure, is Bill Frindall. Dubbed 'the Bearded Wonder' by Brian Johnston, his every scorecard is a work of art revealing all sorts of esoteric detail, and with his travelling library of reference books he has made himself an essential part of the team. He is very much his own man, always eating his own lunch and tea rather than one provided by the sponsors, carefully prepared for him, to his fastidious specifications, by one of his doting 'handmaidens', as Arlott aptly called the large collection of female helpers who perform for Frindall by rota through the summer. For many years he has played and helped with the public address at charity cricket matches – he is a useful all-rounder still despite a growing midriff – and since the advent of 'phone-in' cricket commentaries has been a regular commentator on county matches.

He is also responsible for several of the most essential reference books on the game, and he needs no persuasion to join in on TMS whenever a record is approaching or something unusual like an all-run four occurs. He took his own initiative when, hearing of the death of Arthur Wrigley in 1965, he wrote to Charles Max-Muller, having just finished a short-service commission in the RAF. After an interview and a few county trials, he was entrusted with the Old Trafford Test the following summer and has never looked back. He lists the essentials of his job, apart from his books, as 'files, stop-watches, binoculars, pens, pencils, ruler, scoring sheets and frames, coffee-flask and cushion'.

The scorer's path had first been beaten by Arthur Wrigley, an accountant from Manchester and former leg-spinner on the Lancashire groundstaff (Arlott recalled that he would spot a googly from the commentary box with the greatest of ease), who had been recommended to BBC North Region by Lancashire when Howard Marshall asked for a scorer in 1935. He had found, not surprisingly, that the need to score at the same time as commentating had inhibited his flow, although a few local radio commentators have achieved this since, notably the fluent Londoner, Norman De Mesquita.

From 1950 until his death, Wrigley travelled to all the home Test matches, as Rex Alston recalled, 'plying us with all the statistical data we could ever require or desire as well as sometimes passing us notes with some shrewd Lancashire comment'.

His most famous television counterpart was Roy Webber who, like Frindall, was an industrious compiler of excellent books of records. He, in turn, was succeeded by Irving Rosenwater and then, when Rosenwater received from Channel Nine television in Australia an offer he could not refuse, by the mild but sharp-minded and efficient Kentish man Michael Fordham, who married Webber's widow and also, alas, died suddenly and young. That scoring on the air is a stressful job is not in any doubt at all. I once had to take over from Michael for a few balls, during the famous Headingley Test of 1981 when, during the unbearable excitement of the final day, he had to spend a penny or burst.

Rosenwater is perhaps the most remarkable of them all when it comes to carrying enormous historical and statistical knowledge in his head. A man of firm principles and extraordinary verbosity, he cares deeply for the game, though he never played it, something which might be said of many devoted scorers over the years. Those who do play of course owe them an immense debt.

One of the more unlikely of those who have done some

scoring for radio or television is John Woodcock, later the distinguished cricket correspondent of *The Times* and editor of *Wisden*, who did some TV scoring at the outset of his career as well as some work as a cameraman.

What of the listeners themselves? The number of them can never be precisely gauged but on television in the 1980s they have generally ranged between four million and under half a million, depending on the time of day and the attraction of the match, and on Radio Three between two million and 200,000, although audience 'reaction', one of the chief BBC guides to a programme's acceptability, is unusually high at an average 'Reaction Index' of 85, with positive response from all ages and all social groups.

Amongst the most dedicated devotees of Test Match Special are the travelling salesmen who tell me to a man that, whether their interest in the game is deep or shallow, they find the commentaries easily the most pleasurable thing to listen to as they fly or grind their way up and down the motorways in their executive cars. Increasingly, too, there has been a female interest, as the huge number of letters which arrive every day during a Test match – far more to the radio box than the television one – proves.

The subjects raised in the letters are almost unlimited. The majority preface whatever point the writer wishes to make with some appreciative comment about the service. Some tell jokes, others ask quiz questions or technical ones, many make points relating to the current Test series, the problems of the game and of English cricket or ancillary matters raised during commentaries. Henry Blofeld, for example, once received a time-table at Leeds for the local buses to which he constantly refers, whatever ground he is on, and Brian Johnston was taken to task by a schoolmistress, feigning indignation, for saying in the presence of the pupils during a West Indies Test commentary: 'The bowler's Holding, the batsman's Willey.' This, in fact, was one of the few *faux pas* which Brian has not committed. Some of his genuine ones have been well aired, including the immortal moment when he resumed commentary after a delay in play due to Glenn Turner of New Zealand being hit in the box by a very fast delivery from Alan Ward. 'Ward to bowl again to Turner then', B.J. continued innocently as play recommenced, 'one ball left.'

Some idea of the scale of interest and the range of subject covered may be gleaned from my own post-bag during the final Test at The Oval in 1989. On counting the letters I am amazed to find that I received no fewer than 84, for some reason more than my usual share. They all had to be answered either on the air or directly, with the help of a patient BBC secretary.

The largest pile concerned various reactions to the one-sided Ashes series and what could be done to improve the England team. Most were serious, some flippant. There was a suggestion from Russell Collingham in Derbyshire that there should be a regional championship in place of the Sunday League involving South-East, West, Midlands and North, while David Donner of Hove suggested that there should be provision for Test trials. H. J. Hardy suggested that England should field Russell and Smith plus nine bowlers with Gower as 12th man. Martin Roberts, a regular correspondent from the unlikely cricketing venue of Whins of Fordie in Scotland, wanted Ian Botham back as captain.

Any number of writers wanted either less limited-overs county cricket or a four-day championship or both. Keith Andrew wrote from the National Cricket Association to deny allegations that it was official policy at Lord's to encourage young players to stand with their bats off the ground à la Brearley or Gooch. J. T. R. Cooper of Sunderland bemoaned the high cost of tickets at Trent Bridge. David Blackmore of the Keep Sunday Special Campaign wrote strongly against seven-day-a-week professional cricket. Several reflected the multiracial nature of modern British society by commenting on the number of South African-, West Indian- and Asian-born players coming into the England team. There were three letters about the forthcoming cricket tour to South Africa and the usual split of opinion both on this issue and on whether there should be fewer overseas players in county cricket.

The new regime at the top of English cricket – Dexter, Stewart and Gower – came in for some criticism, but Gower also had his defenders. Needless to say, he was the one who lost his job soon afterwards.

Some people simply wanted to say who they thought ought to be playing for England, or what the best way of winning in the West Indies during the coming winter would be. Kip Stewart of Faversham and Vivian Woodhams of Boscastle both felt the Australians had been over-aggressive.

Other topics included floodlit grounds in England; the need always to play the best wicket-keeper, even in One-Day Internationals; Somerset's ability to attract the very best overseas players, including Richards, Garner, Greg Chappell, Gavaskar, Waugh, Crowe and Cook – indeed a remarkable success story; lighter bats; Hertfordshire's tactics in delivering six successive deliberate no-balls in the final over to keep Northumberland interested in victory; the abilities of Peter Roebuck of Somerset; and a suggestion from Raymond Groom of Harrogate that players under 25 should not be allowed to play in the Sunday League.

Perhaps the most ingenious suggestion was that the fairest way of differentiating between two sides in the limited-overs game would be to say that one side had won by so many balls – not runs or wickets. I think this is absolutely right in so far as it relates to the side batting second, and I resolved in future to use this method.

The next most popular 'category' of letter came under the heading of reaction to things said during the commentaries. Again, some examples will demonstrate the variety of topics.

Philip Pasterfield, a retired parson, wrote to me with memories of players like Hobbs and McCabe whom he had seen in his youth and, in response to my suggestion that bowlers these days seem to get injured more than before (according to Micky Stewart, half the fast bowlers in England had been unable to guarantee their fitness before this particular Test), John Bradley of Blackpool quoted a catalogue of injuries to England and Australian bowlers in 1956.

Other matters picked up and commented upon included criticisms made by Trevor Bailey and Fred Trueman of particular players; information about the village finalists, Hambledon and Toft – and the semi-finalists Bomersund; Alan Igglesden's school (Churchill School, Westerham, now closed) and the fact that, coming from West of the Medway, he is a Kentish man not a man of Kent; the use of the term 'sweeper', which John Sevenoaks of Hereford felt should be confined to soccer; the pronunciation of Mike Atherton's surname and also that of Steve Waugh; a letter from Bulleen in Victoria sympathizing with my difficulty with elementary mathematics; the plight of David Gower; and an entertaining letter from Peter Pritchard of Eastbourne taking Fred Trueman and Trevor Bailey to task for maligning the current England team and selecting for purposes of comparison an 'ordinary' team from the Bailey/Trueman era. It was: J. G. Dewes, B. C. Rose, N. D. Howard, G. A. Smithson, D. W. Richardson, M. F. Tremlett, A. C. Smith, K. E. Palmer, F. E. Rumsey, R. Berry and J. J. Warr.

The selection of Rose seemed to be dubious because he played later, but the point was very well made and I decided not to risk the fury of our two great pundits by reading it over the air.

Letters reflecting the fact that we had a lot of rain during this match, and therefore strayed far and wide at times, included one from Dr P. J. Sleight of Ippleden Cricket Club in Devon, informing me that one of his players had failed to turn up for their match on Saturday because his car had been dented by a wallaby near Teignmouth. A subsequent letter told me that I had mispronounced Teignmouth when I read this remarkable piece of news to the nation. (It should be 'Tinmouth'.) Peter Foley of Essex also wrote to me with the following succinct note: 'While on a Devon theme, I saw a notice on a farm gate in Devon which said: PORK SAUSAGES FOR SALE. 200 YARDS LEFT.'

In response to my mention of the old English teacher's ally

('James, where John had had had, had had had had. Had had had
had the master's approval') during a break for rain, Mr G.
Ramsay of Hackney followed it up by giving me an example of
five 'ands' in a row: A publican wrote to complain to the
signwriters that his new sign for The Pig and Whistle had been
ruined because the craftsman had painted the correct name but
all in one word. There should, he wrote, be a space between 'Pig'
and 'And', and 'And' and 'Whistle'.

When some accuse Test Match Special of triviality or irrele-
vance, they should perhaps reflect on this fact that so many
listeners react with positive enjoyment and interest to the various
sidelines which find their way quite naturally, if often eccentric-
ally and apparently irrelevantly, into a day's commentary. They
would not do so if they did not enjoy the fact that we talk about
more than just the cricket match itself. It is perhaps worth
repeating that this only becomes culpable if the flow of the match
is interrupted.

Other letters I received in this one sample batch included
requests for information, such as a father writing to ask whether
a coach should look at his son's unorthodox bowling action, or
questions as to whether there are any back-of-the-hand left-arm
spinners left in first-class cricket; whether any biographies of
Ken Barrington have been written; or whether there is any
reason for batsmen being given the benefit of the doubt (there is,
it is in the laws). Several people wrote in with interesting facts. I
was told, for example, about a batsman called Lawrie Scott of
Charondon in Hampshire who had hit 28 sixes in an innings of
279 in a local match and about Chris Loggin who had taken all
ten wickets earlier in the season for Brackley, Northamptonshire.

Two correspondents wanted benefit or charity matches mentioned to try to boost spectators (we try to mention such games
at least once during a Test when they are in a good cause), four –
including one from Sierra Leone – wrote about BBC policy on
cricket, and three – David Peters of Harpenden, Paul Cartwright
of Emsworth and Sureshkumar Pareeh of Rajkot in India – wrote

asking for advice about their ambition to write or broadcast on cricket. Finally there were eleven letters of simple appreciation for our efforts as the season drew to its close, including one from Eileen Turner of Reigate sending me a beautifully knitted pair of white woollen cricket socks because I was the only commentator still trying to play some cricket and, nicest of all, a short one from Robin Rimmington of Reading saying: 'When you said farewell at the end of your summary I really felt you were talking directly to me.'

I was!

One final letter, sent to me before this random collection at The Oval, may serve to demonstrate the extraordinary appeal of Test Match Special and the affection for it which exists as much as anything because of the fascination cricket holds for many who have hardly played the game. The writer, Harvey Heavener, was born and bred in County Wicklow in Ireland and introduced himself as a '46-year-old farmer running a beef and dairy village farm here in Wicklow where cricket is rarely mentioned'.

Cricket came first to his notice when he was ill in bed as a child, his father leaving a wireless by his side during a series between England and South Africa whilst he went out haymaking. Young Harvey was instructed to keep occasional note of the score:

I immediately became fascinated with Test match cricket as seen through the eyes of Rex Alston, John Arlott, E. W. Swanton, Norman Yardley etc. It is an interest that I have consistently maintained down through the years, except for a brief period when I found girls almost equally attractive.

I have listened enthralled by the mental pictures conjured up by the commentators whenever I possibly could. As we could not get it on television until 1974 it was radio cricket that I grew up with, and I have never found TV cricket as interesting or enjoyable, although I must admit that my idea of heaven is to watch it on TV with the sound down and your good self and the others on TMS, hopefully with a plentiful supply of Guinness to hand.

I am, of course, looked on locally as being rather odd and fanatic about the game because in winter I regularly set my alarm to awake me in the early hours so that I can tune in to listen to you telling me how hot and sunny it is. And in summer I often go about the farm with a transistor radio tied round my neck with a piece of baling twine.

Recently I was absolutely horrified to learn that TMS may be somewhat curtailed and made to share with other sports in the future. I think that if the continuous ball-by-ball commentary is interfered with the tremendous appeal of TMS would be greatly diminished.

What, indeed, does the future hold for cricket broadcasting on radio?

◀━▶

CHAPTER TWELVE

The Future

On August Bank Holiday 1990 cricket broadcasting on radio was due to enter a brave new era when the BBC, deprived by the Government of two of its eight wavelengths, launched its Radio Five service.

Operating on the old Radio Two medium waveband, the new service was planned to combine education and sport, with Test Match Special as its eventual flagship. (Ball-by-ball commentary was not due to move to Radio Five until, at least, 1991 or at whatever date the BBC lost Radio Three medium wave.) The technical quality of the output was likely to be far better than the old Radio Three medium wave, which had always been difficult to receive in some areas and, with more time for sport in midweek, county cricket was confidently expected to recover much of the airtime lost since the 1960s. Although there would no longer be the guaranteed ball-by-ball coverage of home Test matches which had been in force for 33 years, the Managing Director of Radio, David Hatch, countered widespread cries of alarm from (ironically) Cabinet ministers to coalmen by estimating that Test Match Special would continue exactly as before, covering 'every ball or every raindrop' on some 26 of the 35 or so days on the cricket calendar: 75 per cent in all. 'On the other days (25 per cent),' he said in a speech in 1989, 'other sport will have to challenge TMS for airtime by being of significance or importance . . . So on this 25 per cent of days not every ball of every Test will be covered, but somewhere between 80 and 90 per cent will be.'

Moreover the disappointment felt by devotees at the diminution of TMS on some days was softened by the prospect of an improved service on county cricket with proper commentary on the County Championship returning in place of the brief updates and occasional score service which had become the norm on Radio Two.

These changes were brought about by the Broadcasting Bill introduced into Parliament by Mrs Thatcher's Conservative Government in December 1989. The BBC was due to lose two medium wave frequencies to commercial operators, and with no realistic means of switching to another network when other major sporting events clashed with Test matches, BBC managers reluctantly concluded that ball-by-ball commentary could no longer be sacrosanct.

The 1990s thus presented the cricket commentators of BBC Radio with an exciting new challenge. The imprecation from the managers, quite rightly, was to be positive. The near future was both healthy and exciting, although there was inevitably a danger, once the principle of guaranteed coverage had been conceded, that future BBC managers might look less kindly on TMS than might those in whose hands it was due to be when Radio Five was inaugurated – Pat Ewing, the first chief of the new service, and her successor as head of Radio Outside Broadcasts, Larry Hodgson. Both made abundantly clear their commitment to maintaining what Hodgson called the 'special place and prominence of TMS'.

They were aware that this was a sensitive public issue. As many as 140 MPs signed a House of Commons motion in 1989 deploring the proposed changes to ball-by-ball coverage. The more astute amongst them recognized that there was no real threat to the programme itself, but that there was an unavoidable one to its character, to that strange paradox that many people seemed to enjoy listening to the 'commentaries' more when there was no cricket being played. The unique feature of TMS was that it carried on come rain or shine, not always reaching great heights by any means but generally, by popular consent, reliable, friendly, informative and enjoyable. Gillian Reynolds said of it in the *Daily Telegraph*: 'It has become a national institution, a piece of radio which is very British yet which transcends class, age and gender.'

In *The Times* Charles Nevin, after a day of observation from the back of the commentary box at Leeds in 1989, concluded:

Like any institution, TMS is baffling to the outsider, but it seems to work. Despite rumours to the contrary, they never miss a ball and between them they provide considerable technical expertise and, on occasion, real insight, particularly from Fred. Any number of dour Yorkshire people around Headingley all warmed to it and wouldn't have it changed. Denis Read, from Ramsbottom in Lancashire, said: 'It's cricket and it's England and it's marvellous. It wouldn't be the same without it. It just makes me feel good and it always has done.'

In the *Guardian* the Shadow Home Secretary, Roy Hattersley, asked, with suitable political drama: 'Where will it all end? If one national institution is proved mortal, how many more will die a commercial death?'

A more regular *Guardian* columnist, Frank Keating, pinpointed the one real area of worry in an article during the 1989 Ashes series:

You only have to take a look at any summer's sporting diary to see how vulnerable will be TMS's continuity – which, like it or squirming lump it, is its very essence. With all sport on one station, how will TMS get remotely into its non-stop chuntering stride when, say, Wimbledon 1991 clashes with the second Test? Or the fourth Test with the Open golf? Or the fifth Test in 1992 with the unending synchronized swimming from the Barcelona Olympic Games?

Last weekend was an easy illustration: the Wentworth golf and the Hampden soccer sharing Radio 2: cricket non-stop on Radio 3. Soon they will all be on Radio 5. Whose finger will be on the button when each event is at the kill? A golf nut, a soccer bod, or a cricket chap? Recordings have no vibrancy on radio. Liveness is all, certainly in 'crumbs chaps!' cake-eating.

The proof of the new cake will be in the eating, but the BBC has no intention of relinquishing its 'national institution'. 'For heaven's sake, we invented it,' remarked an understandably exasperated David Hatch. And Pat Ewing did not hesitate to use that most influential of public forums, the letters page of *The Times*. Hence this exchange of letters in October 1988:

CRICKET COVERAGE

From Mr N. W. P. Cole

Sir, I am writing to express my fears for the future of cricket broadcasting in the UK, following the announcement that Test Match Special is to move from Radio 3 to the proposed Radio 5 in 1990. The current proposals would mean TMS sharing radio time with a variety of sports, education and current affairs programmes. Thus the traditional ball-by-ball coverage of matches, which has helped millions to follow Test cricket over the years, would be lost.

Doubtless there are those who say cricket fans should not be so greedy, and should be prepared to surrender all-day broadcasting. This, however, would be to miss the point. The essence of a Test match, and what makes it a unique event in the world of sport, is the manner in which the drama unfolds continuously throughout the match, as fortunes swing to and fro.

If one went to the theatre to see a play by Shakespeare, one would not expect to see it presented in the form of a half-hour sitcom. In the same way, coverage of a Test match cannot be reduced to a series of abbreviated reports if the essence of the event is not to be totally destroyed.

Furthermore, TMS has itself developed into a unique form of entertainment, based as much on the characters and conversation within it as on the cricket. It is a programme which has not only delighted millions of cricket fans over the years, but which has also introduced countless listeners to cricket who otherwise may not have become involved in our national game.

The cheerful, non-stop banter, the fund of anecdotes and the clear enjoyment of a day at the cricket have enabled the TMS team to establish a rapport with their listeners unrivalled in modern broadcasting. To disrupt TMS in the manner which is proposed would inevitably destroy the atmosphere that has made this one of the most popular of all radio programmes.

In recent years the television coverage of Test matches has been increasingly interrupted by other programmes, despite the availability of a second BBC channel. Consequently, the coverage and enjoyment of the cricket has suffered. This must not be allowed to happen to radio coverage as well. TMS has existed for 40 years and is now more popular than ever. There is no reason why it cannot continue in its present form on Radio 3 for the next 40 years.

This will not happen, though, without the support of all those who care about cricket broadcasting. May I therefore urge all of your readers to write to Patricia Ewing, Head of BBC Radio Sport and Controller Designate of Radio 5, to beg her to retain TMS in its entirety, and thus preserve what is for so many their only regular access to Test cricket in this country.

Yours faithfully,
N. W. P. COLE

SPECIAL SERVICE

From Head of Sport and Outside Broadcasts, Radio, and Controller, Radio 5 (Designate), BBC

Sir, May I have the opportunity to respond to Mr N. W. P. Cole's letter (October 27) expressing his concern for the future of *Test Match Special*.

Test Match Special will be found unimpaired on Radio 3 Medium Wave next year and possibly, too, in 1990, depending on the speed at which BBC Radio is required to surrender frequencies following the Broadcasting Bill next year.

Only when the BBC is required to surrender Radio 3 Medium Wave will *Test Match Special* move to the new network, Radio 5. As has been reported, this network will carry all the education and sports output but there is no reason why *Test Match Special* should find itself competing for air-time with educational programmes as there will be more than enough air-time for all.

Nevertheless, it is true to say that Radio 5 will be covering all the sports output and consequently there will be a few occasions when there will be a clash of major sports events – such as Wimbledon. On such occasions, the Sports Editor will have the difficult task of trying to balance the output to provide all that our listeners would want.

However, *Test Match Special* is as much loved by the BBC Radio Sport unit as it is by its listeners and I can promise you we will be doing our very best to retain its unique style and character and indeed for the majority of the time I cannot see any reason why it should differ from its current form.

I hope this goes some way to reassuring Mr Cole and all *Test Match Special* fans.

Yours faithfully,
PATRICIA EWING,

Head of Sport and Outside Broadcasts, Radio, and Controller Radio 5 (Designate), BBC

Six months later, another barrage of letters necessitated another public response in *The Times*:

STILL AT THE WICKET

Dear Sir,

I would like to reassure your readers that there is no possibility of Test Match Special (TMS) ending (leading article, 25 May), or even of its unique character being dramatically changed, when BBC Radio loses Radio 3 medium wave, due to the Government's desire to release wavelengths to news broadcasters, and TMS moves to Radio 5.

The very reason for creating Radio 5 is to ensure that programmes like TMS continue.

It will be given the same air time, sun or rain, as it always has been, which will allow for full coverage of all the Test Matches, one-day internationals and the quarter-finals, semi-finals and finals of the domestic one-day competitions.

In fact, with Radio 5 there could be more cricket coverage than ever. Sometimes TMS will have to share that air time with other sports, but Larry

Hodgson, Radio's head of sport, says that these other sports will have to compete against TMS, not the other way round.

TMS devotees will not be let down, and all they will have to do is to listen to Radio 5 to know that.

Yours faithfully,
PATRICIA EWING
Controller
BBC Radio 5

A number of letters received by commentators were from blind people, who seem especially to appreciate the companionable qualities of the programme. William Smith, a severely physically handicapped man of great character from Seer Green in Buckinghamshire, wrote:

When I lay in a hospital bed in the early 1950s one of my only links with the outside world was listening to John Arlott on the small radio which was controlled from the matron's office. The summer voice of John Arlott somehow kept me going through some very difficult years. Laying in that bed I used to play my own games of cricket in my mind. To keep my brain active, I used to jump from one end of the bed to the other – the length of the bed was the pitch and each of the ends were the wickets.

It is always moving when people unable to play cricket follow Test matches on the radio and feel the commentators to be their friends, and to both listeners and performers alike the reassurances of the BBC management were very welcome.

They did not, however, stop the press from commenting. *The Independent* went so far as to devote a leader to the forthcoming 'demise' of non-stop ball-by-ball commentary, aimed at the responsible lady – not Miss Ewing but Mrs Thatcher:

BENT-ARM DELIVERY FROM THATCHER

'... COMES in to bowl, past Umpire Constant, and Boycott pushes it out on the leg side. No run. Six overs, one maiden, none for 15. A Mrs M. Thatcher writes from Downing Street, and we'll let you know what she has to say at the end of the over. Lillee comes in again from the pavilion end, bowls, and Boycott lets that one go through. Lillee hasn't really found his line today, has he, Trevor?'

'To be honest, Brian, he hasn't bowled well at all. I may say this is exactly the start England need, because the last thing the Australians want is to hang about trying to dislodge the England openers. Not that Lillee looked awfully impressive in the first innings.' [*Roar in background*]

'And Boycott is gone, caught behind off Lillee for eight, an easy catch to first slip off a full-length delivery which didn't do much at all. Boycott made what I can only describe as an uncharacteristic prod at it . . .'

'Not that Boycott has looked entirely happy at any time during the last hour and a half.'

'The Australian fielders are jubilant, they're converging on Lillee as Boycott starts his walk back to the pavilion. [*Discussion of Boycott's mistake, Lillee's action and the task facing England.*] And while we wait for the next batsman to emerge, we turn to the letter from Downing Street.'

'From the Prime Minister, perhaps.' [*Laughter*]

'Well, the writer does refer to herself as Mrs M. Thatcher. She says the Government is going to take two medium-wave frequencies from the BBC and give them to national commercial channels, so Radio 3's continuous ball-by-ball coverage of Test matches will stop after the 1990 season.'

'I think you've got what is known as a spoof there.'

'It's been beautifully done. The paper is embossed with a crest, and she says in a PS that once the stations are commercial, people will be able to listen to what they want.'

'But some of them like listening to us. Here's a letter from another lady, she sent it in with some delicious shortbread [*crunching sound*]. She says: "Test Match Special is the one undoubted triumph of radio sports broadcasting. My friends tell me you are experts, but I love listening to you even though cricket doesn't generally appeal to me. You're part of our summer." Hmmm. Seems a bit boastful to read that out.'

'You've forgotten about Denis.'

'Denis Compton?'

'Denis Thatcher would never let her do a thing like that. Otherwise what's the point of him?'

'And now, with the new batsman about to come out, it's over to Fred Trueman.'

'Yes, well, I don't know what all this nonsense is about taking us off the air. I should think there's the odd Tory will want to have a word or two with Margaret Thatcher about that. And it's to be David Gower, anybody know what kept him, maybe he had to write a letter to a certain grand personage who's about to lose the next election. Mind you, there's other programmes she could take off and the voters might thank her.'

'Lillee comes in to bowl his first ball to Gower, who pushes it out on the leg side. No run.'

The debate about the future of the programme had been intense ever since the publishing of the Government White Paper in 1988. Fears were expressed that what had happened to Sunday cricket on BBC 2 might, in time, become the sad fate of TMS. TV cricket on Sundays had been gradually whittled down by other sports once it had been decided to interrupt the continuous broadcasting of one match, until eventually rights were sold instead to a commercial station.

No one in BBC radio has any intention of letting this happen to its favourite and most popular sports programme. No one affected by involuntary change likes it very much but the challenge of the 1990s and beyond, especially for those of us who remain once *anno domini* catches up with Brian Johnston, will be to keep standards high and to make Test Match Special as informative, natural and entertaining on Radio Five as it was on Radio Three. *Deo volente*, the show will go on.

Finally, lest I be thought to have taken myself and TMS too seriously, which would hardly be appropriate for a programme renowned for its lightness of touch, here is one listener's view of how the ship will finally sink, sent to The Oval in 1989 by a keen observer of the game called James McCarter with, as he said, 'no offence intended':

THE LAST COMMENTARY: EIGHT BEFORE LUNCH

Extraordinary scenes were reported from Lord's yesterday during the England v. Australia match held to mark the passing of continuous ball-by-call commentary, with Mr Brian Johnston performing the incredible feat of consuming eight full-sized cakes *before* the luncheon interval. Although this took place behind the high-security doors of the commentary box, a witness, who wishes to remain anonymous, described the scene to me:

'Johnners was in absolutely mid-season form and murdered the opposition. I felt the moment that he came in that he was going to mark the day with something special. The first delivery he received was something of a loosener – a date-and-walnut with marzipan icing pitched just outside leg. Johnners was on to it like a shot and with a masterly flick of the knife despatched it in one. Before you could see where it had gone, he was brushing the crumbs from his sleeve and waiting for the next delivery.

'It wasn't long coming, and it was a beauty. It had, as us old-timers used to say, "jam in it and cream on top". It was the kind of fruity one that not many people like to face so early in the day. Johnners watched it on to the table, moved his legs beautifully to give himself room, and it went the inevitable way of the first.

'You could sense the tension rising in the box. The Bearded Wonder crouched more intently over his cobwebbed tomes. CMJ's fingers played nervously with his old school tie. Blowers grasped the nearest bottle of champagne, as much for support as for sustenance. A low growl of "dear, oh dear, oh dear" rose and fell from the far corner.

'The tactics now required were obviously those of containment. A simple Battenburg and a Victoria Sponge in quick succession might have tied a lesser trencherman up, but they were meat and drink to Johnners, who scarcely paused to wipe the cream from his lips.

'The delivery boy was labouring now, and a change was urgently required. Following a quiet word from Blowers, FST rolled up his sleeves and began to measure out his run-up. "I'll soften 'im up wi' a dolly first and then let 'im 'ave it wi' Yorkshire Parkin," he whispered as he strode into the distance.

'Fred's dolly was one of the best I've ever seen. It had chocolate chips and smarties, as well as those little silver balls in hundreds and thousands. It had the lot. There was a knowing smile on Trueman's face as he watched Johnners fall on it. Pitched up in the block-hole as it was, Johnners hardly moved before sweeping it up in a stroke that owed as much to the wrists as to the shoulders.

'However, this was but a prelude to the "Parkin", one of Trueman's favourite deliveries. Fred had polished it until it shone like the seat of a Louis XV commode. From a full run-up which started somewhere near the Gents' lavatory at the foot of the Warner Stand, he came storming in. The Parkin screamed like a banshee as it hurtled from his hand towards the target, swerving in the air like a renegade Blue Streak missile. No one is exactly sure what happened next. Pitch it did (there are scorchmarks on the floor to prove it), and move off the thick seam of compacted currants it did, but Johnners' work with knife and fork was too quick for the eye to follow. Somehow, in a cloud of crumbs and currants, the deed was done: when the air cleared the Parkin was nowhere to be seen. Trueman's head dropped, and he was led away to the refreshment tent, sobbing quietly to himself.

'A stunned silence fell over the box, but then the Boyle rose to step into the firing line. (Blowers later said: "You know, Old Thing, it was just like that poem we used to learn at school. How does it go? 'And up stood proud Horatio, te tum, te tum, te tum ...' Dashed if I didn't quite pipe the eye.")

'The Boyle walked over to the mountain of boxes that had by now arrived in the box and seemed to take his time selecting which to bowl. Eventually he turned, concealing his chosen weapon behind his back. "Quite ready, Brian?", he asked with a smile that could only be described as menacing in the extreme. Johnners replied with a good-natured wave.

'Bailey's approach to the wicket did not seem particularly aggressive, but the delivery was a brute. The projectile seemed to dig into the floorboards before rearing upwards towards the unfortunate Johnston's head. Johnners did well to fend it off, but it took the outside edge of his fork. The Alderman, who took the catch behind, said that it was either a question of catching it or going to meet his Maker there and then. However, as arms everywhere rose in jubilation the stentorian cry of "No Cake!" echoed round the confines of the commentary box.

'All eyes turned on Umpire Bird, who had arrived to give his talk on Late Elizabethan Love Poetry during the luncheon interval.

'"What do you mean, 'No Cake'?" demanded a furious Bailey.

'"Tha knows what I mean, lad," replied the unperturbed Bird.

'"That were a Ten-Year-Old Special Alderman Mosey Melton Mowbray Pork Pie."

'A shame-faced and dejected Bailey slunk from the box and was last seen boarding the boat train for Calais and destinations East.

'This indignity seemed to crush the spirit of the attacking side, and the eighth cake passed almost unnoticed. The Bearded Wonder recorded it as a Black Forest Gâteau, delivered by CMJ from the back of the hand. "Wrong-un" or not, Johnners never even had to open his waistcoat buttons to deal with it.

'And so history was made. Whether or not Johnners would have continued to paste the patisserie all over the box after lunch is something that cricket followers everywhere will argue about for many years to come. Fate, as it so often does in cricket, had the final say.

'Shortly after the luncheon interval a message was relayed over the public address system. (It will be recalled that the Australian innings had ended in the final over, and that England were to commence their innings when play began again.) "Honourable members, gentlemen and ladies, the heavy roller, requested by the England captain, has apparently been sabotaged. Until a replacement can be obtained, start of play will be delayed indefinitely."

'Johnners rose and adjusted his dress. "That was splendid," he said, "just the job. Nice and fruity, but I'd better go and do my duty."

'A distraught Blowers clutched his brow and was heard to mutter: "Good heavens, the man even talks in rhyming cupcakes." As he slumped in his chair a small black fly crawled sedately along the bridge of his nose. You will recall that, thanks to the makeshift roller (which unfortunately became wedged beneath the sightscreen at the Nursery End), play began again on time.'

I decided to go to the commentary box to check the details of this incredible story for myself. At first I thought it was empty, but then I spotted the shrunken figure of Peter Baxter. He was hurrying between a bank of tape-recorders, switching this one on, that one off. His face was ashen and his eyes betrayed a vacancy which I found disturbing. Anticipating the question forming on my lips, he raised a trembling hand and pointed to the rear window which looks down on the back of the Lord's Pavilion. I turned, just in time to see five figures, huddled in grey National Health blankets, being led into waiting ambulances. I looked back at Baxter; there was nothing more anyone could do for him, poor chap. I closed the door softly behind me. From a transistor radio below I heard the words: 'And now we go over to Cleethorpes for the Indoor Leap-Frog Championships.'

Then, carried on the breeze from far away, from somewhere in the north in St John's Wood, I heard the sound of a lone bugler playing. The strains were those of 'The Last Post'. They died away and faded, almost to a chuckle, and then all was quiet.

APPENDIX

Complete List of Commentators on BBC Radio and Television for Test Matches since 1946

(TV producers in brackets)

1946   **ENGLAND V. INDIA** (Light programme)
1. 22, 24, 25/6   Rex Alston, C. B. Fry
LORD'S   TV: Aidan Crawley, Brian Johnston

2. 20, 22, 23/7   Alston, Fry, E. W. Swanton
OLD TRAFFORD   (no TV)

3. 17, 19, 20/8   Alston, Fry
OVAL   TV: Percy Fender, Swanton, Dudley Vernon,
R. C. Robertson-Glasgow, Johnston

1947   **ENGLAND V. SOUTH AFRICA**
(Light programme)
1. 7, 9, 10, 11/6   Alston, Swanton, A. E. R. Gilligan
TRENT BRIDGE   (no TV)

2. 21, 23, 24, 25/6   Alston, Swanton, R. E. S. Wyatt
LORD'S   TV: Crawley, Johnston, Vernon

3. 5, 7, 8, 9/7   Alston, Swanton, George Duckworth, John Arlott
OLD TRAFFORD   (no TV)

1948   **ENGLAND V. AUSTRALIA** (Light programme)
1. 10, 11, 12, 14, 15/6   Alston, Arlott, Alan McGilvray, Swanton
TRENT BRIDGE   (no TV)

2. 24, 25, 26, 28, 29/6   Alston, Arlott, McGilvray, Swanton, Gilligan
LORD'S   TV: Johnston, Swanton, Robertson-Glasgow, W. B. Franklin

3. 8, 9, 10, 12, 13/7   Alston, Arlott, McGilvray, Swanton, Gilligan
OLD TRAFFORD   (no TV)

4. 22, 23, 24, 26, 27/7   Alston, Arlott, McGilvray, Gilligan, Swanton
HEADINGLEY   (no TV)

5. 14, 16, 17, 18/8   Alston, Arlott, McGilvray, Swanton, Gilligan
OVAL   TV: Johnston, Swanton

1949   **ENGLAND V. NEW ZEALAND**
                                 (Light programme)
1. 11, 13, 14/6   Alston, Arlott, Swanton, Roger Blunt, Gilligan
    HEADINGLEY   (no TV)

2. 25, 27, 28/6   Alston, Arlott, Swanton, Blunt, Gilligan
    LORD'S   TV: Johnston, Robert Hudson, Swanton

3. 23, 25, 26/7   Alston, Arlott, Swanton, Blunt, Gilligan
    OLD TRAFFORD   (no TV)

4. 13, 15, 16/8   Alston, Arlott, Blunt, Gilligan, Swanton
    OVAL   TV: Johnston, Swanton

1950   **ENGLAND V. WEST INDIES**
                                 (Light programme)
1. 8, 9, 10, 12/6   Alston, Swanton, Arlott, Gilligan, Bill Bowes,
    OLD TRAFFORD   Michael Laing (of Trinidad Broadcasting Company –
                           billed as being 'on holiday in this country')
                           (no TV)

2. 24, 26, 27, 28, 29/6   Alston, Arlott, Kenneth Ablack, Learie Constantine, Gilligan
    LORD'S   TV: Johnston, Swanton

3. 20, 21, 22, 24, 25/7   Alston, Arlott, Swanton, Ablack, Gilligan
    TRENT BRIDGE   TV: Johnston, Hudson

4. 12, 14, 15, 16/8   Alston, Arlott, Ablack, Constantine, Gilligan
    OVAL   TV: Johnston, Swanton

1951   **ENGLAND V. SOUTH AFRICA**
                                 (Light programme)
1. 7, 8, 9, 11, 12/6   Alston, Charles Fortune (SABC), Arlott, Gilligan
    TRENT BRIDGE   S. C. Griffith
                           TV: Swanton, Johnston

2. 21, 22, 23/6   Alston, Arlott, Fortune, Gilligan, Swanton, Griffith
    LORD'S   TV: Johnston, Swanton

3. 5, 6, 7, 9, 10/7   Swanton, Alston, Arlott, Fortune, Gilligan, George Duckworth
    OLD TRAFFORD   (no TV)

4. 26, 27, 28, 30, 31/7   Alston, Arlott, Fortune, Swanton, Gilligan, Bowes
    HEADINGLEY   (no TV)

5. 16, 17, 18/8   Alston, Arlott, Fortune, Gilligan, Alf Gover
    OVAL   TV: Johnston, Swanton

1952   **ENGLAND V. INDIA** (Light programme)
1. 5, 6, 7, 9/6   Alston, Arlott, Bowes, Duckworth
    HEADINGLEY   TV: Johnston, Swanton

2. 19, 20, 21, 23, 24/6   Alston, Swanton, Arlott, Gilligan, Ernest Eytle
    LORD'S   TV: Johnston, Peter West

3. 17, 18, 19/7   Arlott, Swanton, Gilligan
    OLD TRAFFORD   TV: Johnston, West

4. 14, 15, 16, 18, 19/8   Alston, Gover, Arlott
    OVAL   TV: Johnston, Swanton

1953   **ENGLAND V. AUSTRALIA** (Light programme)

1. 11, 12, 13, 15, 16/6   Alston, Gilligan, W. A. Oldfield, Arlott, Bernard Kerr
TRENT BRIDGE   TV: Swanton, Johnston

2. 25, 26, 27, 29, 30/6   Alston, Swanton, Kerr, Arlott
LORD'S   TV: West, Johnston

3. 9, 10, 11, 13, 14/7   Arlott, Duckworth, Kerr, Alston
OLD TRAFFORD   TV: Swanton, Johnston

4. 23, 24, 25, 27, 28/7   Alston, Swanton, Kerr, Arlott
HEADINGLEY   TV: West, Johnston

5. 15, 17, 18, 19/8   Arlott, Gover, Kerr, Alston
TV: Swanton, Johnston

1954   **ENGLAND V. PAKISTAN** (Light programme)

1. 10, 11, 12, 14, 15/6   Alston, Swanton, Arlott
LORD'S   TV: Johnston, West
(first production credit: TV Presentation: Anthony Craxton)

2. 1, 2, 3, 5/7   Arlott, Johnston, Gilligan, Swanton, Alston
TRENT BRIDGE   TV: Swanton, Johnston

3. 22, 23, 24, 26, 27/7   Swanton, Arlott, Duckworth
OLD TRAFFORD   TV: West, Johnston (Derek Burrell-Davis)

4. 12, 13, 14, 16, 17/8   Alston, Arlott, Gover
OVAL   TV: Johnston, Swanton (Craxton)

1955   **ENGLAND V. SOUTH AFRICA**
(Light programme)

1. 9, 10, 11, 13/6   Arlott, Alston, Fortune, Crawford White
TRENT BRIDGE   TV: Swanton, Johnston

2. 23, 24, 25, 27/6   Arlott, Alston, Fortune, Swanton
LORD'S   TV: Johnston, West (Craxton)

3. 7, 8, 9, 11, 12/7   Alston, Arlott, Fortune, Duckworth, Swanton
OLD TRAFFORD   TV: Swanton, Johnston (William Cave)

4. 21, 22, 23, 25, 26/7   Alston, Arlott, Fortune, Swanton, White
HEADINGLEY   TV: West, Johnston (Cave)

5. 13, 15, 16, 17/8   Johnston, Arlott, Fortune, Gover, Alston
OVAL   TV: Johnston, Swanton (Craxton)

1956   **ENGLAND V. AUSTRALIA** (Home Service and
Light programme)

1. 7, 8, 9, 11, 12/6   Alston, Arlott, Michael Charlton, Norman Yardley, Swanton
TRENT BRIDGE   TV: Swanton, Johnston

2. 21, 22, 23, 25, 26/6   Alston, Arlott, Charlton, Swanton, McGilvray
LORD'S   TV: Johnston, West, Jack Fingleton (Craxton)

3. 12, 13, 14, 16, 17/7   Alston, Arlott, Charlton, Yardley, Hudson
HEADINGLEY   TV: Swanton, Johnston (Ray Lakeland)

4. 26, 27, 28, 30, 31/7   Alston, Arlott, Charlton, Swanton
OLD TRAFFORD   TV: Johnston, West, Fingleton (Lakeland)

5. 23, 24, 25, 27, 28/8   Alston, Arlott, Charlton, Gover
OVAL   TV: Johnston, Swanton, Fingleton (Craxton)

1957

1. 30, 31/5, 1, 3, 4/6
    EDGBASTON

ENGLAND V. WEST INDIES (Light
programme and 'Special Service' – in effect Third programme)
(First billing as 'Test Match Special')
Alston, Arlott, Ablack, Swanton, Gerry Gomez, Bowes
TV: Johnston, West, Gomes (Barry Edgar/David Martin)

2. 20, 21, 22/6
    LORD'S

Ablack, Arlott, Alston, Gomez, Yardley, Roy Lawrence
TV: Johnston, Swanton, Gomez (Craxton)

3. 4, 5, 6, 8, 9/7
    TRENT BRIDGE

Ablack, Alston, Arlott, Gomez, Swanton, Yardley
TV: Johnston, Swanton, Gomez (Martin)

4. 25, 26, 27/7
    HEADINGLEY

Ablack, Alston, Arlott, Gomez, Yardley, Eytle
TV: Johnston, Swanton, Gomez (Lakeland)

5. 22, 23, 24/8
    OVAL

Ablack, Alston, Arlott, F. R. Brown, Gover, Swanton
TV: Johnston, West, Brown (Craxton)

1958

1. 5, 6, 7, 9/6
    EDGBASTON

ENGLAND V. NEW ZEALAND (Light
programme and Special Service)
Alston, Arlott, Brown, Swanton, West, Bill Merritt
TV: Johnston, West, Denis Compton (David Martin)

2. 19, 20, 21/6
    LORD'S

Alston, Arlott, Brown, Yardley, Merritt, Swanton
TV: Johnston, Swanton, Compton

3. 3, 4, 5, 7, 8/7
    HEADINGLEY

Alston, Arlott, Brown, Yardley, Merritt
TV: Johnston, Swanton, Compton (Lakeland)

4. 24, 25, 26, 28, 29/7
    OLD TRAFFORD

Arlott, Brown, Hudson, Swanton, Merritt, Bowes
TV: Johnston, West, Compton (Lakeland)

5. 21, 22, 23, 25, 26/8
    OVAL

Arlott, Brown, West, Yardley, Merritt
TV: Swanton, Johnston, Compton

1959

1. 4, 5, 6, 8/6
    TRENT BRIDGE

ENGLAND V. INDIA (Light programme and
Special Service)
Alston, Arlott, Brown, Pearson Surita, The Maharajkumar of
Vizianagram, Swanton
TV: Johnston, West, Compton (Philip Lewis)

2. 18, 19, 20/6
    LORD'S

Alston, Arlott, Brown, Surita, Yardley, M of V
TV: Johnston, Swanton, Compton

3. 2, 3, 4/7
    HEADINGLEY

Alston, Arlott, Brown, Surita, Yardley, M of V
TV: Johnston, Swanton, Compton (Lakeland)

4. 23, 24, 25, 27, 28/7
    OLD TRAFFORD

Alston, Arlott, Brown, Surita, Yardley, M of V
TV: Johnston, Swanton, Compton (Lakeland)

5. 20, 21, 22, 24/8
    OVAL

Alston, Arlott, Brown, Surita, Swanton, M of V
TV: West, Johnston, Compton (Peter Webber)

1960

1. 9, 10, 11, 13, 14/6
    EDGBASTON

ENGLAND V. SOUTH AFRICA (Light
programme and Special Service)
Alston, Arlott, Brown, Fortune, Swanton
TV: Johnston, West, Compton (Philip Lewis)

2.	23, 24, 25, 27/6 LORD'S	Alston, Arlott, Brown, Fortune, Yardley, Richie Benaud TV: Swanton, Johnston, Compton (Lewis)
3.	7, 8, 9, 11/7 TRENT BRIDGE	Alston, Arlott, Brown, Fortune, Yardley, Benaud TV: Johnston, Swanton, Compton (Lewis)
4.	21, 22, 23, 25, 26/7 OLD TRAFFORD	Alston, Arlott, Brown, Fortune, Yardley, Benaud TV: Johnston, Swanton, Compton (Lakeland)
5.	18, 19, 20, 22, 23/8 OVAL	Arlott, Brown, Fortune, Swanton, Benaud TV: West, Johnston, Compton (Philip Daly)

1961

ENGLAND V. AUSTRALIA (Light programme and Sports Service – Third Network)

1.	8, 9, 10, 12, 13/6 EDGBASTON	Alston, Arlott, McGilvray, Bob Richardson, Brown, Fingleton, Swanton TV: Johnston, West, Compton, Fingleton (TV Presentation: Lewis. Executive Producer: Craxton)
2.	22, 23, 24, 26/6 LORD'S	Alston, Arlott, McGilvray, Richardson, Brown, Fingleton, Yardley TV: Swanton, Johnston, Compton, Fingleton (Craxton)
3.	6, 7, 8/7 HEADINGLEY	Alston, Arlott, McGilvray, Richardson, Brown, Fingleton, Yardley TV: Swanton, Johnston, Compton, Fingleton (Lakeland, Craxton)
4.	27, 28, 29, 31/7, 1/8 OLD TRAFFORD	Alston, Arlott, McGilvray, Richardson, Brown, Fingleton, Yardley TV: Swanton, Johnston, Compton, Fingleton (Lakeland, Craxton)
5.	17, 18, 19, 21, 22/8 OVAL	Alston, Arlott, McGilvray, Richardson, Brown, Fingleton, Swanton TV: West, Johnston, Compton, Fingleton (Craxton)

1962

ENGLAND V. PAKISTAN (Light programme and Third Network)

1.	31/5, 1, 2, 4/6 EDGBASTON	Alston, Arlott, Alan Gibson, Omar Kureishi, Brown, Yardley, Swanton TV: West, Johnston, Compton (Craxton, Lewis)
2.	21, 22, 23/6 LORD'S	Alston, Arlott, Hudson, Kureishi, Brown, Yardley TV: Swanton, Johnston, Compton (Craxton, Lewis)
3.	5, 6, 7/7 HEADINGLEY	Alston, Arlott, Gibson, Kureishi, Brown, Yardley, Swanton TV: Hudson, Johnston, Compton (Lakeland)
4.	26, 27, 28, 30, 31/7 TRENT BRIDGE	Alston, Hudson, Arlott, Kureishi, Brown, Yardley, Swanton TV: West, Johnston, Compton (Lewis)
5.	16, 17, 18, 20/8 OVAL	Alston, Arlott, Hudson, Kureishi, Brown, Yardley, Swanton TV: West, Johnston, Compton (Lewis)

1963

ENGLAND V. WEST INDIES (Third Network)

1.	6, 7, 8, 10/6 OLD TRAFFORD	Alston, Arlott, Gibson, Roy Lawrence, Brown, Yardley, Swanton TV: Johnston, West, Compton (Lakeland)

2. 20, 21, 22, 24, 25/6   Alston, Arlott, Gibson, Lawrence, Brown, Yardley, Swanton
    LORD'S   TV: Johnston, Hudson, Compton (Lewis)

3. 4, 5, 6, 8, 9/7   Alston, Arlott, Gibson, Lawrence, Brown, Yardley, Swanton
    EDGBASTON   TV: Johnston, Hudson, Compton (Lewis)

4. 25, 26, 27, 29/7   Alston, Arlott, Hudson, Lawrence, Brown, Yardley, Swanton
    HEADINGLEY   TV: Johnston, West, Compton, Colin Cowdrey, Swanton
                             (Lakeland)

5. 22, 23, 24, 26/8   Alston, Arlott, Hudson, Lawrence, Brown, Swanton, Yardley
    OVAL   TV: West, Johnston, Compton, Cowdrey (Lewis)

1964   **ENGLAND V. AUSTRALIA** (Third Network)
                             (BBC-1 and 2)
1. 4, 5, 6, 8, 9/6   Arlott, McGilvray, Alston, Fingleton, Ron Roberts, Yardley
    TRENT BRIDGE   TV: Johnston, West, Compton, Benaud, Swanton (Lewis)

2. 18, 19, 20, 22, 23/6   Alston, Arlott, McGilvray, Fingleton, Yardley, Swanton
    LORD'S   TV: Johnston, Hudson, Compton, Benaud (Lewis)

3. 2, 3, 4, 6/7   Alston, Arlott, McGilvray, Fingleton, Yardley, Roberts
    HEADINGLEY   TV: Johnston, Hudson, Compton, Benaud (Lakeland)

4. 23, 24, 25, 27, 28/7   Arlott, McGilvray, Hudson, Fingleton, Brown, Swanton
    OLD TRAFFORD   TV: Johnston, West, Compton, Benaud (Lakeland)

5. 13, 14, 15, 17, 18/8   Arlott, McGilvray, Hudson, Brown, Fingleton, Roberts
    OVAL   TV: Johnston, West, Compton, Benaud, Swanton (Lewis)

1965   **ENGLAND V. NEW ZEALAND** (Third
                             Network)
1. 27, 28, 29, 31/5, 1/6   Arlott, Gibson, Peter Cranmer, Brown, Yardley
    EDGBASTON   TV: Johnston, West, Compton, Benaud (Lewis)

2. 17, 18, 19, 21, 22/6   Arlott, Gibson, Hudson, Brown, Yardley
    LORD'S   TV: Johnston, Swanton, Compton, Benaud (Lewis, John
                             McGonagle)

3. 8, 9, 10, 12, 13/7   Arlott, Gibson, Hudson, Brown, Yardley, Swanton
    HEADINGLEY   TV: Johnston, West, Compton, Benaud (Nick Hunter,
                             Lakeland)

                             ENGLAND V. SOUTH AFRICA
1. 22, 23, 24, 26, 27/7   Arlott, Fortune, Hudson, Brown, Swanton
    LORD'S   TV: Johnston, West, Compton, Benaud (Lewis)

2. 5, 6, 7, 9/8   Arlott, Fortune, Hudson, Brown, Yardley
    TRENT BRIDGE   TV: Johnston, West, Compton, Benaud, Swanton (Lewis)

3. 26, 27, 28, 30, 31/8   Arlott, Fortune, Hudson, Brown, Yardley, Swanton
    OVAL   TV: Johnston, West, Compton, Benaud (Lewis)

1966   **ENGLAND V. WEST INDIES** (Third
                             programme)
1. 2, 3, 4, 6, 7/6   Arlott, Hudson, Lawrence, Brown, Yardley
    OLD TRAFFORD   TV: Johnston, West, Benaud, Compton (Lakeland, Lewis)

2. 16, 17, 18, 20, 21/6   Johnston, Hudson, Lawrence, Yardley, Swanton
   LORD'S   TV: West, Arlott, Compton, Benaud, Swanton (Lewis)

3. 30/6, 1, 2, 4, 5/7   Arlott, Gibson, Lawrence, Brown, Yardley
   TRENT BRIDGE   TV: Johnston, Gilbert Bennett, Compton, Benaud, Swanton
                        (Lewis)

4. 4, 5, 6, 8, 9/8   Tony Cozier, Hudson, Johnston, Swanton, Yardley
   HEADINGLEY   TV: West, Arlott, Compton, Johnston, Benaud (Hunter)

5. 18, 19, 20, 22, 23/8 Arlott, Hudson, Lawrence, Yardley, Brown
   OVAL   TV: Johnston, West, Compton, Benaud, Swanton (Lewis)

1967

ENGLAND V. INDIA (Third Network)

1. 8, 9, 10, 12, 13/6   Surita, Gibson, Arlott, Trevor Bailey, Yardley
   HEADINGLEY   TV: West, Compton, Benaud, Johnston (Lakeland, Lewis,
                        Hunter)

2. 22, 23, 24, 26/6   Gibson, Johnston, Surita, Yardley, Swanton
   LORD'S   TV: West, Arlott, Benaud, Compton (Lewis, McGonagle)

3. 13, 14, 15/7   Hudson, Johnston, Surita, Brown, Ted Dexter
   EDGBASTON   TV: West, Arlott, Benaud, Compton, Swanton (Lewis,
                        McGonagle)

ENGLAND V. PAKISTAN

1. 27, 28, 29, 31/7, 1/8 Arlott, Hudson, Kureishi, Brown, Bailey
   LORD'S   TV: Johnston, West, Benaud, Compton, Swanton (Lewis,
                        McGonagle)

2. 10, 11, 12, 14, 15/8 Hudson, Johnston, Kureishi, Yardley, Swanton
   TRENT BRIDGE   TV: West, Arlott, Benaud, Compton (Lewis, McGonagle)

3. 24, 25, 26, 28/8   Arlott, Hudson, Kureishi, Brown, Swanton
   OVAL   TV: Johnston, West, Benaud, Compton (Lewis, McGonagle)

1968

ENGLAND V. AUSTRALIA (*Radio 3*)

1. 6, 7, 8, 10, 11/6   McGilvray, Arlott, Cranmer, Bailey, Brown, Swanton
   OLD TRAFFORD   TV: West, Johnston, Benaud, Compton, Dexter (Hunter,
                        Lakeland)

2. 20, 21, 22, 24, 25/6 Arlott, Hudson, McGilvray, Bailey, Swanton, Yardley
   LORD'S   TV: Johnston, West, Benaud, Compton, Dexter (McGonagle,
                        Hunter, Lewis)

3. 11, 12, 13, 15, 16/7 Johnston, Arlott, McGilvray, Bailey, Brown, Swanton
   EDGBASTON   TV: West, Benaud, Compton, Dexter (Hunter, Lewis, Bob
                        Duncan)

4. 25, 26, 27, 29, 30/7 McGilvray, Johnston, Arlott, Bailey, Swanton, Yardley
   HEADINGLEY   TV: West, Benaud, Compton, Dexter (Hunter, Lewis)

5. 22, 23, 24, 26, 27/8 Arlott, Hudson, McGilvray, Bailey, Yardley, Swanton
   OVAL   TV: Johnston, West, Benaud, Compton, Dexter (Lewis,
                        Hunter)

1969

ENGLAND V. WEST INDIES (*Radio 3*)

1. 12, 13, 14, 16, 17/6 Lawrence, Arlott, Johnston, Brown, Bailey, Swanton
   OLD TRAFFORD   TV: West, Benaud, Compton, Laker, Hunter (Lakeland)

2. 26, 27, 28, 30/6, 1/7   Lawrence, Arlott, Gibson, Bailey, Yardley, Swanton
    LORD'S   TV: Benaud, Johnston, Compton, Laker, Colin Milburn
                             (Lewis, Hunter)

3. 10, 11, 12, 14, 15/7   Lawrence, Arlott, Johnston, Bailey, Yardley, Swanton
    HEADINGLEY   TV: West, Benaud, Compton, Laker, Milburn (Hunter,
                             Lewis)

ENGLAND V. NEW ZEALAND

1. 24, 25, 26, 28, 29/7   Arlott, Gibson, Neil Durden-Smith, Bailey, Swanton, Merritt
    LORD'S   TV: Benaud, Johnston, Dexter, Compton, Milburn (Lewis,
                             Hunter)

2. 7, 8, 9, 11, 12/8   Arlott, Johnston, Gibson, Bailey, Merritt, Swanton
    TRENT BRIDGE   TV: Benaud, West, Dexter, Compton, Milburn (Lewis,
                             Hunter)

3. 21, 22, 23, 25, 26/8   Arlott, Gibson, D-Smith, Bailey, Merritt, Swanton
    OVAL   TV: Johnston, Benaud, Dexter, Compton, Milburn (Lewis,
                             Hunter)

1970   ENGLAND V. REST OF THE WORLD
                      (S African tour cancelled (*Radio 3*)

1. 17, 19, 20, 22/6   Arlott, Gibson, Johnston, Bailey
    LORD'S   TV: West, Benaud, Laker, Dexter, Compton (Hunter, Lewis)
                             (*NB*: no play on 18th – General Election;
                                    no TV coverage 17th or 19th – Gen. Election and World
                                    Cup)

2. 2, 3, 4, 6, 7/7   Arlott, D-Smith, Johnston, Bailey, Benaud, Swanton
    TRENT BRIDGE   (no TV)

3. 16, 17, 18, 20, 21/7   Arlott, Gibson, Johnston, Bailey, Benaud, Swanton
    EDGBASTON   (no TV)

4. 30, 31/7, 1, 3, 4/8   Arlott, Gibson, Johnston, Bailey, Benaud, Swanton
    HEADINGLEY   TV: West, Laker, Benaud, Compton, Dexter (Hunter, David
                             Kenning)

5. 13, 14, 15, 17, 18/8   Arlott, Johnston, D-Smith, Bailey, Benaud, Swanton
    OVAL   TV: West, Benaud, Laker, Compton, Dexter (Hunter,
                             Kenning)

1971   ENGLAND V. PAKISTAN (*Radio 3*)

1. 3, 4, 5, 7, 8/6   Arlott, Johnston, D-Smith, Bailey, Wazir Mohammad,
    EDGBASTON   Swanton
                             TV: West, Laker, Compton, Dexter (Kenning, Bob Duncan,
                             John Shrewsbury)

2. 17, 18, 19, 21, 22/6   Arlott, Johnston, Gibson, Bailey, Khan Mohammed, Swanton
    LORD'S   TV: West, Laker, Compton, Dexter (Kenning, Shrewsbury)

3. 8, 9, 10, 12, 13/7   Arlott, Johnston, D-Smith, Bailey, K. Mohammed, Swanton
    HEADINGLEY   TV: West, Laker, Compton, Dexter (Kenning, Hunter)

ENGLAND V. INDIA

1. 22, 23, 24, 26, 27/7
   LORD'S
   Arlott, Johnston, Gibson, Bailey, Lt-Col H. R. Adhikari, Swanton
   TV: West, Laker, Compton, Dexter (Kenning, Hunter)

2. 5, 6, 7, 9, 10/8
   OLD TRAFFORD
   Arlott, Johnston, D-Smith, Bailey, Adhikari, Swanton
   TV: West, Laker, Compton, Dexter (Kenning, Hunter)

3. 19, 20, 21, 23, 24/8
   OVAL
   Arlott, Johnston, Gibson, Bailey, Adhikari, Swanton
   TV: West, Laker, Compton, Dexter (Kenning, Bill Taylor)

1972

ENGLAND V. AUSTRALIA (*Radio 3*)

1. 8, 9, 10, 12, 13/6
   OLD TRAFFORD
   Arlott, Johnston, McGilvray, Bailey, Alan Davidson, Swanton
   TV: West, Benaud, Laker, Dexter (Kenning, Hunter)

2. 22, 23, 24, 26/6
   LORD'S
   Johnston, Arlott, McGilvray, Bailey, Davidson, Swanton
   TV: West, Benaud, Laker, Compton (Kenning, Hunter)

3. 13, 14, 15, 17, 18/7
   TRENT BRIDGE
   Johnston, Arlott, McGilvray, Bailey, Benaud, Swanton
   TV: West, Benaud, Laker, Compton (Kenning, Taylor)

4. 27, 28, 29/7
   HEADINGLEY
   Johnston, Arlott, McGilvray, Bailey, Benaud, Swanton
   TV: West, Benaud, Laker, Dexter (Kenning, Richard Tilling)

5. 10, 11, 12, 14, 15, 16/8
   OVAL
   Johnston, Arlott, McGilvray, Bailey, Benaud, Swanton
   TV: West, Benaud, Laker, Compton, Dexter (Kenning, Taylor)

1973

ENGLAND V. NEW ZEALAND (*Radio 3*)

1. 7, 8, 9, 11, 12/6
   TRENT BRIDGE
   Johnston, Alan Richards, Arlott, Gibson, Bailey, Yardley, Swanton
   TV: West, Benaud, Laker, Dexter (Kenning, Shrewsbury)

2. 21, 22, 23, 25, 26/6
   LORD'S
   Johnston, Arlott, Richards, D-Smith, Bailey, Swanton
   TV: West, Benaud, Laker, Compton (Kenning, Shrewsbury)

3. 5, 6, 7, 9, 10/7
   HEADINGLEY
   Johnston, Richards, Arlott, Gibson, Bailey, Yardley, Swanton
   TV: West, Benaud, Laker, Dexter (Kenning, Shrewsbury)

ENGLAND V. WEST INDIES

1. 26, 27, 28, 30, 31/7
   OVAL
   Johnston, Cozier, Arlott, Gibson, Bailey, Yardley, Swanton
   TV: West, Benaud, Compton, Laker (Kenning, Roy Norton)

2. 9, 10, 11, 13, 14/8
   EDGBASTON
   Johnston, Cozier, Arlott, D-Smith, Bailey, Yardley, Swanton
   TV: West, Benaud, Laker, Compton (Kenning, Shrewsbury)

3. 23, 24, 25, 27/8
   LORD'S
   Johnston, Cozier, Arlott, Christopher Martin-Jenkins, Bailey, Yardley, Swanton
   TV: West, Benaud, Laker, Dexter (Kenning, Shrewsbury)

1974

ENGLAND V. INDIA (*Radio 3*)

1. 6, 7, 8, 10, 11/6
   OLD TRAFFORD
   Arlott, Johnston, CMJ, Henry Blofeld, Bailey, Maharaja of Baroda, Swanton
   TV: West, Benaud, Laker, Compton (Kenning, Shrewsbury)

2. 20, 21, 22, 24, 25/6
   LORD'S
   Johnston, Arlott, CMJ, D-Smith, Bailey, Baroda, Swanton
   TV: West, Benaud, Laker, Dexter (Kenning, Shrewsbury)

3. 4, 5, 6, 8, 9/7   Johnston, Arlott, CMJ, Gibson, Bailey, Baroda, Swanton
    EDGBASTON   TV: Peter Walker, Benaud, Laker, Compton (Kenning,
                        Shrewsbury)

ENGLAND V. PAKISTAN

1. 25, 26, 27, 29, 30/7   Arlott, Johnston, Don Mosey, Blofeld, Bailey, Billy Ibadulla,
    HEADINGLEY   Freddie Trueman, Swanton. Producer: Don Mosey
                        TV: West, Benaud, Laker, Dexter (Kenning, Shrewsbury)

2. 8, 9, 10, 12, 13/8   Arlott, Johnston, Blofeld, Mosey, Bailey, Ibadulla, Swanton
    LORD'S   TV: West, Benaud, Laker, Compton (Kenning, Shrewsbury)

3. 22, 23, 24, 26, 27/8   Arlott, Johnston, Gibson, D-Smith, Bailey, Ibadulla, Swanton
    OVAL   TV: West, Benaud, Laker, Dexter (Kenning, Shrewsbury)

1975   ENGLAND V. AUSTRALIA *(Radio 3)*

1. 10, 11, 12, 14/7   Arlott, Johnston, McGilvray, Mosey, Bailey, Trueman
    EDGBASTON   TV: West, Benaud, Laker, Dexter (Kenning, Taylor)

2. 31/7, 1, 2, 4, 5/8   Arlott, Johnston, McGilvray, Blofeld, Bailey, Trueman
    LORD'S   TV: West, Benaud, Laker, Compton (Kenning, Taylor)

3. 14, 15, 16, 18, 19/8   Arlott, Gibson, Johnston, McGilvray, Bailey, Trueman
    HEADINGLEY   TV: West, Benaud, Laker, Ray Illingworth (Kenning, Taylor)

4. 28, 29, 30/8, 1, 2, 3/9 Arlott, Johnston, McGilvray, CMJ, Bailey, Trueman
    OVAL   TV: West, Benaud, Laker, Dexter (Kenning, Taylor)

1976   ENGLAND V. WEST INDIES

1. 3, 4, 5, 7, 8/6   Arlott, Cozier, Johnston, CMJ, Bailey, Trueman
    TRENT BRIDGE   TV: West, Benaud, Laker, Dexter (Kenning, Taylor)

2. 17, 18, 19, 21, 22/6   Arlott, Cozier, Johnston, Mosey, Bailey, Trueman
    LORD'S   TV: West, Benaud, Laker (Kenning, Taylor)

3. 8, 9, 10, 12, 13/7   Arlott, Blofeld, Cozier, Johnston, Bailey, Trueman
    OLD TRAFFORD   TV: West, Benaud, Laker (Kenning, Taylor)

4. 22, 23, 24, 26, 27/7   Arlott, Cozier, CMJ, Johnston, Bailey, Trueman
    HEADINGLEY   TV: Walker, Benaud, Laker, Dexter (Kenning, Taylor)

5. 12, 13, 14, 16, 17/8   Arlott, Cozier, Johnston, Mosey, Bailey, Trueman, Frindall
    OVAL   TV: West, Benaud, Laker, Everton Weekes (Kenning, Taylor)

1977   ENGLAND V. AUSTRALIA

1. 16, 17, 18, 20, 21/6   Arlott, Johnston, Mosey, McGilvray, Bailey, Trueman, Tony
    LORD'S   Lewis
                        TV: West, Benaud, Laker, Dexter (Kenning, Taylor)

2. 7, 8, 9, 11, 12/7   Arlott, Johnston, CMJ, McGilvray, Bailey, Trueman, Lewis
    OLD TRAFFORD   TV: West, Benaud, Laker, Ian Chappell (Kenning, Hunter)

3. 28, 29, 30/7, 1, 2/8   Arlott, Blofeld, Johnston, McGilvray, Bailey, Trueman, Lewis
    TRENT BRIDGE   TV: West, Benaud, Laker, Ian Chappell (Kenning, Taylor)

4. 11, 12, 13, 15/8   Arlott, Johnston, CMJ, McGilvray, Bailey, Trueman, Lewis
    HEADINGLEY   TV: West, Benaud, Laker, Chappell (Kenning, Taylor)

5. 25, 26, 27, 29, 30/8   Arlott, Johnston, Mosey, McGilvray, Bailey, Trueman, Lewis
    OVAL   TV: West, Benaud, Laker, Dexter (Kenning, Taylor)

1978

1. 1, 2, 3, 5/6
   EDGBASTON

ENGLAND V. PAKISTAN
Arlott, Blofeld, Johnston, Mosey, Bailey, Trueman, Lewis
TV: West, Benaud, Laker, Dexter (Kenning, Taylor)

2. 15, 16, 17, 19/6
   LORD'S

Arlott, Blofeld, Johnston, CMJ, Bailey, Trueman, Lewis
TV: West, Benaud, Laker (Kenning, Taylor)

3. 29, 30/6, 1, 3, 4/7
   HEADINGLEY

Arlott, Johnston, CMJ, Mosey, Bailey, Trueman, Lewis
TV: Walker, Benaud, Laker, Dexter (Taylor, Hunter)

ENGLAND V. NEW ZEALAND

1. 27, 28, 29, 31/7, 1/8
   OVAL

Arlott, Johnston, Mosey, Alan Richards, Bailey, Trueman, Lewis
TV: West, Benaud, Laker (Kenning, Taylor)

2. 10, 11, 12, 14/8
   TRENT BRIDGE

Arlott, Johnston, CMJ, Richards, Bailey, Trueman, Mosey
TV: West, Benaud, Laker, Dexter (Kenning, Taylor)

3. 24, 25, 26, 28/8
   LORD'S

Arlott, Johnston, Blofeld, Richards, Bailey, Trueman, Lewis
TV: West, Benaud, Laker (Kenning, Taylor)

1979

1. 12, 13, 14, 16/7
   EDGBASTON

ENGLAND V. INDIA
Arlott, Johnston, CMJ, Blofeld, Bailey, Trueman
TV: West, Benaud, Laker, Dexter (Hunter, Huw Jones)

2. 2, 3, 4, 6, 7/8
   LORD'S

Arlott, Johnston, CMJ, Mosey, Bailey, Trueman
TV: West, Benaud, Laker, Dexter (Hunter, Jones)

3. 16, 17, 18, 20, 21/8
   HEADINGLEY

Arlott, Johnston, Blofeld, Lewis, Bailey, Trueman
TV: West, Benaud, Laker, Dexter, M. J. K. Smith (Hunter, Jones)

4. 30, 31/8, 1, 3, 4/9
   OVAL

Arlott, Johnston, CMJ, Mosey, Bailey, Lewis, Trueman
TV: West, Benaud, Laker, Dexter, Smith (Hunter, Jones)

1980

1. 5, 6, 7, 9, 10/6
   TRENT BRIDGE

ENGLAND V. WEST INDIES
Arlott, Johnston, Mosey, Cozier, Bailey, Trueman
TV: West, Benaud, Laker, Dexter, Smith (Hunter, Taylor)

2. 19, 20, 21, 23, 24/6
   LORD'S

Arlott, Johnston, CMJ, Cozier, Bailey, Trueman
TV: West, Benaud, Laker, Dexter, Tom Graveney (Hunter, Taylor)

3. 10, 11, 12, 14, 15/7
   OLD TRAFFORD

Arlott, Johnston, CMJ, Blofeld, Cozier, Bailey, Trueman
TV: West, Benaud, Laker, Dexter, Smith (Hunter, Taylor)

4. 24, 25, 26, 28, 29/7
   OVAL

Arlott, Johnston, Mosey, Cozier, Bailey, Trueman
TV: West, Benaud, Laker, Graveney, Smith (Hunter, Taylor)

5. 7, 8, 9, 11, 12/8
   HEADINGLEY

Arlott, Johnston, CMJ, Cozier, Bailey, Trueman
TV: West, Benaud, Laker, Dexter, Graveney, Cozier (Hunter, Taylor)

ENGLAND V. AUSTRALIA

28, 29, 30/8, 1, 2/9
LORD'S

Arlott, Johnston, McGilvray, CMJ, Mosey, Bailey, Trueman, Lindsay Hassett, Keith Miller
TV: West, Benaud, Laker, Dexter, Smith, Graveney (Hunter, Taylor)

1981   ENGLAND V. AUSTRALIA

1. 18, 19, 20, 21/6   Johnston, Lewis, Mosey, McGilvray, Bailey, Trueman
    TRENT BRIDGE   TV: Walker, West, Benaud, CMJ, Graveney, Smith (Taylor,
                              Mike Adley, Hunter)

2. 2, 3, 4, 6, 7/7   Johnston, CMJ, Blofeld, McGilvray, Bailey, Trueman
    LORD'S   TV: Walker, Benaud, Lewis, Graveney, Bob Simpson (Taylor,
                              Jones, Hunter)

3. 16, 17, 18, 20, 21/7   Johnston, Mosey, Blofeld, McGilvray, Bailey, Trueman
    HEADINGLEY   TV: West, Benaud, CMJ, Graveney, Dexter (Taylor, Jones,
                              Hunter)

4. 30, 31/7, 1, 2/8   Johnston, Lewis, CMJ, McGilvray, Bailey, Trueman
    EDGBASTON   TV: West, Benaud, Walker, Smith, Graveney (Taylor,
                              Kenning)

5. 13, 14, 15, 16, 17/8   Johnston, Lewis, Blofeld, McGilvray, Bailey, Trueman
    OLD TRAFFORD   TV: West, Benaud, Laker, CMJ, Graveney, Peter Parfitt
                              (Hunter, Jones)

6. 27, 28, 29, 31/8, 1/9   Johnston, CMJ, Mosey, McGilvray, Bailey, Trueman
    OVAL   TV: West, Benaud, Laker, Lewis, Graveney, Dexter (Taylor,
                              Adley, Hunter)

1982   ENGLAND V. INDIA

1. 10, 11, 12, 14, 15/6   Johnston, Lewis, CMJ, Mosey, Bailey, Trueman, Frindall
    LORD'S   TV: West, Benaud, Laker, Graveney, Brian Close (Hunter,
                              Taylor)

2. 24, 25, 26, 27, 28/6   Johnston, CMJ, Lewis, Mosey
    OLD TRAFFORD   TV: Lewis, Benaud, Laker, Graveney (Hunter, Taylor)

3. 8, 9, 10, 12, 13/7   TV: West, Benaud, Laker, Graveney, Dexter (Hunter, Taylor)
    OVAL

                                  ENGLAND V. PAKISTAN

1. 29, 30, 31/7, 1/8   Johnston, Mosey, CMJ, Blofeld, Bailey, Trueman
    EDGBASTON   TV: West, Benaud, Laker, Graveney, Lewis (Hunter, Taylor)

2. 12, 13, 14, 15, 16/8   Johnston, CMJ, Mosey, Blofeld, Bailey, Trueman
    LORD'S   TV: West, Benaud, Laker, Graveney, Close (Hunter, Taylor)

3. 26, 27, 28, 30, 31/8   Johnston, Blofeld, Lewis, Mosey
    HEADINGLEY   TV: West, Benaud, Laker, Graveney, Dexter (Hunter,
                              Kenning)

1983   ENGLAND V. NEW ZEALAND

1. 14, 15, 16, 17, 18/7   Johnston, CMJ, Blofeld, Richards, Bailey, Trueman, Milburn
    OVAL   TV: West, Benaud, Laker, Lewis, Graveney (Taylor, Keith
                              Mackenzie, Hunter)

2. 28, 29, 30/7, 1/8   Johnston, CMJ, Blofeld, Richards
    HEADINGLEY   TV: West, Benaud, Laker, Lewis, Graveney, Dexter (Taylor,
                              Mackenzie, Hunter, Fred Viner)

3. 11, 12, 13, 15/8 Johnston, Mosey, Blofeld, Richards, Bailey, Trueman,
   LORD'S   Graveney
                    TV: West, Benaud, Laker, Lewis, Dexter (Viner, Adley,
                    Taylor)

4. 25, 26, 27, 28, 29/8 Johnston, CMJ, Mosey, Richards, Bailey, Trueman, Lewis
   TRENT BRIDGE   TV: West, Benaud, Laker, Graveney, Jack Bannister (Adley,
                        Mackenzie, Hunter)

1984
ENGLAND V. WEST INDIES

1. 14, 15, 16, 18/6 Johnston, CMJ, Mosey, Cozier, Bailey, Trueman, Lewis
   EDGBASTON   TV: West, Benaud, Laker, Graveney, Ray Illingworth (Adley,
                    Mackenzie, Hunter)

2. 28, 29, 30/6, 2, 3/7 Johnston, Blofeld, CMJ, Cozier, Bailey, Lewis, Illingworth
   LORD'S   TV: West, Benaud, Laker, Dexter, Bannister (Mackenzie,
                        Hunter, Taylor)

3. 12, 13, 14, 16/7 Johnston, Mosey, Lewis, Cozier, Trueman, Bailey,
   HEADINGLEY   Mike Denness
                    TV: West, Benaud, Laker, Graveney, Illingworth (Taylor,
                    Adley, Mackenzie, Hunter)

4. 26, 27, 28, 30, 31/7 Johnston, Mosey, CMJ, Cozier, Trueman, Lewis, Illingworth
   OLD TRAFFORD   TV: West, Benaud, Laker, Dexter, Graveney (Taylor, Adley,
                        Mackenzie, Hunter)

5. 9, 10, 11, 13, 14/8 Johnston, Mosey, Blofeld, CMJ, Cozier, Trueman, Lewis,
   OVAL   Illingworth
                       TV: West, Benaud, Laker, Illingworth, Dexter (Adley,
                       Mackenzie, Taylor)

ENGLAND V. SRI LANKA

23, 24, 25, 27, 28/8 Johnston, Mosey, Lewis, Blofeld, Trueman, Bailey, Gamini
LORD'S   Goonesena
                     TV: West, Benaud, Laker, Graveney, Illingworth (Adley,
                     Hunter, Mackenzie, Taylor)

1985
ENGLAND V. AUSTRALIA

1. 13, 14, 15, 17, 18/6 Johnston, McGilvray, CMJ, Mosey, Lewis, Trueman
   HEADINGLEY   TV: West, Benaud, Laker, Bob Willis, Illingworth
                       (Mackenzie, Adley, Hunter)

2. 27, 28, 29/6, 1, 2/7 Johnston, McGilvray, CMJ, Blofeld, Bailey, Illingworth
   LORD'S   TV: West, Benaud, Laker, Lewis, Dexter (Mackenzie, Adley,
                        Hunter)

3. 11, 12, 13, 15, 16/7 Johnston, Lewis, McGilvray, Mosey, Illingworth, Robin
   TRENT BRIDGE   Jackman
                       TV: West, Benaud, Laker, Graveney, Willis (Mackenzie,
                       Adley, Hunter)

4. 1, 2, 3, 5, 6/8 Johnston, McGilvray, CMJ, Mosey, Bailey, Trueman
   OLD TRAFFORD   TV: West, Benaud, Laker, Lewis, Illingworth (Mackenzie,
                   Adley, Alan Griffiths, Hunter)

5. 15, 16, 17, 19, 20/8   Johnston, McGilvray, Lewis, Blofeld, Trueman, Bannister
    EDGBASTON   TV: West, Benaud, Laker, Graveney, Illingworth (Adley,
                        Griffiths, Mackenzie)

6. 29, 30, 31/8, 2/9   Johnston, McGilvray, CMJ, Lewis, Bailey, Illingworth
    OVAL   TV: West, Benaud, Laker, Dexter, Willis (Mackenzie,
                        Griffiths, Hunter, Adley)

1986   ENGLAND V. INDIA

1. 5, 6, 7, 9, 10/6   Johnston, CMJ, Blofeld, Bailey, Trueman, Farokh Engineer
    LORD'S   TV: West, Benaud, Lewis, Willis, Dexter (Mackenzie,
                        Griffiths, Hunter)

2. 19, 20, 21, 23/6   Johnston, CMJ, Mosey, Illingworth, Jackman, Engineer
    HEADINGLEY   TV: West, Benaud, Lewis, Graveney, Willis (Mackenzie,
                        Griffiths, Hunter)

3. 3, 4, 5, 7, 8/7   Johnston, Mosey, Blofeld, Trueman, Bannister, Engineer
    EDGBASTON   TV: West, Benaud, Lewis, Illingworth, Willis (Mackenzie,
                        Griffiths)

ENGLAND V. NEW ZEALAND

1. 24, 25, 26, 28, 29/7 Johnston, Mosey, Blofeld, Richards, Bailey, Illingworth
    LORD'S   TV: West, Benaud, Lewis, Dexter, Willis (Hunter, Mackenzie)

2. 7, 8, 9, 11, 12/8   Johnston, CMJ, Richards, Trueman, Bannister
    TRENT BRIDGE   TV: West, Benaud, Lewis, Illingworth, Willis (Mackenzie,
                        Griffiths)

3. 21, 22, 23, 25, 26/8 Johnston, CMJ, Mosey, Richards, Bailey, Illingworth
    OVAL   TV: West, Benaud, Lewis, Dexter, Graveney (Mackenzie,
                         Griffiths)

1987   ENGLAND V. PAKISTAN

1. 4, 5, 6, 8, 9/6   Johnston, CMJ, Mosey, Trueman, Bannister, Mushtaq
    OLD TRAFFORD   Mohammad
                        TV: Lewis, Benaud, Illingworth, Graveney, Willis
                        (Mackenzie, Griffiths)

2. 18, 19, 20, 22, 23/6 Johnston, CMJ, Blofeld, Bailey, Milburn, Mushtaq
    LORD'S   TV: Lewis, Benaud, Illingworth, Dexter, Bannister
                         (Mackenzie, Griffiths)

3. 2, 3, 4, 6/7   Johnston, Mosey, Blofeld, Trueman, Jackman, Mushtaq
    HEADINGLEY   TV: Lewis, Benaud, Illingworth, Graveney, Willis
                       (Mackenzie, Griffiths)

4. 23, 24, 25, 27, 28/7 Johnston, CMJ, Mosey, Bailey, Bannister, Mushtaq
    EDGBASTON   TV: Lewis, Benaud, Illingworth, Dexter, Jackman (Mackenzie,
                         Griffiths)

5. 6, 7, 8, 10, 11/8   Johnston, CMJ, Mosey, Bailey, Jackman, Mushtaq
    OVAL   TV: Lewis, Benaud, Illingworth, Graveney, Bannister
                        (Mackenzie, Griffiths)

1988   **ENGLAND V. WEST INDIES**
1. 2, 3, 4, 6, 7/6   Johnston, CMJ, Cozier, Bailey, Jackman
    TRENT BRIDGE   TV: Lewis, Benaud, Bannister, Illingworth, Graveney
                                (Mackenzie, Griffiths)

2. 16, 17, 18, 20, 21/6   Johnston, CMJ, Blofeld, Cozier, Bailey, Mike Selvey
    LORD'S   TV: Lewis, Benaud, Bannister, Illingworth, Jackman
                                (Mackenzie, Griffiths)

3. 30/6, 1, 2, 4, 5/7   Johnston, Mosey, Cozier, Trueman, Jackman
    OLD TRAFFORD   TV: Lewis, Benaud, Bannister, Illingworth, Graveney
                                (Mackenzie, Griffiths)

4. 21, 22, 23, 25, 26/7   Johnston, Mosey, Cozier, Trueman, Milburn
    HEADINGLEY   TV: Lewis, Benaud, Bannister, Illingworth, Dexter
                                (Mackenzie, Griffiths)

5. 4, 5, 6, 8/8   Johnston, CMJ, Cozier, Bailey, Trueman
    OVAL   TV: Lewis, Benaud, Bannister, Illingworth, Ian Botham
                                (Mackenzie, Griffiths)

                               ENGLAND V. SRI LANKA
25, 26, 27, 29, 30/8   Johnston, CMJ, Blofeld, Bailey, Milburn, Goonesena
LORD'S   TV: Lewis, Benaud, Bannister, Illingworth, Graveney
                                (Mackenzie, Griffiths)

1989   **ENGLAND V. AUSTRALIA**
1. 8, 9, 10, 12, 13/6   Johnston, CMJ, Mosey, Neville Oliver, Bailey, Trueman
    HEADINGLEY   TV: Lewis, Benaud, Bannister, Illingworth, Alan Knott
                                (Mackenzie, Griffiths)

2. 22, 23, 24, 26, 27/6   Johnston, CMJ, Blofeld, Oliver, Bailey, Selvey
    LORD'S   TV: Lewis, Benaud, Bannister, Illingworth, Graveney
                                (Mackenzie, Griffiths)

3. 6, 7, 8, 10, 11/7   Johnston, Mosey, Blofeld, Oliver, Trueman, Phil Edmonds
    EDGBASTON   TV: Lewis, Benaud, Bannister, Illingworth, Knott (Mackenzie,
                                Griffiths)

4. 27, 28, 29, 31/7, 1/8   Johnston, CMJ, Mosey, Oliver, Trueman, Jackman
    OLD TRAFFORD   TV: Lewis, Benaud, Bannister, Illingworth, Graveney
                                (Mackenzie, Griffiths)

5. 10, 11, 12, 14, 15/8   Johnston, CMJ, Blofeld, Oliver, Bailey, Jackman
    TRENT BRIDGE   TV: Lewis, Benaud, Bannister, Illingworth, Graveney
                                (Mackenzie, Griffiths)

6. 24, 25, 26, 28, 29/8   Johnston, CMJ, Blofeld, Oliver, Bailey, Selvey
    OVAL   TV: Lewis, Benaud, Bannister, Illingworth, Graveney
                                (Griffiths, Simon Wheeler, Mackenzie)

PICTURE CREDITS

INDEX